# THE COMPLETE GUIDE TO HEALTHY COOKING AND NUTRITION FOR COLLEGE STUDENTS:

## How Not to Gain 17 Pounds at College

By J. Lucy Boyd, RN, BSN

# THE COMPLETE GUIDE TO HEALTHY COOKING AND NUTRITION FOR COLLEGE STUDENTS: HOW NOT TO GAIN 17 POUNDS AT COLLEGE

Library of Congress Cataloging-in-Publication Data

Boyd, J. Lucy, 1966-
  The complete guide to healthy cooking and nutrition for college students : how not to gain 17
pounds at college / by J. Lucy Boyd.
     p. cm.
  Includes bibliographical references and index.
  ISBN-13: 978-1-60138-357-0 (alk. paper)
  ISBN-10: 1-60138-357-6 (alk. paper)
  1. College students--Health and hygiene. 2. College students--Nutrition. I. Title.
RA777.3.B69 2009
613.2084'2--dc22
                          2009035934

Printed in the United States

PROJECT MANAGER: Melissa Peterson • mpeterson@atlantic-pub.com
ASSISTANT EDITOR: Angela Pham • apham@atlantic-pub.com
INTERIOR DESIGN: Antoinette D'Amore • addesign@videotron.ca
COVER DESIGN: Meg Buchner • meg@megbuchner.com
JACKET DESIGN: Jackie Miller • sullmill@charter.net

Printed on Recycled Paper

We recently lost our beloved pet "Bear," who was not only our best and dearest friend but also the "Vice President of Sunshine" here at Atlantic Publishing. He did not receive a salary but worked tirelessly 24 hours a day to please his parents. Bear was a rescue dog that turned around and showered myself, my wife, Sherri, his grandparents

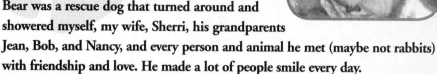

Jean, Bob, and Nancy, and every person and animal he met (maybe not rabbits) with friendship and love. He made a lot of people smile every day.

We wanted you to know that a portion of the profits of this book will be donated to The Humane Society of the United States.  *–Douglas & Sherri Brown*

---

The human-animal bond is as old as human history. We cherish our animal companions for their unconditional affection and acceptance. We feel a thrill when we glimpse wild creatures in their natural habitat or in our own backyard.

Unfortunately, the human-animal bond has at times been weakened. Humans have exploited some animal species to the point of extinction.

The Humane Society of the United States makes a difference in the lives of animals here at home and worldwide. The HSUS is dedicated to creating a world where our relationship with animals is guided by compassion. We seek a truly humane society in which animals are respected for their intrinsic value, and where the human-animal bond is strong.

Want to help animals? We have plenty of suggestions. Adopt a pet from a local shelter, join The Humane Society and be a part of

our work to help companion animals and wildlife. You will be funding our educational, legislative, investigative and outreach projects in the U.S. and across the globe.

Or perhaps you'd like to make a memorial donation in honor of a pet, friend or relative? You can through our Kindred Spirits program. And if you'd like to contribute in a more structured way, our Planned Giving Office has suggestions about estate planning, annuities, and even gifts of stock that avoid capital gains taxes.

Maybe you have land that you would like to preserve as a lasting habitat for wildlife. Our Wildlife Land Trust can help you. Perhaps the land you want to share is a backyard— that's enough. Our Urban Wildlife Sanctuary Program will show you how to create a habitat for your wild neighbors.

So you see, it's easy to help animals. And The HSUS is here to help.

**THE HUMANE SOCIETY**
**OF THE UNITED STATES.**

**2100 L Street NW • Washington, DC 20037 • 202-452-1100**
**www.hsus.org**

# TRADEMARK DISCLAIMER

All trademarks, trade names, or logos mentioned or used are the property of their respective owners and are used only to directly describe the products being provided. Every effort has been made to properly capitalize, punctuate, identify, and attribute trademarks and trade names to their respective owners, including the use of ® and ™ wherever possible and practical. Atlantic Publishing Group, Inc. is not a partner, affiliate, or licensee with the holders of said trademarks.

The "George Foreman" name and logo are trademarks and property of Salton, Inc.

The "Miracle Whip" name and logo are registered trademarks and property of Kraft Foods, Inc.

The "Chinet" name and logo are registered trademarks and property of Huhtamaki Company Manufacturing.

The "Alli" name and logo are registered trademarks and property of SmithKline Beecham Corporation.

The "Stove Top" name and logo are trademarks and property of Kraft Foods Holdings, Inc.

The "Toll House" name and logo are registered trademarks and property of Societe des Produits Nestle S.A.

The "Mrs. Dash" name and logo are registered trademarks and property of Alberto-Culver Company.

The "Food Network" name and logo are registered trademarks and property of Television Food Network, G.P. Cable Program Management Co.

The "HGTV" name and logo are registered trademarks and property of Scripps Networks, Inc.

The "Fine Living" name and logo are registered trademarks of Scripps Networks, Inc.

The "US Weekly" name and logo are registered trademarks and property of Us Weekly LLC.

The "WebMD" name and logo are registered trademarks and property of WEBMD LLC.

The "Working Mother" name and logo are registered trademarks and property of McCall Publishing Company.

The "Clif Bar" name and logo are trademarks and property of Clif Bar & Company.

The "Rice Krispies" name and logo are trademarks and property of Kellogg Company.

The "Save-A-Lot" name and logo are registered trademarks of MORAN FOODS, INC.

# DEDICATION

*I wish to thank my husband and best friend, Sammy, for his endless patience, support, and taste-testing. To our beautiful children, Chris, Bridgett, and Ayesha. Thank you, Ayesha, for all your input about college life. May this book show all the grandbabies — Anna, Jinnah, Cole, Emma, and Madelyn — that you can do anything you set your mind to. Thank you to Granny, who taught me that cooking is ultimately a venture of love. To my grandmother and mother, for all their excellent recipe advice.*

*I dedicate this book to all the patients I have ever cared for, who taught me more than I could possibly teach them.*

# TABLE OF CONTENTS

# FOREWORD

**"W**hat have you had to eat today, Zach?" I asked the pale young man seated on my exam table. He had come to see me for help with some stomach problems.

He ran a hand through lank hair, considering.

"Um, well, I didn't have breakfast. Never do. No time. Let's see...I grabbed a soda after class and a bag of chips. Then for lunch, around three, I got a burger and some fries across the street."

Sadly, this is a common story. Many college students just do not take good care of themselves. This is a very busy time in their lives; most of them enter college just out of high school. For the first time, they are living away from the comforts of home, away from home-cooked meals. They are making new friends, stretching their independent wings, learning, and studying. Their highest priorities are often academic and social success, not what food they put in their bodies. As a result, their nutrition is likely to suffer.

So what, you ask? They are young and resilient — they will bounce back. It is true that students tend to be young and resilient, but nutrition does matter in the short and long run. Look at Zach. His stomach problems were directly related to his poor diet. I see too many patients like him. Digestive problems, anemia, obesity, and low energy; these problems, and many more, can be caused by unhealthy eating habits.

College students are not stupid. If they were, they would not be in college. They know when they are not eating well — I hear it from my patients all the time. But often, they do not know what to do about it. They never learned to cook back home. They are only allowed a microwave and a hot plate in their dorm. They think cooking takes too much time; it is easier to get fast food on the go. Shopping and cooking is expensive, and they are on a budget. These are all valid points — or they were until *The Complete Guide to Healthy Cooking and Nutrition For College Students* came along.

If you are a student, this book is for you, whether you are a comfortable cook or have never even cracked an egg. If you are a beginner, you can learn right here. Author J. Lucy Boyd starts with the very basics of cooking, from what utensils you need in your kitchen, through the types of vegetables, to how to stir fry. She even walks you through your trip to the grocery store. Her recipes are simple and healthy, and she clearly understands what it means to be a student who is short on money and even shorter on time.

If you already know the basics of cooking, this book still offers much for you. Boyd will help you expand your culinary horizons and broaden your skill set. Her upperclassmen chapters introduce more sophisticated forms of food preparation, while maintaining the ease of preparation using readily available ingredients that she establishes from the beginning.

If you are a parent, or friend of a college student, this book will make a great gift. Mom, you can feel comfortable sending your kid off to college without those cozy cooking sessions you kept meaning to share. Uncle Bob, this is a more useful freshman gift than that fishing rod you were eyeing. Students will keep this book on a handy shelf, probably in the kitchen, and refer to it often.

This book is not just about balanced nutrition. It is also about living a balanced life in college. The author understands that health is multifaceted, and she is clearly knowledgeable about other issues facing college students. She discusses sleep, exercise, alcohol use, and weight management. She offers advice about schedule planning, dignity and self worth, relationships, and more. Boyd's wisdom is warmly accessible, shared in a friendly, non-judgmental tone.

I am thrilled to have this addition to my own bag of tricks to offer students in my practice — and I cannot wait to give it to Zach.

Peggy Spencer, MD
University of New Mexico

## Foreword Author Biography

*Dr. Peggy Spencer is a graduate of the University of California with a BA in biology with honors and the University of Arizona College of Medicine with an MD. She is certified by the American Board of Family Practice. She serves as a staff physician at University of New Mexico (UNM) Student Health and Counseling and holds an adjunct faculty position at the UNM School of Medicine.*

*Spencer is the recipient of numerous professional honors and awards. She writes a column for the* New Mexico Daily Lobo *newspaper answering reader-submitted health questions and contributes articles to the* UNM Parent Matters *and* UNM Today. *She is the co-author of* 50 Ways to Leave Your 40s *with Sheila Key and serves as Plain Language Medical Editor for Hope Health. Spencer is a member of the American Academy of Family Physicians and SouthWest Writers.*

# PREFACE

**Y**ou enter college to gain new knowledge and learn new skills. This book is a primer for your new adult life outside the classroom. Healthy eating habits truly set the stage for your college career and your life beyond.

This book has been created to help young adults begin a healthy lifestyle. It covers everything one needs to know to begin cooking basic recipes and expands into restaurant and cafeteria eating. You will learn how to shop, where to shop, and how to prepare the foods you love — and the foods you do not yet know about.

Many young adults gain unneeded weight during their years of college, an undesirable consequence of improper diets. But you will learn that it can be fun, easy, and delicious to prepare your own meals and avoid excess calories. Good nutrition will help you feel good, perform at your best, and graduate with a strong body and mind.

Written by a professional registered nurse, who is also an amateur chef, this book makes an excellent gift for children or grandchildren who are headed to college. It begins at a basic cooking level and encourages healthy nutrition from beginning to end.

Spoken in practical, everyday language, it walks the new adult through every aspect of their daily meals. The book also covers eating disorders — prevalent on college campuses — and reasons to avoid unhealthy eating choices. Exercise and proper sleep are discussed at length, as well as time management, organization, and stress management. Bon appétit.

# INTRODUCTION

L ike college, this book is divided into Freshman, Sophomore, Junior, and Senior sections to walk you through the healthy eating process. Each of the sections includes basic recipes — most of them appropriate for making one serving. They can easily be multiplied if needed. Read through the book, then revisit the chapters as you need to. A handy recipe index is available at the end of the book to help you find just what you are looking for.

Begin with the Freshman recipes, as they are the easiest. We will show you how cooking can be simple, economical, and fun. There are even options available for those who only have a George Foreman™ grill or a microwave. You will also find healthy versions of many of your favorite foods included in these recipes.

# FRESHMAN SECTION

# CHAPTER 1

# The Basics

L et us begin with a discussion of the basics of nutrition, a cal-
culation of your needs, and a look at where your nutrition
stands today.

## Good Nutrition Basics

Our bodies need several nutrients for healthy growth. These include protein, fat, carbohydrates, fiber, water, vitamins, and minerals. We will take a look at each of these nutrients, but do not
be overwhelmed, as you will soon learn how to easily meet your
daily requirements.

### Protein

Protein is essential for human life. It consists of amino acids. Our
bodies need 20 different amino acids, some that our bodies produce on their own, and others that we must receive from our food.
Some sources of protein contain all the essential amino acids, such
as foods that come from animals. Other food sources are considered incomplete proteins, as they do not contain all the essential

amino acids. This only gets tricky if you follow a vegan diet. If you do not eat any animal products, you will have to plan your diet to meet your protein needs. This involves pairing various foods to give you the full range of amino acids. Refer to Chapter 17 to learn more about a proper vegetarian diet.

Protein is found in beans, soy, and nuts, and there is a small amount in grains. Protein gives your body energy and allows you to heal from wounds and infections. It is necessary for the growth of your body, muscles, and cells. But most Americans consume much more protein than their body needs to function properly. This can be hard on the kidneys and, eventually, on the cardiac system. Keep in mind the amount of protein you need each day, and try not to consume more than necessary. On the list of things to worry about, it does not need to be near the top. Still, most people can tolerate a little too much protein without ill effect.

## Fats

Fat, while considered the enemy by many of us, actually has some necessary functions. It helps us with long-term energy, pads our organs, is a component of all of our cells, and transports some of our vitamins. Too much time spent on a faddish, low-fat diet can have many harmful effects, including the loss of a female's menstrual cycle and gall bladder problems. Most of us consume much more fat each day than our body needs.

Understanding the different types of fat is important. The good fats we should be consuming include plant oils — such as olive oil and avocados. Nuts also contain good fat. Bad fats include those that are solid at room temperature, such as the classic, old-fashioned products of shortening, lard, and tallow. These are called saturated fats. The worst fat is called trans fat, and many food companies and restaurants are beginning to phase it out of their products. It is an unnaturally made fat that our body simply does not know how to process, causing it to build up inside our arteries. There is no healthy consumption level of trans fat, and it should be avoided. It is easy to look at food labels to make sure it is not present, and to stay away from restaurants that still use it.

Cholesterol, found in animal products — especially eggs and liver — is good for you, but only in small quantities. If you eat one egg per day and a small piece of chicken, you will have eaten as much cholesterol as you should consume daily. Staying away from fatty meat, such as hamburger and meat with obvious marbling, will help you avoid saturated fat and too much cholesterol. And it is possible to find margarine and shortening without trans fat. Look for products that are low in calories and saturated fat. There is a hot debate as to whether to eat butter, or the improved margarines. Current research indicates that the best advice is to eat the margarines for everyday use, with butter for occasional use, such as holiday cooking.

## Carbohydrates

Carbohydrates (carbs) give us quick energy. They are what we think of as sugars and starches. Though they sometimes get a bad rap, foods containing carbs give us many vitamins and antioxidants necessary for good health. They also give energy to the central nervous system. Complex carbohydrates digest more slowly and assist the body in a more long-term fashion, while simple carbohydrates give quick energy, followed by a fall in blood sugar. Foods high in carbohydrates include vegetables, fruits, and grains. Stay away from empty carbs, such as soda, chips, and pastries. You should focus on whole grains, and raw or minimally-processed fruits and vegetables. Avoid foods swimming in sweet sauces. Most Americans consume more than enough carbohydrates each day. Although low-carb diets are not usually harmful because of a lack of carbs, they can cause damage by giving the body too much protein and fat.

## Fiber

While technically a carbohydrate, fiber deserves its own mention in the list of essential nutrients. There are two types of fiber: soluble and insoluble. They are both important. Soluble fiber binds with fatty acids and ensures that sugar is released and absorbed more slowly; it also lowers cholesterol levels and regulates blood sugar. Insoluble fiber stays in your gastrointestinal tract and functions to sweep out and move along waste. This activity helps to prevent colon cancer, constipation, and other conditions. Insoluble fiber performs a similar task inside your blood vessels; it helps to prevent dangerous plaque buildup that can lead to heart attack and stroke. You need both types of fiber, around 25 grams per day total.

Most Americans fall far short of their needed fiber per day. A bowl of oatmeal in the morning makes an excellent start to the day. Try to improve your regular consumption of oats, whole-grain cereals, and other whole grains, beans, veggies, and fruits. Stay away from grains that are made from white flour as much as possible. Consider white bread, buns, rolls, and non-whole-grain cereals as pretty much junk. For the same calories, you could be eating something that helps your body immensely. It is an easy habit to begin, by buying whole grains at the grocery store and eating them when offered at a sub shop, for example.

## Water

Water is essential for human life. Exactly how much we need to drink is a topic of medical debate, but a good guideline is eight 8-ounce glasses per day, unless you are performing athletically, in which case you may need considerably more. Pure, old-fashioned water is best. It flushes out your body without requiring your kidneys or liver to do any extra work that additives might necessitate. It can be cold or room temperature, tap, filtered, or bottled. A good habit to develop is carrying a bottle around with you at all times and using it as your only between-meal drink. You *do* get used to it. Water helps your bowels to move regularly and helps prevent dehydration, fatigue, and headaches.

## Vitamins

You need an adequate intake of the following vitamins:

**Vitamin A:** This vitamin is needed for healthy vision, bone development, and healthy mucous membranes. It is found in deep yellow and orange fruits and vegetables, liver, fish liver oils, dairy products, and egg yolks.

**Vitamin D:** This vitamin is needed for healthy bones and to increase the absorption of calcium and other minerals. It is found in sunshine and fish liver oils, and is frequently added to milk.

**Vitamin E:** This vitamin works with other nutrients to keep your blood cells and other body components running smoothly. It is found in vegetable oils, nuts, green leafy vegetables, and wheat germ.

**Vitamin K:** This vitamin helps your blood to clot properly. It can be found in green, leafy vegetables and alfalfa.

Vitamins A, D, E, and K are all fat-soluble, meaning they need to be eaten with a little fat in order for your body to absorb them properly. It also means your body stores them in fat, and it is possible to get too much A, D, and K. If you take a supplement of these vitamins, be careful not to take too much more than 100-percent of the U.S. Recommended Daily Allowance (RDA).

**Vitamin B1 (thiamine):** Scientists used to believe there was just one B vitamin, but over time, they discovered that it was actually many different nutrients. Thus, we have the various B vitamins you see listed. This vitamin is needed for metabolizing carbohydrates, and things can get pretty grim without it (depression, cardiac failure, and kidney problems to name a few). It can be found in meats, including organ meats, fish, and poultry, and in nuts and whole grains. Enriched cereals and flour frequently contain thiamine and some of the other B vitamins.

**Vitamin B2 (riboflavin):** This vitamin helps to keep your lips, eyes, and mouth healthy. It can be found in organ meats, milk, eggs, and green leafy vegetables.

**Vitamin B3 (niacin):** This vitamin helps to rid the body of harmful chemicals, improves circulation, and lowers your cholesterol level. It can be found in meat, poultry, fish, nuts, and whole grains.

**Vitamin B5 (pantothenic acid):** This vitamin helps to metabolize carbohydrates, protein, and fats. It is found in whole grains, nuts, meat, and eggs. The word *pantothenic* comes from a Greek word meaning "from everywhere," because this vitamin is easy to find.

**Vitamin B6 (pyroxidine):** This vitamin is important for your nervous system and complex body functions. It can be found in meat, poultry, fish, and vegetables, including potatoes.

**Vitamin B7 (biotin):** This vitamin helps to metabolize fat and protein and is necessary for the growth of your cells. Fortunately, bacteria in your intestines produce more than enough of this vitamin, but just in case, it is also in tomatoes, romaine lettuce, and carrots, among other foods.

**Vitamin B9 (folic acid):** This vitamin helps to mature your red blood cells and keep your nervous system healthy. It is found in liver, eggs, poultry, fish, and green leafy vegetables.

**Vitamin B12 (actually a group called cobalamins):** This vitamin group helps with forming your blood and works with your nervous system, including your brain. Some people do not process it properly and have a condition known as pernicious anemia. It is found in liver, shellfish, and milk.

**Choline (one of the B vitamins, without its own number):** This vitamin helps the liver to function properly. It is found in egg yolk, soy, and liver.

**Vitamin C:** This vitamin helps your immune system and also helps with iron absorption. Without it, your wounds would heal poorly and you would bleed too easily. It is found in many foods, including citrus fruits, strawberries, melon, tomato, and broccoli.

The B vitamins and vitamin C are water-soluble. This means you are not as likely to overdose on them because if you consume too much, you will generally pass the excess when you void. If you are wondering what happened to the other B vitamins, they turned out not to be vitamins after all and were disqualified.

There are also higher B numbers, which have not yet been proved to be vitamins.

The main thing to remember about vitamins is that it is important to eat a variety of foods and not think of meat, milk, and eggs as bad foods. They become deleterious to your health when eaten in excess, not in moderation.

## Minerals

Minerals are inorganic substances from the earth, in contrast to vitamins, which are of plant, animal, or bacterial origin. You need an adequate intake of the following minerals:

**Calcium:** Your body needs calcium to build strong bones and teeth. It is also necessary for your cells, muscles, nerves, and heart. A deficiency can cause numerous problems, including osteoporosis and tetany. Good sources are milk products, oysters, salmon, and sardines.

**Chloride:** Chloride is involved in the body's metabolism and in keeping a proper acid-base balance in the blood. Almost all Americans get plenty of chloride in table salt.

**Copper:** Copper helps your bones, immune system, and circulatory system. Most Americans are never deficient in copper because it leaks into our water system through copper piping. It can be found in beef, nuts, liver, mackerel, beans, and lentils.

**Iodine:** This mineral helps our body regulate our metabolism. In the past, many Americans were deficient in iodine, but it is now added to most table salt. It is also found in seafood.

**Iron:** Iron is necessary to keep our blood healthy. A deficiency can lead to anemia. It is found in organ meats, including liver, and in egg yolks, meat, poultry, and dark green vegetables.

**Magnesium:** This mineral is necessary for healthy bones, teeth, muscles, and nerves. It is also involved in metabolism. It can be found in milk products, meat, nuts, and legumes.

**Manganese:** Manganese helps us with enzyme processes, metabolism, wound healing, and bone development. Good sources of manganese include tofu, nuts, seeds, oysters, whole grains, and chocolate.

**Molybdenum:** This mineral is an enzymatic component that helps our bodies turn food into energy. There has never been a known deficiency in this mineral. Beans, lentils, nuts, and milk products are good sources.

**Nickel:** Nickel assists the functioning and distribution of other nutrients, including iron, in our bodies. It can be found in lentils, oatmeal, nuts, and cocoa.

**Phosphorus:** This mineral plays several important roles in our bodies, including helping in the development of bones and teeth. A deficiency can lead to stunted growth. It can be found in milk products, eggs, meat, poultry, fish, and nuts.

**Potassium:** Potassium is critical in nerve and muscle health, among other functions. A serious deficiency can lead to a heart arrhythmia. It can be found in most fruits and vegetables, especially citrus, melons, and bananas.

**Selenium:** This mineral is involved in metabolism and thyroid functions. Good sources of selenium include butter, garlic, whole grains, nuts, seeds, fish, and liver.

**Sodium:** Sodium is essential for fluid balance and healthy nerves and muscles. Americans consume plenty of sodium in table salt.

**Sulfur:** This mineral helps to create our hair, skin, and nails. It is found in meat, milk products, eggs, fish, and nuts.

**Zinc:** Zinc is important to the immune system, muscle growth, and healthy skin. Good sources include meat, poultry, seafood, whole grains, nuts, and eggs.

# USDA Food Pyramid

The United States Department of Agriculture (USDA) has created a food pyramid to help us get the right nutrition without over-consuming the wrong foods. You are probably pressed for time and realize you cannot count out the amount of proteins, fats, carbohydrates, fiber, calories, and various vitamins and minerals you need each day, and this is where the food pyramid will come in handy. If you follow its simple guidelines, which can be tailored exactly to your situation, you can feel confident that you are properly nourishing your body. The food pyramid can be found by visiting **www.mypyramid.gov**. Let us look quickly at the components of the pyramid.

The food pyramid divides our nutritional needs into different food groups: the grain group; the vegetable group; the fruit group; the milk, yogurt, and cheese group; the meat, poultry, fish, dry bean, egg, and nut group; and the oil group. They also add physical activity to the pyramid. The following information is from the USDA Web site:

## The grain group:

Any food made from wheat, rice, oats, cornmeal, barley, or another cereal grain is a grain product. Bread, pasta, oatmeal, breakfast cereals, tortillas, and grits are examples of grain products.

Grains are divided into two subgroups: whole grains and refined grains.

Whole grains contain the entire grain kernel — the bran, germ, and endosperm. Examples include:

- Whole-wheat flour
- Bulgur (cracked wheat)
- Oatmeal
- Whole cornmeal
- Brown rice

Refined grains have been milled, which is a process that removes the bran and germ. This is done to give grains a finer texture and improve their shelf life, but it also removes dietary fiber, iron, and many B vitamins. Some examples of refined grain products are:

- White flour
- Degermed cornmeal
- White bread
- White rice

Most refined grains are *enriched*. This means certain B vitamins (e.g., thiamin, riboflavin, niacin, and folic acid) and iron are added back after processing. Fiber is not added back to enriched grains. Check the ingredient list on refined grain products to make sure that the word "enriched" is included in the grain name. Some food products are made from mixtures of whole grains and refined grains.

Some commonly eaten grain products are:

**Whole grains:**

- Brown rice
- Buckwheat
- Bulgur (cracked wheat)
- Oatmeal
- Popcorn
- Ready-to-eat breakfast cereals
- Whole-wheat cereal flakes
- Muesli
- Whole-grain barley
- Whole-grain cornmeal
- Whole rye
- Whole-wheat bread
- Whole-wheat crackers
- Whole-wheat pasta
- Whole-wheat sandwich buns and rolls
- Whole-wheat tortillas
- Wild rice

**Less common whole grains:**

- Amaranth
- Millet
- Quinoa
- Sorghum
- Triticale

**Refined grains:**

- Cornbread
- Corn tortillas
- Couscous
- Crackers
- Flour tortillas
- Grits

**Pasta:**

- Spaghetti
- Macaroni

**Ready-to-eat breakfast cereals:**

- Corn flakes

**Others:**

- Pitas
- White rice

- Pretzels
- White bread

- White sandwich buns and rolls

## Tips to help you eat whole grains:

**At meals:**

- To eat more whole grains, substitute a whole-grain product for a refined product — such as eating whole-wheat bread instead of white bread, or brown rice instead of white rice. It is important to *substitute* the whole-grain product for the refined one, rather than *adding* the whole-grain product.

- For a change, try brown rice or whole-wheat pasta. Try brown rice stuffing in baked green peppers or tomatoes, and whole-wheat macaroni in macaroni and cheese.

- Use whole grains in mixed dishes, such as barley in vegetable soups or stews, and bulgur wheat in casserole or stir-fries.

- Create a whole-grain pilaf with a mixture of barley, wild rice, brown rice, broth, and spices. For a special touch, stir in toasted nuts or chopped dried fruit.

- Experiment by substituting whole-wheat or oat flour for up to half of the flour in pancake, waffle, muffin, or other flour-based recipes. They may need a bit more leavening.

- Use whole-grain bread or cracker crumbs in meatloaf.

- Try rolled oats or a crushed, unsweetened whole-grain cereal as breading for baked chicken, fish, veal cutlets, or eggplant Parmesan.

- Try an unsweetened, whole-grain, ready-to-eat cereal instead of croutons in salad, or in place of crackers with soup.

- Freeze leftover cooked brown rice, bulgur, or barley. Heat and serve it later as a quick side dish.

**As snacks:**

- Snack on ready-to-eat, whole-grain cereals, such as toasted oat cereal.

- Add whole-grain flour or oatmeal when making cookies or other baked treats.

- Try a whole-grain snack chip, such as baked tortilla chips.

- Popcorn, a whole grain, can be a healthy snack with little or no added salt or butter.

## What to look for on the food label:

- Choose foods that name one of the following whole-grain ingredients first on the label's ingredient list: brown rice, bulgur, graham flour, oatmeal, whole-grain corn, whole oats, whole wheat, whole rye, or wild rice.

- Foods labeled with the words "multi-grain," "stone-ground," "100% wheat," "cracked wheat," "seven-grain," or "bran" are not always whole-grain products.

- Color is not an indication of a whole grain. Bread can be brown because of molasses or other added ingredients. Read the ingredient list to see whether it is a whole grain.

- Use the nutrition facts label and choose products with a higher percentage daily value (%DV) for fiber — the %DV for fiber is a good clue to the amount of whole grain in the product.

- Read the food label's ingredient list. Look for terms that indicate added sugars (sucrose, high-fructose corn syrup, honey, and molasses) and oils (partially hydrogenated vegetable oils) that add extra calories. Choose foods with fewer added sugars, fats, or oils.

- Most sodium in the food supply comes from packaged foods. Similar packaged foods can vary widely in sodium content, including breads. Use the nutrition facts label to choose foods with a lower %DV for sodium. Foods with less than 140 mg sodium per serving can be labeled as low-sodium foods. Claims such as "low in sodium" or "very low in sodium" on the front of the food label can help you identify foods that contain less salt (or sodium).

## The vegetable group:

Any vegetable or 100-percent vegetable juice counts as a member of the vegetable group. Vegetables may be raw, cooked, fresh, frozen, canned, or dried/dehydrated, and may be whole, cut up, or mashed.

Vegetables are organized into five subgroups, based on their nutrient content. Some commonly eaten vegetables in each subgroup are:

### Dark green vegetables:

- Bok choy
- Broccoli
- Collard greens
- Dark green leafy lettuce
- Kale
- Mustard greens
- Romaine lettuce
- Spinach
- Turnip greens
- Watercress

- Mesclun

**Orange vegetables:**

- Acorn squash
- Butternut squash
- Carrots
- Hubbard squash
- Pumpkin
- Sweet potatoes

**Dry beans and peas:**

- Black beans
- Black-eyed peas
- Garbanzo beans (chickpeas)
- Kidney beans
- Lentils
- Lima beans (mature)
- Navy beans
- Pinto beans
- Soybeans
- Split peas
- Tofu (bean curd made from soybeans)
- White beans

**Starchy vegetables:**

- Corn
- Green peas
- Lima beans (green)
- Potatoes

**Other vegetables:**

- Artichokes
- Asparagus
- Bean sprouts
- Beets
- Brussels sprouts
- Cabbage
- Cauliflower
- Celery
- Cucumbers
- Eggplant
- Iceberg (head) lettuce
- Mushrooms
- Okra
- Onions
- Parsnips
- Tomatoes
- Tomato juice
- Vegetable juice
- Turnips
- Wax beans

- Green beans
- Green or red peppers

- Zucchini

## Tips to help you eat vegetables:

### In general:

- Buy fresh vegetables in-season. They cost less and are likely to be at their peak flavor.

- Stock up on frozen vegetables for quick, easy cooking in the microwave.

- Buy vegetables that are easy to prepare. Pick up prewashed bags of salad greens, and add baby carrots or grape tomatoes for a salad in minutes. Buy packages of veggies, such as baby carrots or celery sticks, for quick snacks.

- Use a microwave to quickly "zap" vegetables. White or sweet potatoes can be baked quickly this way.

- Vary your veggie choices to keep meals interesting.

- Try crunchy vegetables raw or lightly steamed.

### For the best nutritional value:

- Select vegetables with more potassium, such as sweet potatoes, white potatoes, white beans, tomato products (paste, sauce, and juice), beet greens, soybeans, lima beans, winter squash, spinach, lentils, kidney beans, and split peas.

- Sauces or seasonings can add calories, fat, and sodium to vegetables. Use the nutrition facts label to compare the calories and %DV for fat and sodium in plain and seasoned vegetables.

- Prepare more foods from fresh ingredients to lower sodium intake. Most sodium in the food supply comes from packaged or processed foods.

- Buy canned vegetables labeled "no salt added." If you want to add a little salt, it will likely be less than the amount in the regular canned product.

## At meals:

- Plan some meals around a vegetable main dish, such as a vegetable stir fry or soup. Add other foods to complement it.

- Try a main-dish salad for lunch. Go light on the salad dressing.

- Include a green salad with your dinner every night.

- Shred carrots or zucchini into meatloaf, casseroles, quick breads, and muffins.

- Include chopped vegetables in pasta sauce or lasagna.

- Order a veggie pizza with toppings like mushrooms, green peppers, and onions, and ask for extra veggies.

- Use pureed, cooked vegetables, such as potatoes, to thicken stews, soups, and gravies. These add flavor, nutrients, and texture.

- Grill vegetable kabobs as part of a barbecue meal. Try tomatoes, mushrooms, green peppers, and onions.

**Make vegetables more appealing:**

- Many vegetables taste good with a dip or dressing. Try a low-fat salad dressing with raw broccoli, red and green peppers, celery sticks, or cauliflower.

- Add color to salads by adding baby carrots, shredded red cabbage, or spinach leaves. Include in-season vegetables for variety through the year.

- Include cooked dry beans or peas in flavorful mixed dishes, such as chili or minestrone soup.

- Decorate plates or serving dishes with vegetable slices.

- Keep a bowl of cut-up vegetables in a see-through container in the refrigerator. Carrot and celery sticks are traditional, but consider broccoli florets, cucumber slices, or red or green pepper strips.

## The fruit group:

Any fruit or 100-percent fruit juice counts as part of the fruit group. Fruits may be fresh, canned, frozen, or dried, and may be whole, cut up, or pureed. Some commonly eaten fruits are:

- Apples
- Apricots

- Avocado
- Bananas

**Berries:**

- Strawberries
- Blueberries

- Raspberries
- Cherries

**Melons:**

- Cantaloupe

- Watermelon

- Honeydew

**Mixed fruits:**

- Fruit cocktail

**100-percent fruit juice:**

- Orange
- Apple
- Grape
- Grapefruit

**Others:**

- Grapefruit
- Kiwi fruit
- Lemons
- Limes
- Mangoes
- Nectarines
- Oranges
- Peaches
- Grapes
- Pears
- Papaya
- Pineapple
- Plums
- Prunes
- Raisins
- Tangerines

## Tips to help you eat fruits:

### In general:

- Keep a bowl of whole fruit on the table or counter, or in the refrigerator.

- Refrigerate cut-up fruit to store for later.

- Buy fresh fruits in season when they may be less expensive and at their peak flavor.

- Buy fruits that are dried, frozen, and canned, as well as fresh, so that you always have a supply on hand.

- Consider convenience when shopping. Buy pre-cut packages of fruit (such as melon or pineapple chunks) for a healthy snack in seconds. Choose packaged fruits that do not have added sugars.

**For the best nutritional value:**

- Make the most of your choices with whole or cut-up fruit rather than juice, for the benefits that dietary fiber provides.

- Select fruits with more potassium, such as bananas; prunes and prune juice; dried peaches and apricots; cantaloupe; honeydew melon; and orange juice.

- When choosing canned fruits, select fruit canned in 100-percent fruit juice or water, rather than syrup.

- Vary your fruit choices. Fruits differ in nutrient content.

**At meals:**

- At breakfast, top your cereal with bananas or peaches; add blueberries to pancakes; drink 100-percent orange or grapefruit juice; or try a fruit mixed with low-fat or fat-free yogurt.

- At lunch, pack a tangerine, banana, or grapes to eat, or choose fruits from a salad bar. Individual containers of fruits, like peaches or applesauce, are easy and convenient.

- At dinner, add crushed pineapple to coleslaw, or include mandarin oranges or grapes in a tossed salad.

- Make a Waldorf salad, with apples, celery, walnuts, and dressing.

- Try meat dishes that incorporate fruit, such as chicken with apricots or mango chutney.

- Add fruit like pineapple or peaches to kabobs as part of a barbecue meal.

- For dessert, have baked apples, pears, or a fruit salad.

**As snacks:**

- Cut-up fruit makes a good snack. Cut them yourself or buy pre-cut packages of fruit pieces, like pineapple or melon. Also try whole, fresh berries or grapes.

- Dried fruits also make a good snack. They are easy to carry and store well. Because they are dried, ¼ cup is equivalent to ½ cup of other fruits.

- Keep a package of dried fruit in your desk or handbag. Some fruits that are available dried include apricots, apples, pineapple, bananas, cherries, figs, dates, cranberries, blueberries, prunes (dried plums), and raisins (dried grapes).

- As a snack, spread peanut butter on apple slices, or top frozen yogurt with berries or slices of kiwi fruit.

- Frozen juice bars (100-percent juice) make healthy alternatives to high-fat snacks.

**Make fruit more appealing:**

- Many fruits taste good with a dip or dressing. Try low-fat yogurt or pudding as a dip for fruits like strawberries or melons.

- Make a fruit smoothie by blending fat-free or low-fat milk or yogurt with fresh or frozen fruit. Try bananas, peaches, strawberries, or other berries.

- Try applesauce as a fat-free substitute for some of the oil when baking cakes.

- Try different textures of fruits. For example, apples are crunchy, bananas are smooth and creamy, and oranges are juicy.

- For fresh fruit salads, mix apples, bananas, or pears with acidic fruits, like oranges, pineapple, or lemon juice to keep them from turning brown.

## The milk, yogurt, and cheese group:

All fluid milk products, and many foods made from milk, are considered part of this food group. Foods made from milk that retain their calcium content are part of the group, while foods made from milk that have little to no calcium, such as cream cheese, cream, and butter, are not. Most milk group choices should be fat-free or low-fat.

Some commonly eaten choices in the milk, yogurt, and cheese group are:

**Milk:**

- All fluid milk
- Fat-free (skim)
- Low-fat (1 percent)
- Reduced-fat (2 percent)
- Whole

**Flavored milks:**

- Chocolate
- Strawberry

**Milk-based desserts:**

- Puddings made with milk
- Ice milk
- Frozen yogurt
- Ice cream

**Others:**

- Lactose-reduced milks
- Lactose-free milks

**Cheese:**

**Hard, natural cheeses:**

- Cheddar
- Mozzarella
- Swiss
- Parmesan

**Soft cheeses:**

- Ricotta
- Cottage cheese

**Processed cheeses:**

- American

**Yogurt:**

- Fat-free
- Low-fat
- Reduced-fat
- Whole-milk

**Selection tips:**

Choose fat-free or low-fat milk, yogurt, and cheese. When choosing milk or yogurt that is not fat-free, or cheese that is not low-fat, the fat in the product counts as part of the discretionary calorie allowance.

If sweetened milk products are chosen (e.g., flavored milk, yogurt, drinkable yogurt, or desserts), the added sugars also count as part of the discretionary calorie allowance.

**Tips for making wise choices:**

- Include milk as a beverage at meals. Choose fat-free or low-fat milk.

- If you usually drink whole milk, switch gradually to fat-free milk to lower saturated fat and calories. Try reduced fat (2 percent), then low-fat (1 percent), and finally, fat-free (skim).

- If you drink cappuccinos or lattes, ask for them with fat-free (skim) milk.

- Add fat-free or low-fat milk instead of water to oatmeal and hot cereals.

- Use fat-free or low-fat milk when making condensed cream soups (such as cream of tomato).

- Have fat-free or low-fat yogurt as a snack.

- Make a dip for fruits or vegetables from yogurt.

- Make fruit-yogurt smoothies in the blender.

- For dessert, make chocolate or butterscotch pudding with fat-free or low-fat milk.

- Top cut-up fruit with flavored yogurt for a quick dessert.

- Top casseroles, soups, stews, or vegetables with shredded low-fat cheese.

- Top a baked potato with fat-free or low-fat yogurt.

**Keep milk safe to consume:**

- Avoid raw (unpasteurized) milk or any products made from unpasteurized milk.

- Chill (refrigerate) perishable foods promptly, and defrost foods properly. Refrigerate or freeze perishables, prepared foods, and leftovers as soon as possible. If food has been left at temperatures between 40° and 140° F for more than two hours, discard it, even though it may look and smell good.

- Separate raw, cooked, and ready-to-eat foods.

**For those who choose not to consume milk products:**

If you avoid milk because of lactose intolerance, the most reliable way to get the health benefits of milk is to choose lactose-free alternatives within the milk group, such as cheese, yogurt, or lactose-free milk, or to consume the enzyme lactase before consuming milk products.

Calcium sources for those who do not consume milk products include:

- Calcium-fortified juices, cereals, breads, soy beverages, or rice beverages

- Canned fish (e.g., sardines and salmon with bones)

- Soybeans, and other soy products (e.g., soy-based beverages, soy yogurt, and tempeh), and some other dried beans

- Some leafy greens (e.g., collard and turnip greens, kale, and bok choy)

The amount of calcium that can be absorbed from these foods varies.

## The meat, poultry, fish, dry beans, eggs, and nuts group:

All foods made from meat, poultry, fish, dried beans or peas, eggs, nuts, and seeds are considered part of this group. Dried beans and peas are part of both this group and the vegetable group.

Most meat and poultry choices should be lean or low-fat. Fish, nuts, and seeds contain healthy oils, so choose these foods frequently instead of meat or poultry.

Some commonly eaten choices in the meat and beans group, followed by selection tips, are:

**Lean cuts of:**

- Beef
- Ham
- Lamb
- Pork
- Veal

**Game meats:**

- Bison
- Rabbit
- Venison

**Lean ground meats:**

- Beef
- Pork
- Lamb

**Organ meats:**

- Liver
- Giblets

**Poultry:**

- Chicken
- Duck
- Goose
- Turkey
- Ground chicken and turkey

**Eggs:**

- Chicken eggs
- Duck eggs

**Dried beans and peas:**

- Black beans
- Black-eyed peas
- Chickpeas (garbanzo beans)
- Falafel
- Kidney beans
- Lentils
- Lima beans (mature)
- Navy beans
- Pinto beans
- Soy beans
- Split peas
- Tofu (bean curd made from soy beans)
- White beans

**Bean burgers:**

- Soy-based burgers
- Veggie burgers

**Other protein:**

- Tempeh
- Texturized vegetable protein (TVP)

**Nuts and seeds:**

- Almonds
- Cashews
- Hazelnuts (filberts)
- Mixed nuts
- Pumpkin seeds
- Sesame seeds
- Peanuts
- Peanut butter
- Pecans
- Pistachios
- Sunflower seeds
- Walnuts

**Finfish:**

- Catfish
- Cod
- Porgy
- Salmon

- Flounder
- Haddock
- Halibut
- Herring
- Mackerel
- Pollock
- Sea bass
- Snapper
- Swordfish
- Trout
- Tuna

**Shellfish:**

- Clams
- Crab
- Crayfish
- Lobster
- Mussels
- Octopus
- Oysters
- Scallops
- Squid (calamari)
- Shrimp

**Canned fish:**

- Anchovies
- Clams
- Tuna
- Sardines

**Selection tips:**

- Choose lean or low-fat meat and poultry. If higher fat choices are made, such as regular ground beef (75 to 80 percent lean) or chicken with skin, the fat in the product counts as part of the discretionary calorie allowance.

- If solid fat is added in cooking, such as frying chicken in shortening or frying eggs in butter or stick margarine, this also counts as part of the discretionary calorie allowance.

- Select fish rich in omega-3 fatty acids, such as salmon, trout, and herring, more often.

- Liver and other organ meats are high in cholesterol. Egg yolks are also high in cholesterol, but egg whites are cholesterol-free.

- Processed meats, such as ham, sausage, frankfurters, and luncheon or deli meats, have added sodium. Check the ingredient and nutrition facts label to help limit sodium intake.

- Fresh chicken, turkey, and pork that have been enhanced with a salt-containing solution also have added sodium. Check the product label for statements such as "self-basting" or "contains up to __% of __," which mean that a sodium-containing solution has been added to the product.

- Sunflower seeds, almonds, and hazelnuts (filberts) are the richest sources of vitamin E in this food group. To help meet vitamin E recommendations, make these your nut and seed choices more often.

Tips to help you make wise choices from the meat and beans group:

**Go lean with protein:**

→ The leanest beef cuts include round steaks and roasts (i.e., round eye, top round, bottom round, or round tip), top loin, top sirloin, and chuck shoulder and arm roasts.

→ The leanest pork choices include pork loin, tenderloin, center loin, and ham.

→ Choose extra lean ground beef. The label should say it is at least 90 percent lean. You may be able to find ground beef that is 93 or 95 percent lean.

→ Buy skinless chicken parts, or take off the skin before cooking.

→ Boneless, skinless chicken breasts and turkey cutlets are the leanest poultry choices.

→ Choose lean turkey, roast beef, or ham, or low-fat luncheon meats for sandwiches instead of luncheon meats with more fat, such as regular bologna or salami.

→ Trim away all the visible fat from meats and poultry before cooking.

→ Broil, grill, roast, poach, or boil meat, poultry, or fish instead of frying.

→ Drain off any fat that appears during cooking.

→ Skip or limit the breading on meat, poultry, or fish. Breading adds fat and calories. It will also cause the food to soak up more fat during frying.

→ Prepare dry beans and peas without added fats.

→ Choose and prepare foods without high-fat sauces or gravies.

**Vary your protein choices:**

• Choose fish more often for lunch or dinner. Look for fish rich in omega-3 fatty acids, such as salmon, trout, and herring. Some ideas are:

→ Salmon steak or fillet

→ Salmon loaf

→ Grilled or baked trout

- Choose beans or peas as a main dish or part of a meal often. Some choices are:

  → Chili with kidney or pinto beans

  → Stir-fried tofu

  → Split pea, lentil, minestrone, or white bean soups

  → Baked beans

  → Black bean enchiladas

  → Garbanzo or kidney beans on a chef's salad

  → Rice and beans

  → Veggie burgers or soy burgers

  → Hummus (chickpeas) spread on pita bread

- Choose nuts as a snack, on salads, or in main dishes. Use nuts to replace meat or poultry, not in addition to them.

  → Use pine nuts in pesto sauce for pasta.

  → Add slivered almonds to steamed vegetables.

  → Add toasted peanuts or cashews to a vegetable stir fry instead of meat.

  → Sprinkle a few nuts on top of low-fat ice cream or frozen yogurt.

→ Add walnuts or pecans to a green salad instead of cheese or meat.

**Reading the food label:**

- Check the nutrition facts label for the saturated fat, trans fat, cholesterol, and sodium content of packaged foods.

  → Processed meats, such as hams, sausages, frankfurters, and luncheon or deli meats, have added sodium. Check the ingredient and nutrition facts label to help limit sodium intake.

  → Fresh chicken, turkey, and pork that have been enhanced with a salt-containing solution also have added sodium. Check the product label for statements such as "self-basting" or "contains up to __% of __."

  → Lower-fat versions of many processed meats are available. Look on the nutrition facts label to choose products with less fat and saturated fat.

**Keep it safe to eat:**

- Separate raw, cooked, and ready-to-eat foods.

- Wash cutting boards, knives, utensils, and countertops in hot, soapy water after preparing each food item and before going on to the next one.

- Store raw meat, poultry, and seafood on the bottom shelf of the refrigerator so juices do not drip onto other foods.

- Cook foods to a safe temperature to kill microorganisms. Use a meat thermometer, which measures the internal temperature of cooked meat and poultry, to make sure that the meat is cooked all the way through.

- Chill (refrigerate) perishable food promptly, and defrost foods properly. Refrigerate or freeze perishables, prepared foods, and leftovers within two hours.

- Plan ahead to defrost foods. Never defrost food on the kitchen counter at room temperature. Thaw food by placing it in the refrigerator, submerging air-tight packaged food in cool running tap water, or defrosting on a plate in the microwave.

- Avoid raw or partially cooked eggs, or foods containing raw eggs and raw or undercooked meat and poultry.

- Women who may become pregnant, pregnant women, nursing mothers, and young children should avoid some types of fish and eat types lower in mercury. Call 1-888-SAFEFOOD for more information.

## The oils group:

Oils are fats that are liquid at room temperature, like the vegetable oils used in cooking. Oils come from many different plants and from fish. Some common oils are:

- Canola oil
- Corn oil
- Cottonseed oil
- Olive oil
- Safflower oil
- Soybean oil
- Sunflower oil

Some oils are used mainly as flavorings, such as walnut oil and sesame oil. A number of foods are naturally high in oils, like:

- Nuts
- Olives
- Some fish
- Avocados

Foods that are mainly oil include mayonnaise, certain salad dressings, and soft (tub or squeeze) margarine with no trans fats. Check the nutrition facts label to find margarines with 0 grams of trans fat.

Most oils are high in monounsaturated or polyunsaturated fats, and low in saturated fats. Oils from plant sources (vegetable and nut oils) do not contain any cholesterol. In fact, no foods from plants sources contain cholesterol.

A few plant oils, however, including coconut oil and palm kernel oil, are high in saturated fats and, for nutritional purposes, should be considered to be solid fats.

Solid fats are fats that are solid at room temperature, like butter and shortening. Solid fats come from many animal foods and can be made from vegetable oils through a process called hydrogenation. Some common solid fats are:

- Butter
- Beef fat (tallow, suet)
- Chicken fat
- Pork fat (lard)
- Stick margarine
- Shortening

## Discretionary calories:

You need a certain number of calories to keep your body functioning and to provide energy for physical activities. Think of the calories you need for energy as money you have to spend. Each person has a total calorie budget. This budget can be divided into essentials and extras.

With a financial budget, the essentials are items like rent and food; the extras are things like movies and vacations. In a calorie budget, the essentials are the minimum calories required to meet your nutrient needs. By selecting the lowest fat and no-sugar-added forms of foods in each food group, you make the best nutrient buys. Depending on the foods you choose, you may be able to spend more calories than the amount required to meet your nutrient needs. These calories are the extras that can be used on luxuries, like solid fats, added sugars, and alcohol, or on more food from any food group. They are your discretionary calories.

Each person has an allowance for some discretionary calories, but many people have used up this allowance before lunchtime. Most discretionary calorie allowances are small, between 100 and 300 calories, especially for those who are not physically active. For many people, the discretionary calorie allowance is used by the foods they choose in each food group, such as higher fat meats, cheeses, whole milk, or sweetened bakery products.

You can use your discretionary calorie allowance to:

- Eat more foods from any food group than the food guide recommends.

- Eat higher calorie forms of foods — those that contain solid fats or added sugars. Examples are whole milk, cheese, sausage, biscuits, sweetened cereal, and sweetened yogurt.

- Add fats or sweeteners to foods. Examples are sauces, salad dressings, sugar, syrup, and butter.

- Eat or drink items that are mostly fats or caloric sweeteners, such as candy and soda.

For example, assume your calorie budget is 2,000 calories per day. Of these calories, you need to spend at least 1,735 for essential nutrients, if you choose foods without added fat and sugar. This would mean you have 265 discretionary calories left. You may use these on "luxury" versions of the foods in each group, such as higher-fat meat or sweetened cereal. Or, you can spend them on sweets, sauces, or beverages. Many people overspend their discretionary calorie allowance, choosing more added fats and sugars than their budget allows.

## Physical activity:

Physical activity simply means movement of the body that uses energy. Walking, gardening, briskly pushing a baby stroller, climbing the stairs, playing soccer, or dancing the night away are all good examples of being active. For health benefits, physical activity should be moderate or vigorous, and add up to at least 30 minutes a day.

**Moderate physical activities include:**

- Walking briskly (about 3½ miles per hour)
- Hiking
- Gardening/doing yard work
- Dancing
- Golf (walking and carrying clubs)
- Bicycling (less than 10 miles per hour)
- Weight training (general light workout)

**Vigorous physical activities include:**

- Running/jogging (5 miles per hour)
- Bicycling (more than 10 miles per hour)
- Swimming (freestyle laps)
- Aerobics
- Walking fast (4½ miles per hour)
- Heavy yard work, such as chopping wood
- Weight lifting (vigorous effort)
- Basketball (competitive)

Some physical activities are not intense enough to help you meet the recommendations. Although you are moving, these activities do not increase your heart rate, so you should not count these toward the 30 or more minutes a day that you should strive for. These include walking at a casual pace, such as while grocery shopping, and doing light household chores.

## Pyramid primer:

The USDA MyPyramid Web site is incredibly easy to use. When you input your information, you get recommendations such as these:

*Each day, you should eat the following and have 60 minutes of moderate to vigorous exercise:*

- *6 ounces of grains*
- *2.5 cups of vegetables*
- *2 cups of fruit*
- *3 cups of milk*
- *5.5 ounces of meat and beans*
- *6 teaspoons of oil*

Your recommendations will be tailored just for you. It does not get much simpler than that. Write down or print off your list, and keep it with you until you memorize it. If you prefer, the Web site has worksheets to make it even more fun. If you are extremely nutrition-focused, you can add every single thing you eat into an online journal, and the worksheets will show you your exact nutrients for the day. You can do the same with journaling your exercise; it is all up to you. At a minimum, find out what your basic recommendations are, and follow them daily.

## Calculating Your Needs

A calorie is the amount of heat needed to raise the temperature of one kilogram of water by 1 degree Celsius. We burn calories 24 hours a day. The amount we burn at rest is called our *basal metabolic rate*. That is added to the amount of calories we expend during activity to compute the amount our bodies need each day. To stay the same weight, eat exactly the number of calories your body needs; to lose weight, eat fewer; and, to gain weight, eat more. We must eat 3,500 calories fewer than our bodies need to lose one pound of weight. If your body needs 2,000 calories per day to sustain you and you eat 1,500 calories each day, you will lose one pound per week. That said, in reality, you must also keep up your metabolism, or your body will adjust to the new diet and quit burning the fat. See Chapter 12 for plenty of fun ways to keep your metabolism revved up.

Follow the instructions to determine your caloric needs from the USDA MyPyramid Web site, or you can use the following:

1. Multiply your current weight by 10. If you are sedentary, multiply that figure by .9. If you are moderately active,

keep that figure. If you are extremely active, multiply that figure by 1.25.

Example: You weigh 180 pounds. 180 x 10 = 1,800. You are sedentary. 1,800 x .9 = 1,620. You should consume approximately 1,620 calories per day to maintain your weight.

2. Next, you may wish to look at what you should ideally weigh. This Web site will show you what you should weigh for your height, weight, and age: **www.halls.md/ ideal-weight/body.htm.**

Most Americans weigh far more than their ideal weight. You must take your bone structure into consideration, and if the guideline shows you to be overweight when you feel you are not, ask your primary care provider for their guidance. If you are not the weight you wish to be, decide how many pounds you wish to lose, and use the following method:

Example: You are a female who weighs 180 pounds. You wish to weigh 123 pounds. You are sedentary. As we noted earlier, you need to consume 1,620 calories per day to maintain your current weight. You need to become more active, having 30 to 60 minutes per day of moderate to intense physical activity. At that point, you would need to consume 1,800 calories to maintain your weight. You should try to lose one pound per week. To lose one pound per week, you need to consume 3,500 calories fewer per week than your body needs. So, you need to eat 500 calories fewer per day than you need. 1,800 − 500 = 1,300 calories.

Up your activity level and decrease your calories, and you should be able to lose one pound per week. You should reach your desired weight in 57 weeks — just over one year. An exception to this rule is that you should never go below 1,200 calories per day without a physician's advice. Most people need at least that many calories to get all their essential nutrients and be healthy. Ignore fad diets that suggest otherwise.

## How Many Calories You Currently Eat

If you are curious how many calories you currently eat, fill in the food journal available at the USDA MyPyramid Web site, or look up the calories you eat each day online. Do this for at least three days and average the amounts to get a rough idea of your current daily consumption. See how your results compare to what you should be consuming. If you are on track, good. If you are not, follow the guidelines discussed throughout this book to reach your healthy weight.

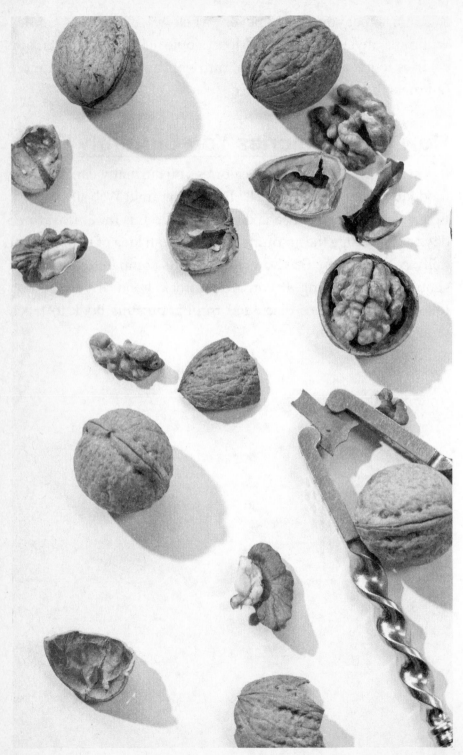

# CHAPTER 2

## Evaluate Your Surroundings

**W**e will now look at the availability of cooking appliances, the college cafeteria, grocery stores, restaurants, and more.

## The Dorm or Apartment Kitchen

Now is the time to look around your kitchen. See whether you have a dedicated kitchen sink, a refrigerator, a freezer compartment, a stove, a microwave, cabinets or shelves, and counter space. The more of these you have, of course, the more cooking you can do for yourself. It is also important to know the facility rules for your living arrangement. If you do not know, find out whether you can have a hot plate (if needed) and a small indoor grilling machine.

## College Cafeteria

We will talk more thoroughly about the cafeteria later, but for now, you need to make a simple evaluation. Is the food available to you through the cafeteria basically healthy or unhealthy? Are good choices available all day long? Is it open for three meals a day, or early morning until late night? Is it open all weekend? These answers will help you determine how often you wish to cook for yourself.

# Grocery Stores

What mode of transportation do you have? If you have an automobile, shopping will be fairly simple. If you use public transportation, ride a bicycle, or walk, you will need to get precise about the location of the stores and where you can feasibly travel to each week. You will naturally be limited in the number of groceries you can carry as well.

## Convenience stores

Convenience stores are traditionally poor choices for buying groceries because they generally charge much more for items and do not have as many healthy choices, such as fresh fruits and vegetables. Do not fall into the trap of shopping at them on a regular basis because they are closer or open during certain hours. Plan your trips and go to a traditional, discount, or bulk grocery store instead.

## Traditional stores

Traditional grocery stores are perfect places to buy your weekly groceries. Find out where the stores are located around you, and go with the closest proximity, unless one has significantly lower prices. Your parents will generally know which stores have the most economical prices.

## Discount stores

These are frequently small grocery stores with good prices, limited produce, and all-generic products. They can be an excellent place to buy eggs, milk, bread, coffee, soup, and many other basic items. Experimentation will tell whether you like each item they offer as well as a name-brand item. The paper products are frequently inferior. Many of the food items, such as pies, biscuits, and so on, may be made with trans fat and may not be healthy options. The cereals may not be whole grain. If you shop at these stores, you may need to make a second stop at a produce market or a traditional store to buy more fruits and vegetables.

## Bulk stores

Whether you should shop at bulk stores depends on several factors, such as whether you have a car to get the large items home and the space to store large quantities. If you have both, you still need to be careful that the prices are indeed lower. It is probably not the time to join a club you have to pay to purchase items at. Only buy bulk items that will not go bad in six months or so, such as toilet tissue, paper towels, cleaners, canned goods, and some boxed items.

# Local Restaurants and Takeout

You need to determine which restaurants are available to you given your transportation constraints. Is takeout available? Do they charge for delivery? Can you order takeout with friends or roommates? Do these restaurants have healthy menu options that you like?

# Must-Have Comfort Foods

No look at your food needs is complete without considering your comfort foods. Do you love Chinese buffets? Is life incomplete without a Friday-night pizza? Are you unable to watch a Saturday ball game without barbecue? Do you need chicken and dumplings after a horrible day? You must put these necessary items into your food budget to help you adjust to the changes of college life, and possibly, being away from home for the first time. You must keep some consistencies at times of change, and this is a fairly simple one to maintain.

# How Much You Can Spend

Determine how much money you can spend on food each week. The following is an example of a proper food budget:

Jesse has $100 a week to spend on food. After thorough evaluation, he decides to buy lunch Monday through Friday in the cafeteria ($4 a day), have a must-have Chinese buffet on Sunday afternoon ($7), and divide the remainder of his funds ($73) by spending $50 at the grocery store and $23 at restaurants, vending machines, and on similar treats.

Compile a similar budget for yourself, mainly so that you will know how much money you wish to spend at the grocery store. Do not forget to budget for cleaning products, such as cleansers and detergent, and paper items, garbage bags, and anything else you might need. Maintaining a stock of these items should not exceed $5 per week once you have bought everything for the first time.

# CHAPTER 3

## Obtaining Basic Supplies

It is time to stock your own kitchen. If you possibly can, it is an excellent idea to take a chef along, such as Mom or Dad. They know the foods you like and also have experience in what will and will not hold up for years. By all means, take along a list of what you plan to purchase, and have a rough idea of what you want to pay for each item.

## Stocking Your Kitchen

### Microwave oven

This is almost a necessity. It heats almost any kind of item, including frozen dinners, with ease. A small one is usually fine, but try to avoid the miniature ones that are too small to hold a frozen dinner. An inner carousel is a nice addition, as the food will cook more evenly. You do not need one with many buttons and choices. If it has at least two speeds — medium and high — it should be fine. A microwave that only functions on high is much better than nothing, also. Do not buy these used, and if you get one from family or friends, purchase a safety checker to make sure that it is not leaking radiation. A microwave should never have dings or other signs that it has been dropped or abused.

Place the microwave where the vents are not obstructed, clean it inside with a damp cloth only, and never run it with foil or metal inside. Keep the area around the door clean so that the door can shut completely. It is best not to leave the vicinity of the microwave while it is running. Occasionally, the microwave may trip a circuit breaker, and you will need to learn what to do if this happens.

## Hot plate

If you do not have a stove, you may need a hot plate. It functions as a one-eye burner and can be used with a saucepan to heat or cook small quantities. Buy it new, and make sure the cord is the appropriate length for where you intend to place it.

## George Foreman® grill

These items are handy for cooking one or two pieces of steak, chicken, hamburger, or fish, and small quantities of vegetables. Once again, you may not need the most deluxe model. A basic one that will hold two pieces of chicken should suffice. You will want to make sure you have cooking oil spray to coat it each time you use it.

## Crock-Pot® slow cooker

You may wish to purchase a small or medium-size slow cooker if you love homemade soups, roasts, stews, or chili. They cook food slowly, often overnight, and are simple to use. These are especially fun to use in the cold months.

## Blender

Many home cooks function quite well without a blender, but if you plan to make many juices or smoothies, you will probably want to purchase a small blender. Some of them have food processor qualities, such as chopping, which can be handy (although unnecessary). This may be something you request as a gift.

## Mixer

Whether you need a mixer depends on how much dessert baking you intend to do. Cake batter mixed with a mixer, instead of by hand, produces better cakes. It is almost a requirement for beating egg whites for meringue. They are also handy for mixing mashed potatoes and other mashed fruits and vegetables. They are inexpensive and take up less space than most of the other appliances. Always be safe and unplug them immediately after use (and before removing the blades). Keep them away from water, and never get the blades near your fingers. If you purchase a mixer, make sure you have a bowl deep enough to use as a mixing bowl.

## Large appliances

Your room or apartment may come furnished with a stove (burner eyes and oven) and a refrigerator with freezer space. Clean and rinse these well before using them for the first time.

## Other appliances

You may wish to purchase a coffee maker, tea-maker, toaster oven, toaster, griddle, deep fryer, or hot-air popcorn popper, according to your tastes. You should only purchase these if you have the space and plan to use them at least once a week, as you can perform their functions with a traditional stove, if you have one.

## Cookware

A basic set of two saucepans with lids (one 1-quart and one 3-quart in size) plus two skillets (one 6-inch and one 9-inch) is perfect for one-person cooking. They can be stainless-steel or non-stick. If you purchase non-stick, be careful not to overheat them or leave them on a hot stove eye without food in them. You will need two mixing bowls and possibly a plate just for cooking. You will want a non-stick cookie sheet, a 9- by 13-inch pan, and a smaller round or square pan in glass or aluminum. An investment in glass is usually worthwhile. You will want a non-stick muffin pan for several of the recipes in this book. You may want a pie plate, depending on your personal tastes. Some people get by with aluminum-foil-type pans, but they do not hold up indefinitely and may not produce the best baking results. A wok is a nice investment, if you can afford it and like to eat Chinese dishes or other stir-fries. You may want to get a cutting board, although you can use your cooking plate, if necessary.

## Utensils

You will want a basic silverware set. They usually come in a set of eight, although you can probably get by with four. Included should be teaspoons, tablespoons, dinner forks, salad forks, and butter knives. You will also want a large metal spoon, a big plastic spoon, a small and large knife, and at least one plastic spatula. You may even want to purchase tongs and a special slotted metal spoon designed to get food out of a deep fryer. Do not forget a can opener, and a glass measuring cup is handy, too. Measuring spoons are nice, but not necessary.

## Spices and other essentials

Unless you hate any of them, you should purchase salt, pepper, cinnamon, parsley, minced garlic, garlic powder or salt, chili powder, and oregano. By all means, get any other spices you like, such as nutmeg, allspice, basil, rosemary, or paprika. It is a good idea to ask for a fresh spice rack as a gift, if you have the space.

This is also the time to buy a small bag of plain flour or self-rising flour (whole wheat is good, or regular, if you are not that brave yet), cornmeal, sugar, brown sugar, baking soda, oil (canola or corn are both good choices), non-stick cooking oil spray (not butter-flavor),  and a small container of olive oil. The cooking oil spray will be critical to many of the recipes you prepare.

## Plates, cups, and bowls

Think of how often you plan to entertain. If you will be cooking mostly for yourself, you will probably want to get at least four plates, four bowls, and four cups or glasses. These can frequently be purchased as an inexpensive matching set. The saucers that may come with the set are unnecessary, but can make good small plates for bread or a snack. If you purchase a set that comes with small teacups, consider whether you want to buy two tall glasses (glass or plastic). If time is a concern, but money is not, you may want to buy disposable paper or foam plates and cups. But keep in mind that this is not your most environmentally friendly option.

## Dishcloths, towels, and more

Purchase two thick potholders. You will want to own at least two dishcloths for cleaning up after cooking. Two towels are also handy to have, and you may want to purchase a sponge or two for quick cleanups. Many people prefer to use paper towels, as they are more sanitary. You may want to buy a package of napkins for entertaining or everyday use, and a bottle of dishwashing detergent is a must. Also consider buying a small box of plastic wrap and a box of aluminum foil. Foil bags can also be purchased for some of the recipes in this book, and Baggies® plastic bags of varying sizes are nice for leftovers or taking a lunch or snack with you. Buy plastic bags for the freezer if you plan to buy foods in quantity or freeze leftovers.

# The First Trip to the Grocery Store

## Purchasing the fundamentals

Carefully plan your first trip to the grocery store. Assuming you have purchased the spices and staples mentioned earlier, you can mainly focus on what you wish to eat the first week.

Consider your breakfast items first. Will you be eating breakfast from home seven days a week, five days a week, or only on the weekends? Some items to consider are frozen breakfasts, frozen waffles, whole-grain cereal, oatmeal (instant or regular), bread, biscuits (or bagels or muffins), and yogurt. Do you feel ambitious enough to try eggs, bacon, sausage, or hash browns? It may be best to wait a couple of weeks before getting too complicated. Make sure that you have enough breakfast items to last as many days as you plan to eat at home this week. Do not forget syrup for pancakes, and any other items you require.

Now, look at lunch. If you are eating lunch at home on the weekends only, do you want a sandwich, soup, or frozen dinner? Think through each item that you plan to eat, and what you will need to go with it. This will get easier as you gain experience in shopping.

Dinnertime can be the most creative and enjoyable experience. Many things you buy may last for two meals. Bags of frozen vegetables and fruits are excellent choices, and canned goods are an economical option as well.

### Fruits and vegetables

Buy some fresh fruit that you know you like to eat. Experimentation can come in a few weeks when you have the basics down pat. Only buy what you will eat at mealtime or snacktime for the week. Also, buy some fresh veggies for snacking or as an appetizer or a side dish to a meal. Keep it simple for now, such as carrot or celery sticks. Always having a tomato on hand is wise because it makes a nice addition to sandwiches, salads, omelets, and many other foods. Always make a point to purchase some fresh fruits and vegetables each week.

### Beverages

If you love coffee, buy a bag or container of instant. Do not forget sweetener and creamer, if you use them. Teabags are also nice to have on hand, for yourself or company. Consider whether you will want fruit or vegetable juices. Look into a purchase of milk, either a gallon or half-gallon, depending on how much you will be drinking at home. Skim milk is best, of course. You may want to buy a small container of buttermilk occasionally, which is often used in cooking and will last beyond a week. It would be a wise choice to avoid buying soda or diet soda, and drink them only on rare occasions at a restaurant. Buy bottled water if you do not wish to drink tap or filtered water.

### Condiments and other stuff

Now is the time to think of what you add to your food. Do you like mayonnaise, mustard, ketchup, salad dressing, or croutons?

Try to buy the fat-free or low-fat varieties in mayonnaise and salad dressing. You will want a small tub of the healthiest margarine you can find. Do you like pickles or olives? Consider what you may need for food that you bring home or order in. You may not think of everything the first week, but you can keep adding to your staples during future shopping trips.

When you go to the grocery store during subsequent visits, it will be easy to purchase the few things you have run out of, along with your menu items for the coming week.

Watch expiration dates, and make a point to purchase the freshest items possible. That often means reaching to the back of the shelf or getting the jug of milk at the back. Fresher food tends to equal more nutritious food.

## Reading food labels

The first things to notice on a food label are the serving size and number of servings per container. For most items, these may be fairly in proportion to the amount most people actually eat at one sitting. Yet some are notoriously deceptive. A can of condensed soup is a good example. The servings per container are typically two and a half, yet few people take two and a half meals to eat a can of soup. Small bags of potato chips can be deceiving as well. Make a point to decide how many "servings" you will be eating, and multiply the calories and nutrients accordingly.

Next are calories. If you plan to eat 1,500 calories per day, you may want to have 450 calories per meal and save 150 calories for snacks. A frozen dinner that is 450 calories is a good choice. If it is 375 calories, you may want to add a small salad. You will probably create a number over which you never go at one meal. For many people, it may be 1,000 calories; more than that can be hard on your body when it hits your bloodstream.

Look at the total fat and saturated fat percent daily value. Try to stay at or below 35 percent for these, as you should ideally consume 33 percent of your nutrients at each of three meals. If you find a snack that is 35 percent of your saturated fat for the day, it is probably not a good choice. Get in the habit of watching the sodium percents also. Do not forget to multiply the number by the actual number of servings you anticipate consuming at one sitting. If an item is more than 50 percent of your sodium allotment for the day, it probably should not be eaten.

Dietary fiber is important. You should be approaching near 100-percent of your fiber needs each day. Compare two loaves of bread, making sure that each label says that one slice of bread equals one serving. If one bread brand has 4 percent of your fiber for a slice, and the other has 8 percent per slice, you will naturally want to go with the higher fiber. While this may seem to take a long time, you will learn which brands you trust and will not have to do this every time you go to the store.

As far as the vitamins and minerals, these readings are mainly good for comparison. If you are comparing two cereals, for example, take a quick look at which one gives you more nutrition. This is one small consideration in your purchase. If you do not get enough calcium, you may want to prioritize finding good calcium sources.

Look at the ingredient list. See whether words like whole, vegetables, beans, or sugar are near the top. Use your common sense about what you want to put into your body. Avoid foods high in sugar, glucose, high fructose corn syrup, flour (other than whole-grain), animal fat, and shortening. Many people also try to avoid eating many artificial ingredients.

## Coupons and sales

Almost every grocery store has weekly sales. You need to learn on what day of the week sales begin for the stores you will be frequenting. Many begin their sale week on Wednesday. Most chain stores have discount cards, and you should get one if it is available. It is often the only way to purchase items at the sale price. Log on to the grocery store Web site, if available, as you are planning your weekly grocery list. Learn whether "buy one get one free" means you have to get two items, or whether you can get one item for half-price. This will vary by store. The buy-one-get-one-free deals are often the best deals you will find for the week. If you are flexible and buy many of the items that are on sale, you can have significant savings. Never buy an item just because it is on sale; it will simply go bad and be money wasted. Some grocery stores will double your coupons' value, up to a certain price. This may occur on certain days, or every day. If you use coupons frequently, you may want to ask about specific policies.

Your college years may not be the best time to find coupons. They frequently come in the mail or newspaper to suburban locations. You can, however, sign up at various Web sites to get magazines or other literature from food companies that will also send coupons. Many coupons are also available to print off the Internet, and you can join Web sites or clubs to gain access to coupons offering substantial savings. Search for coupon clubs for major food companies to find the best ones for you. Many people use a special e-mail address just to get coupons so that it does not interfere with their regular e-mail.

## How to eat on a tight budget

- **Use dollar menus at restaurants wisely.** Sandwiches for a dollar can be a bargain. Look for chicken, roast beef, and turkey sandwiches. Ask for no mayonnaise, and add mustard and ketchup if you like. Also, watch for chili and salad on a dollar menu. Avoid the burgers and fries, except for rare treats.

- **Watch for opportunities where food is served free.** Many organizations near campus offer free meals to students.

- **Eat an occasional mid-week lunch buffet.** This can be from your college cafeteria, a family restaurant, a chicken restaurant, or a Chinese restaurant, among others. Eat a variety of the foods you are not eating at home.

- **When considering grocery shopping, find out whether there is a discount grocery store near you, such as Save-A-Lot® or Aldi.** You may need to bring your own carryout bags to avoid extra fees. Look for the following:

  1. **Vegetables.** Seek out low-cost, fresh vegetables. Frozen boxes or bags of vegetables are good as well. Purchase varieties of canned goods for foods you cannot find fresh or frozen. Look at the store brand of vegetable juice, if you like it. Buy condensed vegetable soups, particularly vegetarian vegetable, if it is available. Canned tomatoes are especially healthy as well.

  2. **Fruits.** Try to have two fruits or cups of fruit juice for each day. An example would be to buy a half gallon of orange juice, two servings of grapes, two apples, and two small bananas. The next week, you might purchase a half gallon of apple juice, two pears, two tan-

gerines, and two plums. Applesauce can be a thrifty way to eat fruit. Frozen fruit is frequently expensive, but may be the best way to purchase berries off-season. Canned fruit is another inexpensive option. Consider shopping with a friend and sharing large bags of potatoes, sweet potatoes, apples, oranges, onions, carrots, celery, and so forth. If fruits and vegetables are in short supply at the discount store, you need to seek a local produce market.

3. **Breads.** See whether the discount store offers whole-grain bread. One loaf per week will help meet your nutritional needs. Keep a box of oatmeal for breakfast, and purchase boxes of whole-grain cereals as you need them.

4. **Meat and protein.** Tuna is frequently a good value at discount grocery stores and can be eaten two to three times a week. Buy canned salmon and peanut butter if you like them. Buy bags of raw beans if you have time to prepare them, or cans of cooked beans if you do not. You will find that certain cuts of chicken are less expensive than others. This usually includes drumsticks and thighs. You may also find that whole fryer chickens are economical. Cut them up carefully, or cook them whole, if you have an oven. Eggs are another inexpensive protein source. Compare the prices between the small, medium, large, extra large, and jumbo. There is usually around a $.10 cent gap in prices between the sizes. Watch for bargains on one size.

5. **Dairy.** Purchase and consume one gallon of skim milk per week. If you are in danger of not getting enough calories, purchase the 2 percent milk instead.

Avoid the unhealthy, cheap snacks at the discount store. They are frequently laden with trans fat and saturated fat. Likewise, avoid the biscuits and similar items, as well as fatty cuts of meat. Being on a restrictive budget is no reason to eat ramen noodles every day. Follow the above principles, and you just may emerge a healthier graduate than your well-fed peers.

# CHAPTER 4

## Attitude, Baby

## Organization

Do you feel that organization is important to you? Do your dirty clothes lay scattered all over your room, or are they neatly in the hamper? Do you know what time you plan to go to bed tonight and get up tomorrow morning? Are your chores neatly apportioned throughout the week so that you do not dread doing so many at once? Everyone is different, of course, but it is true that being organized will contribute to feeling good.

## Time management

Let us talk first about your time management. Do you ever look at your week as having 168 hours in it? Every few months, it is a good idea to look at how you spend your time and figure out what your time-wasters are. First, make a chart of what you do each day. For example, six hours in class, five days a week is 30 hours of class. Perhaps you spend an average of five hours on homework each week, and work in the bookstore on Saturdays for five hours. You sleep for six hours a night during the week, and seven hours a night on Friday and Saturday nights. You spend an hour getting ready each day. You have now spent 91 hours for the week. How do you spend the rest? Do you spend an hour each weekday going to classes and back? Do you spend an hour eating each day? Perhaps you play basketball for two hours each Sunday afternoon and take a two-hour nap each Saturday afternoon. Do you spend an hour on the computer each day? That accounts for 114 hours each week. You still have 54 hours left. Spend some time looking at where your time goes. Remember that time spent relaxing is not necessarily time wasted; we all need some down time. Once you have determined where your hours are going, perform the following exercise.

Determine how many hours a week you wish to devote to different activities:

- Let us say you continue the 6 hours of class each week plus 5 hours of homework.
  Class related: 35 hours

- You want to try to get 8 hours of sleep each night.
  Sleep: 56 hours

- Transfer time and getting ready for the day may be non-negotiable.
  Transfers: 5 hours
  Self-care: 7 hours

- Perhaps you want to slow down your eating a bit, especially on the weekends when you can relax with friends.
  Eating: 10 hours

- You want to increase your exercise to 7 hours per week.
  Exercise: 7 hours

- You want to spend less free time on the computer.
  Computer time: 4 hours

- Your job stays the same.
  Work: 5 hours

You now have 39 hours left. You may want to block in socialization at 7 hours each week.

- Socialization: 7 hours

- Do you have some favorite TV shows?
  Television: 4 hours

Now, you have 28 hours left. But we still have housecleaning and laundry to consider.

- Domestic chores: 7 hours

And, of course you want to begin to do much more cooking.

- Food preparation plus grocery shopping: 9 hours

Now, you have 12 hours left; let us delegate that to free time.

- Free time: 12 hours

Prepare your chart neatly, and refer to it for several weeks as you begin to organize your time. You may want to check off hours each day to see how close you come to your ideal. Remember to block in a minimum of one hour of free time each day, as we frequently lose time running errands and waiting on other people. As you organize your time, you will begin to feel less stress, and likely more energy.

### Keep a calendar

You have probably already noticed that a calendar is a must-have, whether it is on paper or electronic. Something you can carry with you is much handier than something only on the wall or a desktop computer. Keep up with exams, special occasions, bill due-dates, birthdays, things to do, and appointments you have. When you place a birthday or anniversary on the calendar, make a note around five days earlier reminding you to send a card or gift. Get in the habit of placing dates on it as soon as you know about them.

### Make trips count

Go to the grocery store with a list. When you go to the library or bookstore, think of everything you will need for the next week or so. Consider it a victory when you do not have to make repeat trips over forgotten items.

## Good housekeeping

Whether you are keeping up half of a room or an entire house, it helps to have a plan for housekeeping. Write down each chore you must perform and how often you will be doing it. Keep in mind dusting, mopping, sweeping, vacuuming, cleaning sinks, surfaces, toilets, and bathtubs or showers. Also add taking out trash, doing laundry, changing sheets, and any other chores you perform on a weekly basis. Your chores can be divided by the day. Think about whether you want one or two days off from chores entirely, or whether you want to divide them up evenly among the seven days. Then, make a chart for yourself, dividing them up into fairly even amounts based on time and labor (and dread). If you have chores that must be done once a month, season, or year, add them at the bottom of the chart, and delegate a particular week to do them. Never allow your chores to get behind, as it takes a toll on your mental health and creates a situation in which you dread to be at home. Always keep your home relaxing, free from the cares of the world.

### Timesaving and other tips

Buy multipurpose cleaners. It is possible to find one cleaner that will work for all your household cleaning. Watch for cleaners that do not require rinsing, which automatically saves you time. Consider wipes if they are within your budget. At any rate, keep all your cleaning items together, or at least the kitchen-type items together, and the bathroom and other types together. Do not waste time searching for cleaning items. Put on some of your favorite music, think of something you are looking forward to, and get to cleaning. Do the chores you dread first. And make it fun by using pleasant-smelling cleaners, because you will enjoy both the look and smell when you are done.

# Dignity and Self-Worth

Having healthy self-esteem is crucial to taking care of yourself. If you do not think highly of yourself, you will not be interested in self-care because you will not see yourself as worthy of it. This is when poor nutrition and many other problems can crop up. How much junk food do you eat? Do the reasons you eat junk food have to do with finances, time constraints, or addiction — or do you just do not care? Abusing your body with the wrong foods calls for a long, hard look at your motives.

Ask yourself the following questions:

- Do you allow others to abuse you physically, verbally, or emotionally?
- Do you hold your feelings inside instead of stating how you feel?
- Do you beat yourself down with negative self-comments, such as, "That was so stupid," "I'm so fat," or "I'll never get it right?"
- Do you fear the future?
- When something goes wrong, do you automatically think of how it might be your fault?
- Do you wake up in the morning and immediately begin thinking of what you need to worry about?
- Do you base how you feel about yourself on the opinions of those around you?
- Are you up when others encourage you, and nervous or down if others are not praising you?
- Do you violate your own principles to fit in with the crowd?

If you answered "yes" to any of these questions, you probably realize that your self-esteem could use a boost. If you are dealing with any of these issues, perform the following exercises:

- Write down the five things you like best about yourself.
- Write down three unselfish things you have done in your life.
- Write down your five biggest accomplishments.
- Now, consider your goals for the future. What do you want your life to look like in ten years? Give a thorough description of what you see for yourself.
- What do you want your life to look like in one year? How

do you envision yourself?
- What changes do you need to make to get there? Define actionable steps to meet your one-year goal. Take the first step today, and put any others on your calendar.

Watching yourself meet your goals will improve your sense of self-worth. Work on your self-discipline, and do the things you originally intend to. If you plan to get up early Saturday morning and clean your apartment or take a jog, do it. Do you plan to say no the next time your friends ask you to do something you do not believe in? Then say no. Follow through, and you will reap huge benefits.

Self-worth is contingent on seeing accomplishments in your life, however small. Get in the habit of praising yourself, and if you need to, keep a journal, and write down each accomplishment at night. Follow up by setting new goals each morning. Here are a few examples:

- I will smile at three strangers who seem to need a smile.
- I will not overeat.
- I will try one healthy new food today.
- I will work out for 30 minutes.
- I will get to bed by 10 p.m.
- I will spend an hour studying my hardest subject.
- I will take a long, relaxing bath tonight.

Do not be afraid to say to yourself, "I am proud of you!" each day. Everyone needs to hear those words. When you mess up, do not beat yourself up. Just start over the next day. As you stick to your plans and your principles, you will learn to value yourself more. Surround yourself with inspirational quotes that have meaning to you. Realize that you are not alone; most people go through these same feelings as they transition to adulthood, but you just cannot always see it. If you feel like you need to talk with someone, do not hesitate to do so, whether a friend, family member, or counselor.

## Stress Management

What do you do to relieve stress? Rate each of these from one to ten (ten being excellent) in terms of how well they relieve your stress:

- Calling your family
- Talking with a friend
- Spending time with an animal
- Taking a nature walk
- Vigorous exercise (e.g., boxing or basketball)
- Reading
- Getting lost in a movie
- Taking a nap
- Making a plan
- Going to a house of worship or praying
- Writing in a journal
- Meditation
- Taking a long bath
- Getting a massage
- Yoga

Which of these did you rate seven or higher? What can you add to your seven-or-higher list? Keep this list of your most effective stress relievers handy for use during stressful times. Now that you have some techniques in hand, let us look closely at what causes you stress.

Rate each of these as to whether they are currently stressing you, and if they are, is it minimally, moderately, or highly stressful?

- Loneliness
- Class work and grades
- Job
- Friends
- Intimate relations
- Family issues
- Roommate or living situation rules
- Safety concerns
- Finances
- The future
- Health (physical or mental)
- Time management

Look at those that highly or moderately stress you. Write them down, as well as anything else that stresses you to those levels. Can you do anything about each of the problems? If you can, write down your possible solutions. For example, if you are afraid you will fail calculus, allow yourself more study time; study with a buddy; try a tutor; talk with your professor and let him or her know you are concerned; and ask for ways to improve your grade. For each situation you can improve, think of practical steps, and put them into motion by taking the first step and placing the follow-up steps on your calendar. Realizing you are taking action can greatly reduce your stress levels.

Stressful aspects that you have no control over whatsoever can be tougher to solve. This is where stress management techniques come in. Refer to your list and pick one to try. If that does not work, try some more.

It is critically important to refrain from unhealthy techniques. Some of these are: overeating, drugs, alcohol, abuse of others, and self-abuse. Replace any of these behaviors with healthy ones from your list. If you are reliant on unhealthy behaviors, it may be difficult at first, but you will feel much better in the long run. Unhealthy things only create more problems that are worse than the stressors you are trying to relieve.

Too much stress creates a high level of cortisol in your body, causing multiple deleterious effects. This harms your entire well-being and even damages your immune system, leaving you vulnerable to illness. If the stress-management techniques do not lower your stress level, get professional help in the form of counseling. Your college should have resources available, but if you do not find any, or do not want to use them for some reason, look in the phone book for psychologists, psychiatric clinical nurse specialists, licensed professional counselors, or similar mental health practitioners.

## Healthy relationships

It is important to study the patterns you have in your current and past relationships. Ask yourself the following questions:

- Do your romantic relationships usually end badly, with extreme bitterness on one or both sides?
- Is it difficult for you to make and keep friends?
- Do you deal with considerable jealousy, either in romantic situations or in friendships?
- Do you tend to thrive on drama and get bored without it?
- Do you only feel loved if your mate is jealous or possessive?
- Do you have a hard time being alone?

- Do you tolerate bad behavior, such as emotional abuse, from your mate or friends?
- Do you frequently feel guilty that you are not providing enough emotional maintenance for others?
- Do you tend to try to place others on "guilt trips?"

If you answered "yes" to any of these questions, you need to closely examine the roots of the issue. Did you have positive relationship role models at home? Do you have good relationships within your family? Realizing that unhealthy patterns are sometimes born within us, and not created by others, is the first step to wellness. Examine why you are drawn to the mates and friends that you surround yourself with. Here are some indicators of healthy relationships:

- The parties enjoy each other's company and respect the other person's privacy and needs.
- The parties do not abuse each other in any way.
- The parties wish to help each other grow as people.
- Each party is happy for the victories of the other party.
- Each party wants the best for the other, and they are happy to see them with other healthy friendships.

Trying to cope in an unhealthy relationship is hard on you physically and mentally, and it impacts your academic performance. If you feel that your relationships are decidedly unhealthy, seek counseling instead of living a life of perpetual unhealthy attachments. Low self-esteem is at the root of many of these problems, as are problematic early relationships. Help is available; there is no need to suffer in silence.

## Medical issues

### Checkups and vaccinations

Now that you are in charge of your health care, you will want to maintain good medical care for the rest of your life. If you are healthy, this means going for a physical once a year during your teens and twenties. Find a primary care provider, if you have not already done so, and get a complete physical, including the taking of your health history and your family's medical history. The provider will inform you about any vaccinations you need to receive. Women will want to get a yearly reproductive examination from their primary care provider or gynecologist.

When seeking medical care, you will want to take a list of all prescription and over-the-counter medications that you take, either regularly or occasionally. Some providers will want you to bring your actual bottles of medicine. Also, take a list of any questions you have, and a pen and paper to record the answers. Repeat any instructions back to the provider to ensure that you understand them.

Get your vision checked on a regular basis and make yearly dental appointments as well. Keep a simple first aid kit in your backpack or purse. It is a good idea to carry a few bandages, sterile pads, sanitary wipes, acetaminophen, and aspirin, at a minimum. You will want a more extensive kit if you have health issues or spend time in the woods.

### Digestive complaints

Irregular hours, stress, and a poor diet can contribute to digestive complaints. If you frequently suffer after eating, try the following tips:

- Avoid spicy foods for a week and see whether you feel better.

- Consider whether you could be lactose intolerant. Monitor whether consumption of dairy products leads to gastrointestinal disturbances.

- Do not go too long without eating. This unhealthy practice is hard on your stomach. It can also cause hypoglycemia, which can lead to fainting and poor performance.

- Do not binge. Not only does it create too many calories in your bloodstream, but it is hard on your gastrointestinal tract as well.

- If you suffer from gas symptoms after certain foods, such as beans, broccoli, or potatoes, you can purchase medications such as Beano® to correct the problem.

- If you consume alcohol, do so in moderation. Alcohol overconsumption can lead to many gastrointestinal problems, as well as other health issues.

- Do not eat and go straight to bed.

**Nausea**

Nausea can be caused by a virus, food poisoning, nerves, or hormones, among other things. Over-the-counter products exist for mild nausea. Your primary care provider can prescribe stronger nausea medications, if needed.

## Vomiting

Vomiting is usually the result of a virus or food poisoning. It can also be the hallmark of other serious medical problems. If you vomit frequently, seek medical advice. Over-the-counter remedies are available, as are prescription drugs.

## Heartburn and indigestion

Heartburn and indigestion can be caused by a mechanical problem with your upper gastrointestinal (GI) tract, and they can be exacerbated by spicy foods. Over-the-counter medications are available. You may need to sleep with the head of your bed elevated. If you suffer from frequent heartburn, you should seek medical advice, as your esophagus can become eroded, with serious consequences. Occasionally, people feel that they have indigestion when they are actually suffering from a heart attack. Always take unrelenting, severe indigestion seriously.

## Constipation

Constipation is usually caused by poor dietary habits. Natural remedies include increasing fiber intake, increasing fluid intake, and ingesting prune juice. A normal pattern for bowel movements in young adults can vary from two times a day to once every two days. Over-the-counter medications are available, but those other than fiber supplements can become addictive. Seek health care consult for ongoing constipation to rule out medical problems.

## Ulcers

Ulcers are serious medical problems that should be handled by professional medical care. They are usually due to a particular bacteria in the gut and can be corrected with a mixture of medications. Untreated ulcers can lead to severe consequences.

### Diarrhea

Diarrhea can be caused by GI problems, viruses, or food poisoning. It is often best to allow it to run its course. Over-the-counter medications are available. Frequent diarrhea should be evaluated by your primary care provider.

Most people have digestive complaints from time to time. Keeping a bottle of anti-diarrheal medication in your room is a good idea.

# CHAPTER 5

# Freshman Year Recipes

I n this chapter, you will find the most basic recipes to get you started on a lifetime of healthy, fun cooking.

## Chicken Wrap

### Ingredients:

- 1 tortilla (any size you like)
- 2 ounces of chicken
- 1 ounce of sliced or diced tomatoes
- 1 ounce of shredded or sliced lettuce
- ½ ounce onions
- ½ ounce bean sprouts or sweet or sour pickles
- 1 ounce of cheddar cheese
- 1 tablespoon of low-fat mayonnaise

### Instructions:

Place your open tortilla on the plate. Spread the condiment thin-

| Nutrition Facts | |
|---|---|
| per serving | |
| makes 1 serving | |
| **Amount per serving** | |
| **Calories** | 504 |
| Calories from fat | 238 |
| | **% Daily Value \*** |
| **Total Fat 26.5g** | 41% |
| Saturated Fat 9.2g | 46% |
| **Cholesterol 86mg** | 29% |
| **Sodium 502mg** | 21% |
| **Total Carbohydrate 36g** | 12% |
| Dietary Fiber 3.1g | 12% |
| **Protein 30.6g** | |
| Percent values are based on a 2,000 calorie per day diet. Your daily values may differ. | |
| <u>**Additional Information**</u> 47.2% of calories from Fat 28.5% from Carbohydrates 24.3% from Protein | |

ly on the tortilla, beginning one inch from the perimeter. Add the meat, which can be cold or heated. Add the cheese, if desired, and top with plenty of veggies. Roll into a wrap and slice down the middle with a sharp knife. Skewer each half with a toothpick for visual effect, if desired.

**Accompaniments:**

Wraps taste great with baked potato chips (try a half-serving) or a half-cup of baked beans.

> **Tips:**
> *Wraps are easy to prepare and a welcome change from sandwiches. Wraps keep well in the refrigerator and are easy to make ahead of time. You may want to make two and have one for lunch the next day.*

# Ham Salad

**Ingredients:**

7.5 ounces lettuce

1 ounce carrots

1 ounce tomatoes (diced large tomatoes or whole baby tomatoes)

1 ounce red onions

1 ounce diced apples

1 chopped slice of American cheese

½ ounce sunflower seeds

2 ounces extra-lean ham

2 tablespoons low-fat Italian dressing

1 ounce seasoned croutons

| Nutrition Facts | | |
|---|---|---|
| per serving | | |
| makes 1 serving | | |
| **Amount per serving** | | |
| **Calories** | | 620 |
| Calories from fat | | 333 |
| | | **% Daily Value \*** |
| **Total Fat 37g** | | 57% |
| Saturated Fat 9.7g | | 48% |
| **Cholesterol 66mg** | | 22% |
| **Sodium 1477mg** | | 62% |
| **Total Carbohydrate 44.9g** | | 15% |
| Dietary Fiber 9.4g | | 38% |
| **Protein 26.8g** | | |
| Percent values are based on a 2,000 calorie per day diet. Your daily values may differ. | | |
| **Additional Information** 53.7% of calories from Fat 29% from Carbohydrates 17.3% from Protein | | |

**Other Optional Additions:**

- Peppers
- Raisins

- Cucumbers
- Radishes
- Purple cabbage
- Cabbage
- Mushrooms
- Squash
- Celery
- Broccoli
- Cauliflower
- Snow peas
- Bean sprouts
- Halved grapes
- Berries (whole, sliced, or dried)
- Pineapple
- Coconut
- Pecans
- Walnuts
- Cashews
- Almonds
- Any seeds

Add meats and protein if desired:

- Boiled egg (diced)
- Turkey strips
- Chicken strips (hot or cold)
- Black beans

For occasional use:

- Bacon bits (real or soy)

**Instructions:**

Place the lettuce in a bowl, add all the other ingredients except the salad dressing, and toss. Add 1 tablespoon of the dressing and wait to see whether you need to add more.

**Accompaniments:**

Salads can be small and complement a meal of steak and potato. It will also complement chicken and a starchy vegetable or pasta.

A large salad makes a good meal by itself. If needed, you can add a serving of crackers or a garlic breadstick.

**Tips:**

*Salad is one of the most nutritious foods you can eat. It should become a regular lunch or dinner menu item for you on most days. Be creative with your salads. Try many different ingredients, and keep salad fixings on hand at all times. Look for different produce on sale. For example, at your favorite store, mushrooms may go on sale once a month. Also, watch for produce stands when you are out; they can be an excellent place to buy fresh vegetables and fruits.*

# Baked Potato

## Ingredients:

1 potato (white, yellow,
    or red)
2 tablespoons low-fat
    sour cream
1 tsp sprinkle of chives,
    salt, or pepper

Add additional toppings
as desired:

1 tablespoon margarine or
    butter
1 ounce shredded cheese
2 tablespoons bacon bits
    (real or soy)
1 tablespoon salad topping (contains seeds)
2 ounces chili (heated)
2 ounces broccoli with 1 ounce nacho-style cheese (both heated)

| Nutrition Facts | |
|---|---|
| per serving | |
| makes 1 serving | |
| **Amount per serving** | |
| **Calories** | 286 |
| Calories from fat | 53 |
| **% Daily Value \*** | |
| **Total Fat 5.8g** | 9% |
| Saturated Fat 5.2g | 26% |
| **Cholesterol 0mg** | 0% |
| **Sodium 45mg** | 2% |
| **Total Carbohydrate 52.9g** | 18% |
| Dietary Fiber 4.8g | 19% |
| **Protein 5.3g** | |
| Percent values are based on a 2,000 calorie per day diet. Your daily values may differ. | |
| **Additional Information** | |
| 18.5% of calories from Fat | |
| 74% from Carbohydrates | |
| 7.4% from Protein | |

## Instructions:

Choose a potato that does not have green on the skin. Thoroughly wash and remove any potato eyes with a knife. There are several ways to prepare a potato:

If you have an oven, they can be baked. Place potato in any oven-safe dish and pierce it with a fork in at least four places. You may want to experiment with wrapping it in foil before cooking, as the peel will come out differently. Preheat oven, place the baking dish on the middle rack, and bake at 400 degrees for 25 minutes to 1 hour, depending on size. Check after 20 minutes to see whether the potato is getting soft, and watch it every 5 minutes after that. When it feels sufficiently soft, pierce a fork through it to make sure it is done, and enjoy.

Potatoes can also be boiled. Take your largest saucepan (up to three quarts) and add enough water that it will be at least 1 inch over the potato. Turn the burner on medium-high and cover until the water begins to boil. Add the potato carefully with tongs or a large spoon so that you do not splash the water on yourself. Cover the pan and leave the burner on medium-high. Cook for 20 to 30 minutes, depending on the size of the potato. Check after 15 minutes, and every 5 minutes after that. When it seems soft, pierce it with a fork to make sure it is done. Carefully remove it from the water.

For more convenience, potatoes can be cooked in the microwave. Pierce the potato with a fork in four places and place on a microwave-safe plate. Place it more on the edge of the plate than in the middle. Your oven may have a baked-potato setting. If it does not, cook the potato on high for 4 minutes, and let it sit in the microwave for 2 more minutes. Check it for softness. If it is nearly done, cook it for 1 more minute. If it is still quite firm, cook it for up to 4 additional minutes, trying 2 minutes first. Two potatoes cooked at once may take slightly longer. Remove the potato, wrap it in aluminum foil, and allow it to sit for 5 minutes while you prepare the toppings.

**For all methods of cooking:** When the potato is done, slice it in half with a knife. Then take your hands and squeeze each half from the bottom, causing the inside of the potato to break apart and rise slightly above the peel. Take a fork and smash the insides so that there are no large parts that are not smashed. Add salt or pepper if desired. Next, add margarine or butter if desired. Then, add the hot ingredients, and finally, the other cold ones. If you find that some of the peel is green inside, do not eat the green part.

## Accompaniments:

Baked potatoes are excellent with chicken, hamburgers, pork, steak, salad, a fancy sandwich, or alone.

**Tips:**

*Be sure to try all different kinds of potatoes — red, white, and yellow. You will like some varieties better than others. Remember to shorten the cooking time for the smaller potatoes.*

# Marinated Chicken

Chicken is tasty, full of protein and other nutrients, and can be prepared with many different flavors.

## Ingredients:

1 boneless, skinless chicken breast
¾ cup of pineapple juice
1 tablespoon of brown sugar
Sprinkle of salt

## Instructions:

Find a shallow bowl and pour the pineapple juice into it. Add the brown sugar, mixing it with a fork until somewhat, but not

| Nutrition Facts | |
|---|---|
| per serving | |
| makes 1 serving | |
| **Amount per serving** | |
| **Calories** | 503 |
| Calories from fat | 74 |
| | **% Daily Value \*** |
| **Total Fat 8.2g** | 13% |
| Saturated Fat 2.3g | 11% |
| **Cholesterol 193mg** | 64% |
| **Sodium 470mg** | 20% |
| **Total Carbohydrate 36.4g** | 12% |
| Dietary Fiber 0.3g | 1% |
| **Protein 70.9g** | |
| Percent values are based on a 2,000 calorie per day diet. Your daily values may differ. | |
| **Additional Information** 14.7% of calories from Fat 28.9% from Carbohydrates 56.4% from Protein | |

entirely, dissolved. Add the chicken breast(s), making sure there is juice completely surrounding each breast. Poke a few holes in each breast with the fork to allow the juice to permeate. Cover the dish with plastic wrap and leave in the refrigerator for 3 to 8 hours. Turn the chicken over at least once during this time, making sure the juice is still surrounding the breast(s).

Lightly spray your Foreman-type grill with oil, then plug in and place the drip pan appropriately. Remove the breast from the marinade and sprinkle with salt. Place on the grill and close the top. Watch closely, because the chicken will cook quickly. Have a plate ready for the chicken when it is done. Cook until it is no longer pink, and remove from the grill. Unplug the grill right away. Discard the marinade or use as sauce with chicken.

**Accompaniments:**

This chicken is excellent with colorful mixed vegetables, whole-grain rice, or a baked potato. You can also serve a small tossed salad, green beans, carrots, or asparagus. You may want to add a small, whole-grain roll or a garlic breadstick on the side.

**Tips:**

*If you do not have a Foreman-type grill, you can bake the chicken in the oven in a glass baking dish on the middle rack. Preheat the oven to 375 degrees and bake for 25 to 40 minutes. Turn the chicken after 15 minutes. Check for doneness after 20 minutes, and every 5 minutes after that. You may want to brush the chicken with olive oil or canola if it is getting dry. It will not be as moist as the Foreman-type grilled chicken.*

*Once you master this dish, think of other marinades you can create. Consider using orange juice, honey, garlic, or Italian spices.*

# Berry Parfait

## Ingredients:

8 ounces French vanilla
   yogurt

¼ cup strawberries, sliced

¼ cup blackberries or
   dewberries

¼ cup blueberries

¼ cup granola

## Instructions:

Mix the berries together. Place 2 ounces yogurt in dessert dish. Add ½ of the berries. Add another 2 ounces yogurt, followed by ¼ cup granola. Add 2 ounces of yogurt. Add the last of the berries, and another 2 ounces of yogurt. Top with the remainder of the granola, and allow to set in the refrigerator for at least 30 minutes before serving.

| Nutrition Facts | |
|---|---|
| per serving | |
| makes 1 serving | |
| **Amount per serving** | |
| **Calories** | 550 |
| Calories from fat | 205 |
| | **% Daily Value \*** |
| **Total Fat 13.5g** | 35% |
| Saturated Fat 4.3g | 50% |
| **Cholesterol 8mg** | 4% |
| **Sodium 126mg** | 19% |
| **Total Carbohydrate 86.9g** | 28% |
| Dietary Fiber 11g | 36% |
| **Protein 20.3g** | |

Percent values are based on a 2,000 calorie per day diet. Your daily values may differ.

**Additional Information**
26.8% of calories from Fat
62.6% from Carbohydrates
10.6% from Protein

## Accompaniments:

This dessert is fairly high in calories and should be eaten after a light meal, such as a healthy frozen dinner, one slice of pizza, or a turkey sandwich half.

 **Tips:**

*Use fresh berries when in season. Use thawed frozen berries the rest of the year. To make your own granola, combine 3 tablespoons of oats, a sprinkle of cinnamon, a dash of salt, a tablespoon of crushed pecans or walnuts, a teaspoon of coconut, a teaspoon of packed brown sugar, and a teaspoon of sunflower seeds. Add a dash of nutmeg or allspice if desired. If you do not have all the ingredients for the granola mix, but you do have oats, feel free to experiment and create your own granola recipe.*

# Microwaved Sweet Potato

## Ingredients:

1 medium sweet potato

1 tablespoon margarine

1 tablespoon brown sugar

¼ teaspoon cinnamon

Dash of salt

## Instructions:

Place sweet potato on a micro-wave-safe plate. Pierce holes with a fork on all sides. Micro-wave on high for 4 minutes. Allow to sit for 2 minutes in the microwave. Microwave on high for 2 more minutes. Allow to sit for 1 minute, and see whether potato is soft. If it is not soft yet, microwave on high at 1-minute increments until soft. Split potato in two with a sharp knife. Lightly salt each half and add margarine, making slight indentations in each side with the spoon. Add cinnamon, sprinkling evenly over potato. Add brown sugar. Wait 3 minutes, and enjoy.

| Nutrition Facts | |
|---|---|
| per serving | |
| makes 1 serving | |
| **Amount per serving** | |
| **Calories** | 326 |
| Calories from fat | 107 |
| | **% Daily Value \*** |
| **Total Fat 11.9g** | 18% |
| Saturated Fat 2.2g | 11% |
| **Cholesterol 0mg** | 0% |
| **Sodium 321mg** | 13% |
| **Total Carbohydrate 52g** | 17% |
| Dietary Fiber 5.7g | 23% |
| **Protein 2.7g** | |
| Percent values are based on a 2,000 calorie per day diet. Your daily values may differ. | |
| **Additional Information** 32.8% of calories from Fat 63.8% from Carbohydrates 3.3% from Protein | |

## Accompaniments:

This sweet potato makes an excellent lunch by itself. If you wish to serve it with other items, consider ham or pork. Add green beans and a small roll to make a large meal. Do not serve with other sweet items, such as sweet vegetables, fruit, or dessert. Do not serve with other starchy vegetables, such as regular potatoes, corn, or peas.

> **Tips:**
>
> *Eat the peeling right along with the flesh of the sweet potato. It is a good source of fiber and adds a nice contrast to the sweet flesh. Be aware that eating a whole sweet potato can cause gas symptoms and may best be avoided prior to social situations. If you do not wish to add brown sugar, you can substitute your favorite sweetener. When serving to guests, you can surround the sweet potato with aluminum foil while whole, or after splitting and adding the toppings.*
>
> *If you do not have a microwave, you can boil the sweet potato or bake it in the oven following the instructions in the recipe "Baked Potatoes."*

# Baked Onion

**Ingredients:**

> 1 large white or yellow onion
> 2 teaspoons of margarine

**Instructions:**

Preheat the oven to 425 degrees. Place a square piece of aluminum foil in the bottom of a baking dish. Peel the onion and place in the center of the foil. Take a knife and make a plus sign in the top of the onion, extending down ¾ of an inch. Put the margarine on top of the onion and bring the foil up to wrap the onion tightly. Place the baking dish on the middle rack of the oven and bake for 30 minutes. Carefully touch the outside of the foil to see whether the onion feels soft. If it is not soft yet, change the position slightly and continue to cook at 10-minute intervals. When the onion feels soft, carefully remove it from the foil and place on a plate. Depending on how long you cook it, the onion may have some browning on the outside. The browning is

### Nutrition Facts

per serving
makes 1 serving

| Amount per serving | |
|---|---|
| **Calories** | 160 |
| Calories from fat | 71 |

| | % Daily Value * |
|---|---|
| **Total Fat 7.9g** | 12% |
| Saturated Fat 1.5g | 8% |
| **Cholesterol 0mg** | 0% |
| **Sodium 7mg** | 0% |
| **Total Carbohydrate 19.6g** | 7% |
| Dietary Fiber 4.1g | 16% |
| **Protein 2.6g** | |

Percent values are based on a 2,000 calorie per day diet. Your daily values may differ.

**Additional Information**
44.4% of calories from Fat
49.1% from Carbohydrates
6.5% from Protein

desirable, as long as the onion is not burnt. It can take as long as 1 hour to bake a large onion to perfection, and practice will teach you exactly how long to cook yours for your taste.

## Accompaniments:

A baked onion should be served with a simple meat or poultry, such as steak or grilled or baked chicken. It is ideal to also be baking something else in the oven while the onion is baking. Add another vegetable on the side, such as broccoli spears or grilled zucchini. Add a garlic breadstick, if desired, and a simple dessert, such as pistachio pudding.

**Tips:**

*For a gourmet touch when entertaining, add butter instead of margarine. Sprinkle the top with parsley prior to baking, and serve while still wrapped in foil.*

# Tuna Salad Pita

## Ingredients:

½ whole-grain pita

½ can tuna in water, drained

½ rib of celery, thinly sliced

½ apple, any color, diced
    into small pieces

1 ounce walnuts, chopped
    to small size

2 pieces of lettuce —
    any kind

1 teaspoon mayonnaise
    or Miracle Whip-type
    salad dressing

| Nutrition Facts | |
| --- | --- |
| per serving | |
| makes 1 serving | |
| **Amount per serving** | |
| **Calories** | 442 |
| Calories from fat | 177 |
| **% Daily Value \*** | |
| **Total Fat 19.8g** | 30% |
| Saturated Fat 2g | 10% |
| **Cholesterol 27mg** | 9% |
| **Sodium 542mg** | 23% |
| **Total Carbohydrate 35.9g** | 12% |
| Dietary Fiber 7.5g | 30% |
| **Protein 30.4g** | |
| Percent values are based on a 2,000 calorie per day diet. Your daily values may differ. | |
| **Additional Information** | |
| 40% of calories from Fat | |
| 32.5% from Carbohydrates | |
| 27.5% from Protein | |

**Instructions:**

Open the pita pocket and add a piece of lettuce to each side. In a small bowl, combine the tuna, mayonnaise, celery, apple, and walnuts. Stir the mixture well, making sure the tuna separates throughout the other ingredients. Stuff the tuna mixture into the pocket.

**Accompaniments:**

Serve this quick lunch sandwich with a half serving of baked potato chips and a pickle spear. You can also add raw carrot sticks on the side. Have iced tea as a beverage. If you desire dessert with this meal, have small, spicy cookies, such as two ginger snaps.

**Tips:**

*You may wish to prepare the tuna mixture ahead of time and keep it chilled. Consider making two days' worth of the mixture at once by doubling the recipe. Always add to the pita right before serving.*
*Consider other ingredients, such as green or black olives, or diced tomato. If you have stored the tuna mixture in the refrigerator and it looks dry, add a few drops of milk and stir.*

# Grilled Cheese English Muffin

**Ingredients:**

1 English muffin

1 small bell pepper, any
    color, cut into strips

1 small onion, any color, cut
    into small, thin rings

1 tablespoon olive or
    canola oil

Dash of salt

Dash of pepper

2 slices of Swiss, Muenster,
    or mozzarella cheese

| Nutrition Facts | |
|---|---|
| per serving | |
| makes 1 serving | |
| **Amount per serving** | |
| **Calories** | 250 |
| Calories from fat | 140 |
| **% Daily Value \*** | |
| **Total Fat 12g** | 21% |
| Saturated Fat 8.1g | 36% |
| **Cholesterol 64mg** | 21% |
| **Sodium 1548mg** | 64% |
| **Total Carbohydrate 37.6g** | 15% |
| Dietary Fiber 3.7g | 20% |
| **Protein 38.7g** | |
| Percent values are based on a 2,000 calorie per day diet. Your daily values may differ. | |
| **Additional Information** | |
| 44.4% of calories from Fat 33.3% from Carbohydrates 22.4% from Protein | |

**Instructions:**

Place oil in a small skillet over medium heat. Add bell pepper and onion. Saute until vegetables begin to lightly brown. Sprinkle with salt and pepper. Remove from heat. Turn the oven on broil at 400 degrees. Split the muffin and place each half, split side up, on a baking sheet. Place one slice of cheese on each muffin half. Place under broiler on the middle rack. Turn oven light on and watch closely. The cheese will begin to melt within 2 minutes. When the cheese melts, carefully remove from the oven and add the veggie mixture evenly to both sides.

**Accompaniments:**

This meal can be eaten for breakfast or lunch. If served for breakfast, add two fresh fruits, such as orange slices and a small bunch of purple grapes. If served with lunch, add a small bowl of beans or tomato soup. Have water or fruit juice and a small scoop of fat-free frozen yogurt, if desired.

**Tips:**

*These muffins can be eaten with a knife and fork, but I recommend picking them up with your hands. Add any spices you like toward the end of the sautéing. These make an excellent quick breakfast when you are headed out the door. Keep your veggies chopped up and in Baggies ahead of time.*

# Grilled Veggie and Cheese Sandwich

## Ingredients:

2 thick slices of your
favorite gourmet bread

1 tablespoon olive oil

3 thin slices of eggplant

3 thin, lengthwise slices of
zucchini or squash

2 thin slices of white onion

2 slices of Swiss, Muenster,
or mozzarella cheese

Dash of garlic salt —
optional

| Nutrition Facts per serving makes 1 serving | |
| --- | --- |
| **Amount per serving** | |
| **Calories** | 679 |
| Calories from fat | 321 |
| **% Daily Value \*** | |
| **Total Fat 35.7g** | 55% |
| Saturated Fat 14.1g | 71% |
| **Cholesterol 64mg** | 21% |
| **Sodium 1225mg** | 51% |
| **Total Carbohydrate 72.6g** | 24% |
| Dietary Fiber 7.4g | 30% |
| **Protein 41.8g** | |
| Percent values are based on a 2,000 calorie per day diet. Your daily values may differ. | |
| **Additional Information** 41.2% of calories from Fat 37.5% from Carbohydrates 21.5% from Protein | |

## Instructions:

Heat the Foreman-type grill. Place the oil in a small bowl and add garlic salt if desired. Brush the vegetables on both sides with oil. Place the veggies on the grill and grill until soft with nice grill marks. You may need to cook the veggies in two batches. Brush both sides of each slice of bread with the oil mixture. Grill bread for one minute. Remove 1 slice of bread and add 1 slice of cheese to the remaining slice of bread. Add the sautéed vegetables and the other slice of cheese. Top with the slice of bread, and grill the sandwich until the cheese has melted. Remove and cut in half. Serve immediately.

## Accompaniments:

Serve this large sandwich alone or with a half serving of baked potato chips and a small serving of coleslaw. For dessert, have a small red apple. For a beverage, consider tea or lemonade.

**Tips:**

*This sandwich makes a tasty lunch any season that you can find fresh eggplant. Find an exciting recipe for the rest of the eggplant, such as the Baked Eggplant recipe, or make more of these sandwiches on subsequent days.*

# Spicy Baked Potato Logs

**Ingredients:**

1 medium to large potato
2 teaspoons dry mix for
    Italian-style dressing

**Instructions:**

Preheat oven to 400 degrees. Spray baking dish with spray oil. Slice the unpeeled potato into logs approximately the size of a hotdog. Spray the logs on all sides with the spray oil and place on a fresh plate. Sprinkle the dry mix over all surfaces of the potato logs. Place logs in baking dish and bake on the lowest rack of the oven for 20 minutes. Check every 5 minutes thereafter. When potatoes are nicely browned, remove from oven and serve.

## Nutrition Facts

per serving
makes 1 serving

| Amount per serving | |
|---|---|
| **Calories** | 197 |
| Calories from fat | 45 |
| | **% Daily Value \*** |
| **Total Fat 4.9g** | 8% |
| Saturated Fat 0.7g | 3% |
| **Cholesterol 0mg** | 0% |
| **Sodium 88mg** | 4% |
| **Total Carbohydrate 34.1g** | 11% |
| Dietary Fiber 2.9g | 12% |
| **Protein 3.9g** | |

Percent values are based on a 2,000 calorie per day diet. Your daily values may differ.

**Additional Information**
22.8% of calories from Fat
69.2% from Carbohydrates
7.9% from Protein

**Accompaniments:**

These potato logs can be served in place of French fries for many lunch and dinner menus. They can accompany a hamburger, hamburger steak, grilled chicken, steak, fish, or a gourmet meat sandwich. Add coleslaw or a small salad if desired. Offer ketchup. Do not serve bread. Serve with milk or iced tea. If you wish to have dessert, consider frozen chocolate mints.

> **Tips:**
>
> *With practice, you will discover just how brown you like your potato logs. These crispy logs can be eaten with a fork or with your hands, if eating a hamburger or sandwich.*

# Tomato with Black Beans and Cheese

**Ingredients:**

1 large tomato that will
    stand on a plate
½ can black beans
2 ounces shredded cheese,
    any type
Dash salt
Dash pepper

**Instructions:**

Heat the black beans to boiling in a small saucepan on medium-high. Add salt and pepper and allow to boil one full minute. Remove from heat and allow to cool. Cut the top from the tomato and remove the insides of the tomato, leaving a ⅓-inch wall all around. Salt lightly inside tomato. Add cooled black beans to the inside of the tomato until almost filled. Add cheese to top.

**Nutrition Facts**

per serving
makes 1 serving

| Amount per serving | |
| --- | --- |
| **Calories** | 468 |
| Calories from fat | 95 |
| | **% Daily Value \*** |
| **Total Fat 10.6g** | 16% |
| Saturated Fat 6.1g | 30% |
| **Cholesterol 32mg** | 11% |
| **Sodium 573mg** | 24% |
| **Total Carbohydrate 60.1g** | 20% |
| Dietary Fiber 14.2g | 57% |
| **Protein 33.2g** | |

Percent values are based on a 2,000 calorie per day diet. Your daily values may differ.

**Additional Information**

20.3% of calories from Fat
51.3% from Carbohydrates
28.4% from Protein

**Accompaniments:**

This dish is perfect with a half-sandwich for lunch. It can also accompany grilled chicken or pork at dinner time. Serve with milk. Add a small piece of frosted cake for dessert if desired.

**Tips:**

*Feel free to add your favorite Italian spices to the beans. When purchasing fresh tomatoes, you may find that you prefer summer and fall tomatoes to those available in the winter.*

# Fruity Gelatin Salad

**Ingredients:**

2 packages sugar-free
  raspberry gelatin

2 cups apple or pineapple
  juice

½ cup pecans or walnuts

Choose 3 of the following fruits:

1 small banana, sliced into
  ⅛-inch wheels

1 small chopped apple

½ cup berries, fresh or
  thawed frozen

½ cup pineapple, canned
  diced or canned crushed

½ cup maraschino cherries

1 small chopped tangerine

| Nutrition Facts | |
|---|---|
| per serving | |
| makes 12 serving | |
| **Amount per serving** | |
| **Calories** | 125 |
| Calories from fat | 33 |
| | **% Daily Value \*** |
| **Total Fat 3.7g** | 6% |
| Saturated Fat 0.3g | 2% |
| **Cholesterol 0mg** | 0% |
| **Sodium 53mg** | 2% |
| **Total Carbohydrate 24.5g** | 8% |
| Dietary Fiber 1.5g | 7% |
| **Protein 1.6g** | |
| Percent values are based on a 2,000 calorie per day diet. Your daily values may differ. | |
| **Additional Information** | |
| 21.6% of calories from Fat 72% from Carbohydrates 6.3% from Protein | |

**Instructions:**

In a medium saucepan, add the juice to 1 cup of water. Bring to a boil and remove from heat. Add gelatin and stir for 2 minutes. Pour into a large glass bowl and refrigerate for 1½ hours. Add fruit and nuts and stir. Place back in refrigerator until firm. Makes 8 servings.

## Accompaniments:

This dish can be served alone as a snack or as the dessert to a country-style meal, such as meatloaf or breaded meat, mashed potatoes, and another vegetable.

> **Tips:**
>
> This gelatin can be taken to a potluck dinner. You may need to take bowls if you feel that only plates will be available. For variety, add one cup of fruit-flavored miniature marshmallows when the fruit is added. Try many different kinds of fresh, frozen, or canned fruit once you have mastered this dish. Make sure you tell anyone considering this dessert that it contains nuts.

# Tuna Salad

## Ingredients:

1 can water-packed tuna, drained, or 1 small packet of tuna
Bread-and-butter pickle slices
1 hardboiled egg
2 tablespoons Miracle-Whip type dressing
½ teaspoon sugar
Dash of salt
2 slices of bread

## Instructions:

Boil the egg according to the instructions in the Cooking Basics — Breakfast section in Chapter 6. Place the drained tuna in a medium-size bowl that has a lid. Slice the egg into ten slices and add. Sprinkle with salt. Place eight pickle slices on a plate or cutting board and cut each one into 16 small pieces. Add to the tuna.

| Nutrition Facts | |
|---|---|
| per serving | |
| makes 1 serving | |
| **Amount per serving** | |
| **Calories** | 627 |
| Calories from fat | 157 |
| **% Daily Value \*** | |
| **Total Fat 17.4g** | 27% |
| Saturated Fat 5.1g | 25% |
| **Cholesterol 326mg** | 109% |
| **Sodium 1762mg** | 73% |
| **Total Carbohydrate 58.3g** | 19% |
| Dietary Fiber 7.8g | 31% |
| **Protein 59.3g** | |
| Percent values are based on a 2,000 calorie per day diet. Your daily values may differ. | |
| **Additional Information** | |
| 25% of calories from Fat | |
| 37.2% from Carbohydrates | |
| 37.8% from Protein | |

Add 1 teaspoon of the juice from the pickle jar. Add the dressing and sugar. Stir gently and taste test. Add more salt, sugar, or pickles if needed. Place ⅓ of the salad on a slice of bread and top with the other slice of bread. Slice diagonally with a sharp knife and enjoy. Promptly refrigerate the leftover salad.

**Accompaniments:**

Serve with sandwich with crunchy raw vegetables, such as baby carrots, bell pepper strips, or celery sticks. You can also slice a Roma tomato for an accompaniment. Have iced tea and a lemon cookie if dessert is desired.

**Tips:**

*This salad can also be eaten on fancy crackers — any type other than saltines. It makes an appropriate hors d'evoure for a casual party and can accompany small blocks of cheese with toothpicks, an offering of mixed nuts, and party mints. Do not leave outside the refrigerator for longer than 1 hour.*

# Angel Food Cake with Berries

**Ingredients:**

    1 slice angel food cake
        from store
    1 cup of raspberries,
        blueberries, or sliced
        strawberries
    Sugar or sweetener

**Instructions:**

Place the berries in a small saucepan. Add just enough water to cover the berries and heat

| Nutrition Facts | |
|---|---|
| per serving | |
| makes 1 serving | |
| **Amount per serving** | |
| **Calories** | 540 |
| Calories from fat | 17 |
| | **% Daily Value \*** |
| **Total Fat 2g** | 3% |
| Saturated Fat 0.2g | 1% |
| **Cholesterol 0mg** | 0% |
| **Sodium 1283mg** | 53% |
| **Total Carbohydrate 119.8g** | 40% |
| Dietary Fiber 6.5g | 26% |
| **Protein 11g** | |
| Percent values are based on a 2,000 calorie per day diet. Your daily values may differ. | |
| **Additional Information** | |
| 3.1% of calories from Fat 88.7% from Carbohydrates 8.1% from Protein | |

on medium-high heat until boiling. Do not leave unattended. Reduce heat to medium-low. If using blueberries, you can add 1 teaspoon of lemon juice to the water, if you have some. Sweeten the liquid as desired with sugar or sweetener. Continue to cook until slightly thickened and remove from heat. Refrigerate for one hour and pour over angel food cake just prior to serving.

**Accompaniments:**

This dish is excellent alone or as an accompaniment to a sophisticated meal, such as grilled chicken breast with mushrooms and rice.

 **Tips:**

*You can easily add a gourmet touch to this dessert, such as a sprig of mint, slivered almonds, shaved chocolate, or a spiral of orange peel. A tablespoon of fat-free, non-dairy topping can be added as well.*

# Marinated Turkey Breast

**Ingredients:**

1 or 2 thick (½ to ¾ inch) slices of boneless, skinless turkey breast

8 ounces of lemon juice

1 ounce of canola oil

¼ cup sugar

1 teaspoon of garlic powder

½ teaspoon of onion powder

½ teaspoon of ginger

½ teaspoon of rosemary

| Nutrition Facts | |
|---|---|
| per serving makes 1 serving | |
| **Amount per serving** | |
| **Calories** | 640 |
| Calories from fat | 272 |
| | **% Daily Value \*** |
| **Total Fat 30.4g** | 47% |
| Saturated Fat 4.4g | 22% |
| **Cholesterol 39mg** | 13% |
| **Sodium 39mg** | 2% |
| **Total Carbohydrate 73.5g** | 24% |
| Dietary Fiber 1.6g | 6% |
| **Protein 18.6g** | |
| Percent values are based on a 2,000 calorie per day diet. Your daily values may differ. | |
| <u>**Additional Information**</u> 42.5% of calories from Fat 45.9% from Carbohydrates 11.6% from Protein | |

## Instructions:

Mix the last seven ingredients in a shallow bowl. Pour ¼ of the mixture into a cup and refrigerate. Place the turkey breast in the marinade and place in the refrigerator for 4 hours. Turn the turkey every hour, making sure the marinade touches the poultry on all sides.

Heat the Foreman-type grill and place the turkey breast on it. Discard the marinade the turkey was in. Take the refrigerated mixture in the cup and baste the breast as it cooks. Turn the poultry several times, basting the top each time. Do not baste for the last 3 minutes of cooking. Remove the breast when the outside is crispy and the inside is done.

## Accompaniments:

When turkey is your entrée, consider any of the side dishes found in a traditional turkey dinner — dressing or stuffing, mashed potatoes with gravy, peas, sweet potatoes, cranberry sauce, and rolls. Turkey can also be served with crisp Asian vegetables and pasta. For a beverage, try milk, iced tea, or apple cider. For dessert, consider a traditional slice of fruit pie.

### Tips:

*Watch for turkey breast to go on sale, and freeze some extra if possible. Boneless, skinless chicken breast can be substituted for the turkey in this recipe.*

*When you have access to an outdoor grill, try this entrée for a delicious, different grilled meal.*

# Blueberry Breakfast Shake

## Ingredients:

½ cup fresh or frozen, thawed blueberries

½ cup fat-free frozen vanilla yogurt

½ cup skim milk

## Instructions:

Place all ingredients in a blender. Blend on medium high at 5 second intervals until smooth.

## Accompaniments:

| Nutrition Facts | |
|---|---|
| per serving<br>makes 1 serving | |
| **Amount per serving** | |
| **Calories** | 164 |
| Calories from fat | 21 |
| **% Daily Value \*** | |
| **Total Fat 2.4g** | 4% |
| Saturated Fat 1.3g | 6% |
| **Cholesterol 10mg** | 3% |
| **Sodium 153mg** | 6% |
| **Total Carbohydrate 24.7g** | 8% |
| Dietary Fiber 2g | 8% |
| **Protein 11.1g** | |
| Percent values are based on a 2,000 calorie per day diet. Your daily values may differ. | |
| **Additional Information**<br>12.8% of calories from Fat<br>60.2% from Carbohydrates<br>27% from Protein | |

This drink is excellent for a light breakfast. For greater sustenance, add a scrambled egg tortilla wrap or other handheld, hot breakfast food.

**Tips:**

*Quick, nutritious, delicious — what more could you ask of a breakfast drink? You can substitute the blueberries with almost any fruit — blackberries, cherries, raspberries, banana, orange, tangerine, strawberries, peaches, or pineapple.*

# Peanut Butter Crispy Rice Treats

## Ingredients:

- 6 cups Rice Krispies™-type cereal
- 10 ounces regular or miniature marshmallows
- 1 tablespoon margarine
- 3 tablespoons smooth peanut butter

## Instructions:

Place the marshmallows and the margarine in a large, microwave-safe bowl. Microwave on high for 1 minute and stir. Microwave on high for another minute and stir. Microwave on high for up to one more minute, until marshmallows are melted. Add the cereal and peanut butter. Sir until the cereal is completely coated. Spray a 9" X 13" pan with spray oil and place mixture into it, pressing until firm and even. Allow to cool for 30 minutes and cut into 12 squares. Makes 12 servings.

## Accompaniments:

This dish makes an excellent treat by itself. It can be served as the dessert for a light, casual meal, such as a hotdog, fries, and coleslaw.

| Nutrition Facts | |
|---|---|
| per serving | |
| makes 12 serving | |
| **Amount per serving** | |
| **Calories** | 162 |
| Calories from fat | 28 |
| **% Daily Value \*** | |
| **Total Fat 3.1g** | 5% |
| Saturated Fat 0.7g | 3% |
| **Cholesterol 0mg** | 0% |
| **Sodium 154mg** | 6% |
| **Total Carbohydrate 31.4g** | 10% |
| Dietary Fiber 0.3g | 1% |
| **Protein 2.2g** | |
| Percent values are based on a 2,000 calorie per day diet. Your daily values may differ. | |
| **Additional Information** | |
| 17.2% of calories from Fat 77.3% from Carbohydrates 5.4% from Protein | |

## Tips:

*You may want to use utensils that you have sprayed with spray oil to move the ingredients from the bowl to the pan. Plan whom you wish to share the treat with so that you are not tempted to overindulge. Tell anyone you are sharing with that it contains peanut butter.*

# SOPHOMORE SECTION

# CHAPTER 6

## Cooking Basics

**W**e will now explore the beginnings of cooking. This topic will be continued in Chapter 11 on advanced cooking.

## No-Prep Food Choices

Searching for healthy, instant-fix foods is fairly simple. Many canned soups are quite healthy, although high in sodium. Vegetable soups and bean soups are good choices. Make sure you read the instructions on the label; condensed soups will require you to add water. Add a small amount of water and do a taste test before adding more water. The larger cans of soup frequently do not need added water. Keep in mind that most cans of soup are intended to be two or more servings. Place the soup in a saucepan and heat until boiling for at least a minute. Alternatively, place in a microwave-safe bowl and heat until bubbling. You may need to loosely cover the container to prevent the soup from splattering in the microwave. You can accompany crackers or a breadstick with your soup, if desired.

The key to frozen dinners is following the instructions. They can usually be placed in the microwave or in the oven on a cookie sheet. The microwave is much faster, of course. Remember to add a small amount of margarine or condiments to add flavor to your meal. Consider adding a small salad or a piece of fruit to your dinner. If you do not have the freezer space for frozen dinners, you can store them in the refrigerator for around three days. Some dinners will not have the same quality if thawed beforehand.

# Cooking Terms

## Baking

Baking an item means to cook it in the oven for a specified period of time. Preheat the oven to the proper temperature first. An item in the oven will often lightly brown as it gets done and must be watched carefully to avoid burning. Purchase a timer or set the timer on your cell phone, microwave, or stove if you are prone to forgetting to check the oven. Items must be placed in the correct place in the oven.

Always place items in the middle, not the front or rear, unless you have a full oven and cannot avoid it. Most items can be placed on a low or middle rack. The top rack can cause items such as biscuits to get too done on top before being completely baked. Watch items on the middle rack, and move them to the bottom if they are getting brown too quickly. If something is already getting too brown, cover it with a piece of aluminum foil, and watch it closely.

## Boiling

Boiling is simple, done atop a stove. You will frequently turn an item on medium-high until it begins to boil, then turn it down to low, where it will continue to boil slowly. It is a good practice to never turn a burner on high. Medium-high is easier on your pots and pans and helps you to avoid burning and boiling dry. Covered items will come to a boil quicker and may boil over, creating a mess and possibly ruining your food. You must stay with a covered pot until you can turn it down to a slow boil. Milk will frequently scald or burn when left to boil, and you will need to stir it almost constantly. Beans are also quick to burn on the bottom if not stirred frequently. You will want to boil most items for at least a few minutes for safety reasons.

## Broiling

Broiling involves the use of the broiler on your oven. The oven broiler is generally turned up to at least 450 to 500 degrees, and this method of cooking in the oven is not used too frequently, as it can create a mess when grease splatters. If you do broil items, turn on the light and watch them constantly, as they can burn in seconds. Be careful as you remove the pans; it is easy to get burned.

## Grilling

Grilled foods are often a welcome change. If you or a friend has a true outdoor grill, it can be used at any time of year for delicious cooking. Do not think that grilling out can only occur in the summer and fall. Follow all safety instructions carefully, especially with gas grills. Fires or explosions can ruin an otherwise nice occasion. Although people used to enjoy blackened chicken, we now know that these foods contain carcinogens and are unsafe to consume, especially for females. Do not allow the food to be blackened from flame. Be careful to see that foods do not drip grease, causing flames to flare up and burn the meat. Go for flavor from marinating or basting instead.

Grilling with a Foreman-type grill is faster than any other meat and poultry preparation method, except microwaving. It provides a simple, quick way to have nutritious protein without adding sauces or oils.

## Sautéing

Sautéing requires a saucepan on a hot burner. Heat the chosen oil, such as olive oil or margarine, until hot, and add the food you intend to sauté. Keep the heat on medium throughout the sautéing. Lightly brown the items you have added. You may keep the oil with the food or dispose of it, depending on your recipe. Chopped onions and mushrooms are two common items used for sautéing.

# Basic Appliance Use

## Stove

By stove, we usually mean four burners and an oven. If the stove uses gas, and you are unfamiliar with gas stoves, ask for a demonstration of its use by your landlord or the person responsible for the apartment. Turn on all the burners and make sure they work properly. Never turn a burner on higher than medium-high. Familiarize yourself with the oven. Does it have a preheat setting? You may like to use it, or you may prefer to simply turn the oven on to the temperature you wish it to cook at and let it heat a few minutes. Does it have a broil setting? Always watch food that is being broiled carefully.

## Refrigerator

Is it frost-free? If it is not, make sure you defrost it as needed. Keep it clean, and never allow spoiled food to sit in it. Follow the instructions in Cooking Basics: Food Safety later in this chapter to keep the refrigerator the proper temperature. Keep a box of open baking soda in the refrigerator and in the freezer compartment, if you have room.

## Microwave

Learn all the specifics for your microwave. Many of them heat by power and by weight. You will use high power most often. Clean it inside with a damp cloth only, and never run it with foil or metal inside. Never run the microwave without food inside. Keep the area around the door clean so that the door can shut completely. It is best not to leave the vicinity of the microwave while it is running.

## Hot plate

A hot plate should only be used if you do not have a stove. It may come on automatically when plugged in, or it may have an on-and-off switch. Never leave it plugged in when not in use.

## George Foreman grill

These function simply, usually lack an on-and-off switch, and cook much more quickly than the oven. Always use the drip tray to avoid making a mess.

## Crock-Pot

These pots may have one, two, or three heat settings. They should be stirred occasionally, especially if you are preparing beans. They can be tricky to wash if the inner chamber is not removable.

## Blender

Blenders frequently have many speed settings. Follow the instructions for your recipe to determine the appropriate setting.

The main thing to remember about the blender is not to get your fingers inside while it is plugged in. Also, keep the lid on to avoid a lengthy cleanup of your kitchen. Generally, you will operate it for three to ten seconds, turn it off, turn it back on, and repeat until the food or liquid is the consistency you wish. Clean carefully around the blades, and always wash and thoroughly rinse after use.

## Mixer

Your mixer may have several settings. You will want to use it near a clock, as most recipes will say something to the effect of "beat the batter on high for two minutes." Make sure your mixing bowl is deep enough to not splatter the ingredients everywhere. Mixers usually have to run longer than you may anticipate. It can take more than five minutes to beat egg whites, for example. Keep the cord out of water and away from the blades. Always unplug a handheld mixer immediately after use, and remove the blades for washing. Replace the blades before you plug it back in next time.

# A Cooking Primer

It is now time to get cooking. The following will explain some basic dishes to get you started.

## Breakfast

Breakfast is a fun, simple meal to fix. It is best to begin learning to cook the things you love, then become experimental.

## Eggs

Eggs can be fried, scrambled, or boiled. To fry eggs, use a small skillet, or a griddle, if you have one. You can use cooking oil spray or a teaspoon of oil or margarine (margarine tastes best) to begin. Spray the skillet or rub the oil into the pan, and heat on medium heat. Swirl the oil or margarine, carefully crack the egg, and open it with both hands to avoid breaking the yolk. This takes practice. Place one or two eggs in the skillet, and allow them to cook. Add salt or pepper if desired. For sunny side up, place a lid on the skillet, and turn the heat down to medium low until the yolk is set. For regular fried eggs, turn them over with a spatula as soon as you are able to. Cook to desired doneness, and remove with the spatula.

Scrambled eggs can be made many different ways. If you like fluffy eggs, crack one or two eggs, and place them in a mixing bowl. Add up to one tablespoon of milk per egg. Some people add a few drops of water instead, and some add nothing. Add salt or pepper if desired. Beat with a fork or whip until it looks consistent. In the meantime, prepare a skillet with spray or fat, as done with the fried eggs. Add the scrambled egg mixture to the skillet with the heat set to medium. Stir with a metal or plastic spoon, depending on your cookware. Cook until done, and remove with the spoon to your plate.

If you like eggs like you find in fast-food restaurants, such as on an egg biscuit, follow the same instructions for the skillet, except use a tablespoon of fat, and be extra careful to swirl it all over the skillet before adding the egg. Do not add milk to your egg mixture. After placing the scrambled egg in the skillet, turn the burner to medium-high. Use a plastic spatula instead of a spoon, and allow the egg to set before turning it over. You may need to turn it two or three times, but try to keep it as intact as possible. When you make eggs this way, you may want to wait and add the salt and pepper after they have cooked.

Boiled eggs are incredibly simple. Place in a pan with enough water to more than cover the eggs. Turn on medium-high and cover the pan. Covering is not necessary, but it will bring the water to a boil more quickly. Some cooks allow the water to boil for a minute or two, and then let the eggs set in the water with the heat turned off for 15 minutes or so. Other cooks, especially those in a hurry, boil the eggs for around seven minutes. Then, carefully drain off most of the water, and add cold water several times to let the eggs begin to cool. Take a finished egg, holding it in one hand, and bang it lightly on one end and then the opposite end, cracking the shell a bit each time. Roll the egg back and forth on a plate or other clean surface, bearing down a bit. Then, break the shell and remove it. You may need to do this near the sink, in case the egg is too hot inside to hold. Rinse the egg to make sure you have removed all the shell, salt if desired, and enjoy.

## Bacon

The simplest bacon is the kind that is already cooked, allowing you to just heat it in the microwave. Do the math, and see how many slices you get for what price; you may be surprised to see that cooked bacon is sometimes the more economical choice. If you decide to cook bacon from scratch, one way to fix it is in the oven. Turn your oven to 400 degrees, and place the slices of bacon, barely touching or not touching at all, on a 9" X 13" pan or on a cookie sheet with raised edges. Place in the oven on the top rack. Watch it closely, and turn after it begins to get done — usually five to ten minutes. Bacon can also be placed in a cold, large skillet and cooked on medium. You may wish to cut the slices in two before placing them in the skillet. They will need to be turned at least once, and frequently, more often. A griddle placed on medium is also an excellent place to cook bacon. Place cooked bacon on a paper towel to allow excess grease to be absorbed.

Bacon can be cooked from scratch in the microwave or under the broiler, but it can be messy and easy to burn, and this method is not recommended. Consider healthier types of bacon, such as turkey or soy, which may have different cooking instructions.

## Sausage

Sausage may be purchased raw or already cooked. Let us begin with raw sausage. It comes in a plastic wrapper and must be used fairly quickly or frozen once it has been opened. Remove the desired amount from the wrapper, and cut it into the amount of slices you wish. It is best not to cut it too thick; about a third of an inch is perfect. Alternatively, if it begins to make a mess when you try to cut it, feel free to shape it like a small, thin hamburger patty. Use a cold skillet or the griddle and spray with the cooking oil spray if it is not a non-stick surface. Cook on medium, turning at least three times with a fork or plastic spatula, until well-done. If you are preparing links or patties that are already cooked, follow the label instructions carefully, as they will vary quite a bit.

## Oatmeal

There are three basic kinds of oatmeal: instant, quick, and old-fashioned. You may want to find out what kind you are accustomed to eating at home, if you do not know. For instant oats, follow the directions, which will generally entail boiling a small amount of water in a saucepan or the microwave and adding it to a bowl with the oatmeal. Stir well, and allow it to sit for a minute. For quick oatmeal, add a little over 1 cup of water to a saucepan and heat on medium-high until boiling. Add ½ cup of oats, and stir frequently until they are the consistency that you like. For old-fashioned oats, add 1¼ cups of water to a saucepan and heat on medium-high until boiling. Add ½ cup of oats, and turn down the head to medium-low. Stir frequently and cook for five minutes or longer. For all types of oatmeal other than flavored, put in your favorite additions after putting the oatmeal in the bowl. You can add margarine, a touch of milk or cream, sugar, sweetener, or cinnamon. Experiment with honey, berries, walnuts, pecans, and any other flavors you think of. Fruit can be also added to the cold water when preparing instant or old-fashioned oatmeal. Add raisins, peaches, or apples for variety. Try to eat oatmeal at least twice a week.

## Toast

Toast is a simple but tasty food for breakfast. To prepare toast, you are hopefully beginning with delicious, whole-grain bread. Turn the broiler on the oven to 450 degrees and place the bread on a cookie sheet. Place the cookie sheet on the top rack. Watch extremely closely, as the toast may be brown in two minutes or less. Turn it over and broil the other side, if desired. Add a tea-spoon of margarine, if desired, all over the toasted side of the bread, and replace the cookie sheet on the lower rack just long enough to allow the margarine to melt. Eat with your favorite fruit spread. Of course, having a toaster handy makes the process even simpler.

## Canned biscuits

Once again, following the instructions on the label is paramount. As a rule, you will preheat the oven to 350 to 425 degrees and place the biscuits on a cookie sheet or in a pan. Some biscuits call for being placed an inch apart, while others should have the sides touching. Cook on the bottom rack of the oven, checking after seven minutes to make sure the bottoms are not getting too done. If the bottom is browner than the rest of the biscuit, place the sheet or pan on the middle rack for the rest of the cooking. Watch carefully, as over-done biscuits are not enjoyable to eat.

Have one large biscuit, or up to two small biscuits at one meal. Eat with margarine, gravy, fruit spread, molasses, honey, or your own favorite topping. It is fun to make a bacon, egg, and cheese mini-biscuit, and they can be given to friends as well. Place the leftover biscuits in a Baggie, and place in the refrigerator if they will not be eaten within 24 hours.

An ideal breakfast will consist of some protein, one or two servings of a whole grain, milk, and some fruit. Cold whole-grain cereal with an added banana or berries is an excellent choice. Yogurt with granola and pears is another. Try to eat bacon or sausage no more than once a week, if you must do so at all. You can have your old favorites occasionally while exploring new, healthy options for the first meal of the day. Plan your breakfast the night before, so that you will not waste valuable time in the morning trying to figure out what to eat.

## Lunch

One of the best ideas for lunch is salad. Look at the recipe for salad in Chapter 5. If you like sandwiches, make them healthier by experimenting with different whole-grain breads. Try to avoid fatty sandwich spreads, such as egg salad or chicken salad, opting instead for fresh meats. Turkey, chicken, and roast beef are a few good choices. Add plenty of veggies, such as tomato, lettuce, pickles, onions, and anything else that you like. If you like condiments, add mustard or a small amount of fat-free mayonnaise. Add cheese (low-fat if possible) occasionally, and you have a quick, healthy sandwich. You may add a few baked potato chips if you cannot eat a sandwich without chips. Try to get accustomed to eating half a serving of chips at one time. Baked beans are a good accompaniment as well. You may wish to make yourself a half-sandwich at times when you are not overly hungry.

Soup is another popular lunch item. Whether canned or home-made, it provides nourishment and helps you to feel full. Opt for soups that are broth-based instead of creamy. Do not eat soup every day, because you will probably be consuming too much sodium if you do.

An ideal lunch consists of protein (unless you are planning for a high-protein dinner), one or two servings of vegetables, and a serving each of grains, fruit, and milk. It is an easy habit to grab a banana or an apple after lunch for a quick dessert. Cottage cheese makes a quick milk serving. Lunch veggies may frequently be raw and dipped in low-fat ranch dressing. If you do not eat a sandwich, you may want to add a small, whole-grain roll to your meal.

## Dinner

Dinner strikes fear in the heart of many a beginner cook. Dinner should contain a protein choice, two veggies, a grain, and some milk (unless you want a milk snack later). A fruit dessert can also be added. What are some of your favorite foods? How about a grilled chicken breast, a sweet potato, broccoli, and a whole-grain mini-muffin? Baked fish with coleslaw, green beans, and a hush-puppy is another good option. They are even easier than they sound. You may want to get accustomed to making enough food for two days at dinnertime. This saves time and is economical as well. One secret to dinner is that it can be anything you like — a bowl of chili, a cold fruit plate, or anything else that is healthy. Variety is important in order to get all your needed nutrients, and it keeps you from getting bored.

## Healthy snacks

Snacks are fun to make. Popcorn can be fixed in a hot-air popper. Small crackers can look and taste great with meat, cheese, veggie, and fruit toppings. Many different things can be done with fruit alone. Forget the admonition of "Don't play with your food." Snack time is the time to experiment and learn what you like. Have you ever tried strawberries with a small piece of dark chocolate? Cashews mixed with granola, seeds, and dried fruit for a trail mix? Cold cherry tomatoes popped into your mouth? How about purple grapes? Snacks are a good way to catch up on nutrition you missed during the day. If you need that extra fruit, veggie, grain, or milk, this is the opportunity.

# Freezing and Storing Foods

Storing and freezing extra food that you prepare is economical and time-saving. Keep a variety of semi-disposable plastic containers in varying sizes handy if you plan to store foods. Invest in a box of freezer bags, and see whether you use them over several months.

Refrigerator storage is simple. Cover the food with a lid, plastic wrap, or aluminum foil, and keep in the refrigerator for up to three days. Alternatively, place in a plastic bag and refrigerate.

The biggest issue when freezing foods is avoiding freezer burn. If you have purchased meat, poultry, or fish in a large quantity, divide it into the portion sizes you will cook at one time, and freeze individually. Remove all the air from the packaging that you can. Using frozen foods within a month is ideal. They will stay safe longer than that, but the risk of freezer burn can become an issue. Freezing leftovers simply involves placing them in a safe container, leaving some room at the top, and freezing. This method works well for soups, stews, casseroles, entrees, and some desserts. Some creative cooks create their own frozen dinners for later use.

To store pantry items, keep them tightly closed and in a pantry or behind a cabinet door. When storing fruits, you will want to refrigerate most of them. Exceptions include apples, oranges, pears, and bananas. It will not hurt anything to refrigerate them if they are in danger of becoming too ripe, but the smell of bananas can leach onto your other refrigerator foods.

When storing vegetables, you should refrigerate everything except potatoes; sweet potatoes; and white, yellow, and red onions. Tomatoes can be left on the counter until ripe, at which point you may want to refrigerate them. It will not hurt hardy vegetables, such as squash, zucchini, and corn, to leave them out of refrigeration for a few days, but they will keep better under refrigeration. Potatoes, sweet potatoes, and the above-mentioned onions should be kept in a dark, cool place. It is recommended that onions be kept away from potatoes, as they put off a gas that rots potatoes. This can be impractical and unnecessary if you will be eating the vegetables within a few weeks.

Keep eggs and dairy products in the refrigerator at all times. Most breads do not require refrigeration. Follow the product labels for any other items.

# Food Safety

The first thing to remember about cooking is to make sure you have a working smoke alarm.

## Food expiration dates

Always search for and follow the expiration dates on food. If an item gives a "purchase by" date, try to eat it within three days of that date. Food poisoning is too dangerous to ever take a chance with. If something is moldy or does not smell or look right, toss it.

## Other food safety rules

- Keep your refrigerator at 40 degrees and your freezer at zero degrees. You may want to purchase or borrow a thermometer for checking occasionally. Any clean thermometer that registers both of those numbers will be fine.

- Cook meat until done. Never eat questionable meat, including poultry. This goes for eggs as well.

- Be extremely careful with raw meat. Do not allow the juices to spill into the refrigerator or onto the countertop. When preparing meat, and it cooks from raw to done, change or wash the utensil you are handling it with. Thoroughly cook any vegetables or beans that have been in contact with raw meat. Do not use liquid that you marinated raw meat in unless you boil it thoroughly.

- It is best to boil products such as canned soup and vegetables. Though technically it is only necessary to heat them, it is a good safety habit to allow them to boil for at least one minute.

- Do not leave cold foods out of the refrigerator. Takeout food ingredients when you need them, and place them back in the refrigerator as soon as possible. Make a habit to put leftovers in the refrigerator right after eating your meal.

- Thaw foods in the refrigerator, sink, or microwave instead of on the counter.

# CHAPTER 7

# The Dreaded (or Beloved) Cafeteria

## Your College Cafeteria — Healthy or Unhealthy?

The first step you need to take is check out whether the food offered at your college cafeteria is basically healthy or unhealthy. This will be a huge consideration in whether, and how much, you invest your food budget to eat there. At breakfast, do you see fresh fruit, oatmeal, whole grains, and veggie omelets? At lunch and dinner, do you see fresh salad bar offerings, healthy poultry and fish, and fresh vegetables and fruits? Or do you see casseroles, meat swimming in grease, and mashed potatoes?

## The Plan

### Semester plan

If you are on a semester plan, you will be able to eat all your meals from the cafeteria, if desired. Watch carefully if you choose this option to make sure you are eating a wide variety of foods and making healthy choices. It is easy to backslide into large portions and old favorites, such as hamburgers. Make your needs known, and ask the head of the cafeteria to replace white bread and rolls with whole grains. If they do not offer skim milk, low-fat cheeses, and fresh fruit, ask them to begin. Make sure that you are eating fish twice a week and not eating red meat more than twice a week. Try to eat beans and peanut butter as substitutes for red meat. If you are eating almost all your meals from the cafeteria, make sure you weigh yourself weekly to ensure your weight does not change with the new foods. Keep fresh fruit and nuts at home for healthy snacks.

## Per-meal plan

At some colleges, meals are charged at a flat fee per meal. This can be a good option for you. Get your money's worth of the healthiest foods you can find, such as salad, fruit, fish, chicken, and milk. Buy items you cannot regularly afford or that are difficult to buy or prepare. Although it may be tempting to overeat at these meals, it is not a good idea, as it is hard for your body to process more food than it needs. Do choose wisely, however, and enjoy the variety.

## Per-item plan

Some college cafeterias serve their meals just as a traditional cafeteria, where you pay for each item you choose. This is a balanced approach, and you can figure out which meals and foods are cheaper to prepare at home versus eating at the cafeteria. Breakfast items, such as oatmeal or cold cereal, are generally cheaper at home. A dish such as spaghetti may be a better bargain from the cafeteria. At least you have the option to grab a meal there when eating at home is impractical. The temptation to purchase unhealthy foods is lowest with this meal plan.

# Navigating Your Way to the Best Choices

## Breakfast

Begin your breakfast with fresh fruit and skim milk. From there, on most days, seek out cereal, oatmeal, or whole-grain bread. Look for mini-muffins, half bagels, or English muffins instead of large, whole ones. Yogurt is a good choice. You may want an egg occasionally, as long as they are not swimming in grease. Limit breakfast meats to no more often than twice a week. Pancakes or waffles are poor choices, especially if traditional syrup is added. A whole-wheat pancake with sugar-free syrup or fruit is a better choice. Items such as veggie or low-fat cheese omelets or burritos can make for excellent variety at breakfast. Biscuits, gravy, and hash browns should be rare indulgences.

## Lunch

Hit the salad bar. Choose a large variety of fresh vegetables and a fruit or two for your salad, a small sprinkling of cheese, and a small amount of low-fat or fat-free dressing. Avoid the creamy salads, such as macaroni salad. Take no more than a tablespoon of bacon bits or a couple of tablespoons of croutons. On most days, this may suffice for your lunch. Add a few crackers or a breadstick if you like. If you want something different, steer away from fatty sauces and too much red meat. Also avoid fried foods, as their nutritional value is minimal. Look for baked or grilled fish or poultry, or have a vegetable plate. Healthy sandwiches are another good option, as are broth-based soups. Get in the habit of avoiding any dessert other than fruit at lunch.

## Dinner

You may want a salad if you did not have one for lunch. This is a good time to think of growing your tastes into the sophisticated tastes of an adult. Try a glass of unsweetened tea (add sweetener if you need to), sample a healthy offering you ordinarily would not try, and eat slowly, as if you were at an important business meeting. Try to eat a protein source, two vegetables, and a grain. Eat a small serving of dessert if you wish. Relax and enjoy your food, company, and surroundings. The most banal of settings can still be excellent places to indulge in people-watching as you relax and eat your dinner.

# How to Find Out Nutritional Values

If you are not sure whether something is healthy or not, ask what it is made with. You may need to make a formal request to the dietician, writing down the particular items you are inquiring about. Ask about ingredients and calorie counts. Any information you receive should be helpful in making wise decisions. Encourage the dietician to provide plenty of healthy choices. If you cannot find out the answers, look on the Internet for calorie counts of various foods. Almost any food can be found, such as macaroni and cheese or broccoli casserole, with all the nutritional information. It should at least give you a rough idea to go by. Carefully watch portion sizes.

# CHAPTER 8

## Eating Out

## Healthy Options at Various Restaurant Types

We will now look at the best choices to try when you go to a restaurant.

### Fast food

Are you a fast-food junkie? Do you love the drive-thru, or just sitting in the casual atmosphere? There are healthy choices you can find at your favorite restaurants. Once you realize which fast food restaurants are near your home, you can find the Web sites of each and review the available nutritional information. It is a good idea to print off the information for your favorite restaurants. Your goal, of course, is to find the most nutrition and flavor for the fewest calories. Let us evaluate the common offerings.

**Grilled chicken** – Look on the menu for grilled instead of breaded chicken. These can be found in wraps and sandwiches. Ask for these items without dressing, and see whether you like them that way. They frequently have so much flavor that you will not miss the mayonnaise or ranch dressing.

**Fish** – While breaded fish is not ideal, it may be the only way you consume enough fish each week. Look at your calorie count and plan accordingly if you eat breaded fish or fish sandwiches. Some of the fast-food fish restaurants now serve grilled salmon (excellent) or other baked fish.

**Salad** – Tossed salads are generally a safe bet at a fast-food restaurant. You will want to avoid the kind that is housed in a shell that is eaten; they are incredibly high in calories and fat. If you choose to get a large salad with grilled chicken or egg, see whether you can eat it without dressing. If you order dressing, go with the low-fat version, and use it sparingly. If you eat a large, calorie-filled salad, you will want to make sure you do not consume any more calories along with it.

**Roast beef** – Most roast beef sandwiches are not a bad choice. Add lettuce and tomato, and avoid mayonnaise.

**Hamburgers** – If you must have a hamburger, order a small one, and consider adding lettuce, tomato, onions, and pickles. Skip the mayonnaise in favor of mustard and ketchup. At restaurants that serve miniature hamburgers, limit yourself to two.

**Fried chicken** – This is not a healthy choice. If you must have some, limit it to one piece, preferably a breast, and avoid eating the skin. As far as strips or nuggets, they are not ideal either, and you will want to eat half of your serving and save the rest for later. Try them without sauce, but if you have to have sauce, seek out the lowest-calorie offering.

**French fries** – French fries, like tater tots, are low in nutritional content and are a bad choice. If you must have some, get the smallest size available, and do not be afraid to throw some away.

**Side dishes** – Good choices include corn on the cob, green beans, and mixed veggies. Fair choices include cold slaw, baked beans, and rice. Poor choices include mashed potatoes and gravy, macaroni and cheese, potato salad, and pasta salad.

**Biscuits** – Biscuits from fast-food establishments are nearly always a bad choice. They are high in fat and calories with almost no nutritional value. Become accustomed to eating your meal without fatty breads. If you need bread, choose crackers or a garlic breadstick.

**Beverages** – Try unsweetened tea, adding some sweetener if needed. If you must have soda, have the diet version, if you are not afraid of the artificial sweetener. It is best to avoid both the sugary sodas and the diet ones. Coffee can be a good choice, if you like it. If you must have a milkshake, make sure it is the only thing you are consuming at that time, and get the smallest one available. Seek out restaurants that have "real milkshakes" or use "real ice cream" instead of the processed ingredients found at other locations.

**Dessert** – Yogurt with fruit and granola is a good dessert idea. Apple wedges and grapes are also good. Stay away from pies and puddings. If you do get an unhealthy dessert, split it with a friend or save half of it. Make dessert a rare treat, and not an everyday purchase.

## Sit-down restaurants

Sit-down restaurants can be a veritable minefield of high calories. You will want to check out the nutritional information on their Web site before you go to a chain restaurant. If the restaurant is a mom-and-pop establishment, you are on your own. Follow these tips for guidance:

- Order the smallest portion size you can. Many restaurants have a small meal or a discount-price meal.

- Look for grilled chicken or grilled or baked fish. These tend to be low in calories.

- Avoid creamy or buttery sauces.

- A small steak is not a bad choice. Do not eat any obvious fat.

- Have a small salad before your meal with low-fat dressing.

- Limit the amount of bread you eat to one or two pieces.

- Go with a baked potato instead of French fries. Get the toppings on the side so that you can control the amount added.

- Order veggies instead of pasta.

- Consider having a broth-based soup as an appetizer. Stay away from fried, greasy items, such as onion rings.

- Split your meal with a friend or take half of it home.

- Avoid high-calorie desserts. If you must have one, pick one with fruit and take half of it home.

## Ethnic restaurants

### Mexican restaurants

One of the healthiest choices at a Mexican restaurant is the chicken fajitas without the tortilla. These contain grilled chicken, onions, green peppers, delicious spices, and sometimes, tomatoes. Black beans or a small amount of refried beans is fine. A small serving of Spanish rice, cheese, or a small salad can be eaten. Limit the number of tortilla chips that you eat, with salsa but without cheese. Have a few, and ask your server to remove the basket. Limit tortillas to one, and have no more than one tablespoon of sour cream or guacamole. Grilled chicken, steak, or shrimp is preferable to beef dishes.

If you decide to order a high-calorie meal, ask for a box to go and pack half of the order away before you begin to eat. You may be able to order the child's plate. Avoid the fried desserts. Your top options at the Mexican restaurant include:

- Chicken fajitas, skipping the tortilla
- Child's plate
- ½ entrée of your favorite dish

## Italian restaurants

Italian restaurants frequently serve incredible salads. Stick with one breadstick. Pasta dishes with marinara sauce are preferable to cheese sauces. Vegetarian dishes are best, followed by chicken. Dishes with ground beef or heavy cheese are high in calories and fat. Consider asking for sauces on the side. The large amounts of tomatoes, olive oil, and healthy spices used in Italian cooking do make the dishes worthwhile.

Sandwiches served at casual Italian restaurants frequently contain fatty meats. Find a veggie sandwich or a grilled chicken sandwich without sauce. For pizza, order a thin-sliced or whole-wheat pizza with extra marinara sauce. Have all the veggies added, and one meat if you like. Have one or two slices, and take the remainder home. Skip the desserts unless Italian ice or sorbet is available. The best options at an Italian restaurant include:

- Salad
- A small pasta dish with marinara sauce
- Veggie pizza

### Chinese restaurants

Chinese restaurants offer a dizzying array of dishes to choose from. The two biggest healthy-eating rules at Chinese restaurants are:

- Avoid the battered, deep-fried items.
- Avoid the heavy, calorie-laden sauces.

The best foods to seek out include all the veggies, such as mushrooms (all kinds), carrots, water chestnuts, snow peas, bamboo shoots, cabbage, cauliflower, broccoli, celery, baby corn, scallions, green pepper, eggplant, green peas, onion, and string beans. Steamed vegetables are best, followed by those stir-fried with a light sauce. Tofu, soybeans, and bean curd are good choices. Choose fish, shrimp, crab, lobster, or scallops that have not been deep fried. Peanuts and cashews are good, as is the black bean sauce. A small bowl of soup is fine. Have fresh fruit for dessert, and by all means, enjoy your fortune cookie.

Poorer choices include beef, pork, and duck. Avoid the noodles and all deep-fried starches. Dodge the egg rolls, or share one with a friend. Avoid the pancake dishes. Eat a minimal amount of the white rice or fried rice. A couple of pieces of sushi, which are often available in both Chinese and Japanese restaurants, are acceptable from a nutritional standpoint.

Using the chopsticks can help you to eat more slowly and, consequently, consume less.

## Buffets

Look at a buffet as an opportunity to try a variety of healthy foods you may not be eating at home. By now, you should have a general idea of what to eat and what to avoid.

- Begin with a veggie salad with low-fat dressing.

- Consider eating a broth-based soup, such as vegetable.

- Look for fish, chicken, or lean meat. Avoid anything fried or covered in sauce.

- Try stir-fried vegetable offerings. These can provide excellent nutrients.

- Avoid mashed potatoes, fried vegetables, macaroni and cheese, or other pastas. Look for brightly colored vegetables.

- Limit bread to one serving.

- Find fruit if you want dessert or have a small cookie or a serving of yogurt or ice cream.

- Do not arrive starving, and stop before you feel completely full.

## Pizzerias

It is usually possible to make fair choices at a pizza restaurant. Begin with a tossed salad with low-fat dressing. Follow these guidelines for your main course:

- Avoid pan pizza. Thin-crust pizza is best. Stay away from calzones and other one-person dishes that have large amounts of breading.

- Eat pizza with tomato-based sauce, not merely cheese. Order your pizza with extra sauce.

- Load up on veggies. Order peppers, onions, mushrooms, olives, tomatoes, and any other veggies offered. Consider pineapple, if you like it on your pizza.

- Eat meat only if you need it to make your pizza complete. Almost all pizza meats are high in fat. If you eat a meaty pizza, you definitely want to limit yourself to one or two slices, and take the rest home.

- Avoid the pasta dishes. Stick with the pizza and salad.

- Do not order the breadsticks or dessert. They are not necessary for your enjoyment and add many calories with few nutrients.

## Sandwich shops

Sandwich shops are often great places to get whole-grain breads and plenty of veggies. Order the smallest sandwich, or take half of a larger one home. Here are some ideas to lower your calorie intake at the sandwich shop.

- Find whole-grain bread.

- Order all the vegetables, and ask for double portions if you like.

- Choose a lean meat if not ordering a veggie sandwich. Go with turkey, chicken, or roast beef. Ham is frequently lean as well. Avoid bologna, salami, and bacon.

- Avoid the "salads" — tuna salad, chicken salad, egg salad, and ham salad, as well as the meatball sandwich.

- Feel free to order a low-fat cheese.

- For condiments, consider the mustard, Parmesan cheese, oregano, and pepper. If you love mayonnaise, ask if it is low-fat, and ask for it to be added lightly or on the side. If you prefer oil and vinegar, ask for it to be added lightly or on the side as well.

- If you must have chips, get the baked variety, and split them with a friend or take half of them home.

- Avoid the desserts.

- Drink water or calorie-free tea or soda.

## Coffee shops

If you love the ambience of coffee shops, here are some tips for having a pleasant visit, without regretting your calories later.

- Do not arrive hungry. The sandwiches and desserts offered can be high in calories. Stick to your coffee.

- Order milk and sweetener instead of creamy, syrupy offerings. If you must have a coffee with unhealthy additives, get the smallest size possible.

- Do not order strong coffee if that causes you to add large amounts of unhealthy toppings to make it drinkable.

- Sip your coffee slowly, and enjoy your surroundings.

Do not make the coffee shop your place to stop for everyday coffee. Get a coffeemaker or find a place to buy an inexpensive cup of coffee, such as the cafeteria. Make the coffee shop an occasional treat, and your budget will thank you.

# CHAPTER 9

## Variety

## The Importance of Eating a Variety of Foods

Variety is truly the spice of life, and necessary for proper nutrition. Do you find yourself eating the same foods each week? Have you always been a picky eater? Do the following exercise.

- What was your favorite food when you were six?
- What do you crave occasionally?
- What foods signify happy times to you?
- What do you consider to be "grown-up" foods?
- If you could eat anything right now, what would it be?
- What did you like from the elementary school cafeteria?

The answers to these questions should help you think about food choices. Review the following list, and rate each food as "hate it," "it's all right," "love it, but haven't had any in a long time," "love it and eat it regularly," or "never tried it."

- Blackberries
- Fresh pineapple
- Cashews
- Ginger snaps
- Figs
- Smoked turkey
- Black olives
- Grilled salmon
- Garlic bread
- Chicken gordita
- Purple grapes
- Cinnamon applesauce
- Pomegranate juice
- Snow peas
- Dates
- Sweet potato casserole
- Popcorn ball
- Candied apple
- Homemade vegetable soup
- Corn on the cob
- Pineapple coleslaw
- Broccoli salad
- Lentils
- Hummus
- Frozen juice bars

Write down your lists of "love it, but haven't had any in a long time" and "never tried it." Put one item on your grocery list each week. If an item is unfeasible for you to make at home, consider ordering it the next time you are at a restaurant that makes it.

It is fun to experiment with different cooking oils. While it is important to eat the healthiest ones most often, it is also good to try new ones occasionally. In addition to olive oil, corn oil, and canola oil, try peanut oil, cottonseed oil, and coconut oil. Coconut oil should be used rarely for extra flavoring; it contains too much saturated fat for regular use.

Experiment with different fruits. Have you ever eaten a kiwi, pomegranate, or plantain? If your grocery store carries a wide selection of fruits, try one new item each week. Look up on the Internet how to open and prepare it if you need to. You can also find many different types of seasonal melons at the larger stores. You might just find a new favorite food.

If you have begun making stir-fries, you may want to try a new veggie each week. Find one that you can purchase a small amount of, and add it to your stir fry, along with your usual favorites.

Experiment with the wide variety of salad greens. The pre-washed bags are ideal for one week's use. Remember, the darker the vegetable, the more nutrition it likely packs.

Consider having a salad party with your friends, where each person brings two or three healthy salad ingredients, and any dressing they have. Add crackers or breadsticks, and you can have a fun meal while you are learning about new veggies you may love. Talk about your favorite work-out routines, and encourage each other to follow good nutrition and a healthy lifestyle. Quiz your friends on how they deal with stress and how they get enough sleep. This is a good time to learn about new recipes or restaurants that carry healthy menu items.

Try a variety of ethnic foods. If you have friends or professors from other countries or cultures, ask them about the foods they prepare. Get a simple recipe, and prepare it on your own. Your grocery store probably has an ethnic food aisle, which is a fantastic resource for items you may have never seen or heard of. Make an effort to try a new ethnic food at least once a month.

Learn about soy, which is an excellent way to supplement your protein. Tofu is available in many forms for cooking. Edamame can be prepared several different ways or added to other foods. One can purchase soy bacon, soy burgers, or many other soy-added items.

# Easy-to-Purchase Options

## Nuts

Any time you add nuts or nut butters to your menu, you are giving your body needed nutrients, including oils and minerals. Nuts are also a good source of fiber. Some popular nuts include peanuts, cashews, almonds, pecans, pistachios, Brazil nuts, hazelnuts, pine nuts, walnuts, and filberts. Although peanuts are not technically nuts, we will call them such for the purposes of this book. Their nutrition and uses mimic the true nuts. You may like to eat nuts one variety at a time, or you may prefer eating a mixture of nuts together. Nuts can be added to many recipes. They are a mainstay in granola, trail mix, and other quick energy foods.

### Ideas for adding nuts to your diet:

- Salads become gourmet with the addition of almonds, pecans, walnuts, pine nuts, or cashews. Walnuts and pecans add a flavorful crunch to fruit salads.

- You can experiment with any kind of nut in stir-fries. Add during the last five to ten minutes of cooking.

- Pecans and walnuts go well with oatmeal and other cereals.

- Almonds go well with green bean dishes.

- Pecans make a delicious topping for sweet potatoes.

- Pecans and walnuts make excellent additions to brownies.

### Purchasing and storing nuts

Peanuts are generally inexpensive, while other nuts can be costly. You can save significant amounts of money by being careful where and when you purchase nuts. Consider buying halves or pieces, as they tend to be less expensive and work fine for everyday use. Compare the number of ounces between different containers to determine the best buy. Be careful buying nuts around holiday time, as the prices are frequently inflated to match the demand for nuts in holiday cooking. Nuts will usually stay fresh for several months. Keep them in a tightly closed container.

### Nut butters

Peanut butter and other nut butters offer variety, but also a high number of calories. It is best to avoid eating more than two tablespoons at a time. Nut butter on a slice of whole-grain bread makes a quick, healthy half-sandwich. Nut butter is also tasty with bananas or apple slices.

## Cheeses

Cheese provides calcium and is a healthy choice when eaten in moderation. Try different types of cheese to learn your favorites.

### Some basic types of cheese

- American cheese slices. These are tasty as sandwich filling and can also be added to omelets, scrambled eggs, and potatoes. Make sure the label has the word "cheese" on the front and not the word "imitation." "Sandwich slices" are sold next to cheese, tricking many unaware consumers, as they contain oil instead of milk and can be devoid of the healthy nutrients of cheese. The flavor of these fake slices can be quite poor.

- Cottage cheese. Try the fat-free variety of cottage cheese. If you feel that it has a good flavor and texture, you may want to make it your regular cottage cheese. If the fat-free type is disagreeable to you, try the low-fat. It tastes similar to the full-fat cottage cheese, with fewer calories.

Fruit and nuts can be added to cottage cheese. Try fruits such as peaches, pears, pineapples, cherries, and berries in your cottage cheese. Add a teaspoon of sugar or your favorite sweetener if you need to.

- Cheddar cheese. Cheddar cheese comes in different varieties from mild to extra sharp. You may prefer mild with some recipes, such as hamburgers or other dishes made with hamburger. Some prefer extra sharp when eating cheese alone or with crackers. If you need to melt cheddar cheese on top of a dish, you may want to shred it first.

- Mozzarella cheese. Mozzarella cheese is used for Italian dishes. It is the cheese generally used to top pizza. Sliced mozzarella also goes well on a sandwich.

- Blue cheese. This cheese is also called bleu cheese. It adds a twangy, exotic flair when added to salads or stuffed inside hamburgers.

- Swiss cheese. Sliced swiss cheese is a welcome addition to submarine or other sandwiches. It can also be melted on chicken or other dishes.

**Purchasing cheese**

**Cheese blocks**

When considering the purchase of blocks of cheese, you will see 8-ounce, 12-ounce, 16-ounce, and perhaps larger blocks. Unless you plan to eat or prepare a large amount, you may wish to buy the 8-ounce block, as cheese can dry out quickly. If the cheese is not in a resealable bag, place it in a zipped bag, or wrap it tightly in saran wrap or aluminum foil. If you like to eat fine cheeses, you may wish to invest in a cheese slicer or grater. This will enable you to buy cheese in blocks and use it for a variety of different purposes.

### Shredded cheese

Make sure that the cheese you purchase looks fresh and is without a white covering or mold. Look at the expiration dates, and pick the one with the longest period of freshness. Avoid any shredded cheese packages with the word "imitation." Be aware that fat-free cheeses may not melt well and are best suited to cold salads. Low-fat shredded cheese is a good option.

## Vegetables

Vegetables require a few basic decisions, raw or cooked being the first. If they are to be cooked, should they be lightly steamed, boiled, stir fried, microwaved, baked, fried, battered, or broiled? Should you have one vegetable or a mixture? How about a salad, soup, stew, or casserole? The possibilities with vegetables are endless. Consider raw vegetables first. Cut them up and keep them handy in the refrigerator, ready for meals or snacks. Add a dip only if you need to. Vegetables that are tasty raw include tomatoes (regular, cherry, or grape), carrots (regular or baby), lettuce, cabbage, celery, broccoli, cauliflower, squash, zucchini, onions, peppers, cucumbers, radishes, snow peas, and mushrooms.

Expand your vegetable palate by purchasing bags of mixed frozen vegetables. Try Asian style, California style, and any other mixtures you can find. Feel free to add teriyaki sauce, brown sugar, garlic, cinnamon, nuts, Italian spices, pineapple, or anything else you wish to try. These mixtures can be boiled, microwaved, baked, or stir fried.

Make vegetable soups beginning with tomato juice, a V-8-type juice, chicken broth, or beef broth. Add any vegetables you like, and simmer for at least one hour. You can include fresh, canned, or frozen vegetables. You may need to add one tablespoon of margarine or oil. Add salt, pepper, or garlic if desired.

Studies have revealed that some vegetables lose part of their nutrients when microwaved. Try to cook them by another method, when possible. When you boil vegetables, use only the amount of water you must have, as extra water pulls out more of the nutrients. Ideally, when boiling vegetables other than potatoes, sweet potatoes, or corn on the cob, the water will absorb while cooking, and there will be little-to-no leftover water.

## Fruits

Whole, fresh fruits are healthiest. Eat a variety of berries, fresh when in season and frozen the rest of the year. Take advantage of the bounty of each season and explore different melons, citrus, and exotic fruits. Drink fruit juices and nectars occasionally. They are a much better option than sodas. Read the labels carefully, and make sure the juices do not have added sugar, glucose, or corn syrup. As with vegetables, seek to eat all the colors of the rainbow for maximum nutrition. If you purchase canned fruit, make sure the label states that it is in juice, and not sugar or corn syrup.

If you tire of whole fruit, you can add it to yogurt, cottage cheese, hot or cold cereal, salad, or vegetables. Here are some other simple ideas:

Apples:

- Make applesauce or buy unsweetened applesauce
- Cook apples and add cinnamon, margarine, and brown or white sugar
- Eat apple slices with sweetened peanut butter
- Bake apples in the oven with cinnamon and cloves

Oranges and other citrus:

- Slice the whole orange and add to poultry dishes, or use as a garnish for meals
- Add to cold tea
- Make home-squeezed juice, and include the pulp
- Use the juice with brown sugar or honey for a marinade
- Add small chunks to salad

Grapes:

- Cut in two and add to salad

Pears:

- Bake with sugar

Pineapple:

- Use as a basting sauce with juice
- Add the fruit and juice to mixed vegetable dishes, including stir fries
- Add to chicken
- Put small pieces in a salad
- Grill on the Foreman-type grill
- Add a slice to a chicken sandwich
- Add the fruit and juice to sweet potatoes

Bananas:

- Add to sweet bread recipes
- Eat with peanut butter
- Eat as a sandwich with a bit of Miracle-Whip-type dressing or mayonnaise

Fruit salad should be a rare treat. Add at least four kinds of fruit to mayonnaise or dressing, milk, sugar, and nuts (other than peanuts). You can add miniature marshmallows, if desired. Some of the best fruits for fruit salad include bananas, grapes, apples, maraschino cherries, and pineapple.

## Whole grains

If you have ever seen a big variety of whole-grain breads and rolls at a buffet, that should give you an idea of the many grains available. Consider trying these different breads:

- Oatmeal bread
- Rye bread
- Whole-wheat bread

Think of grains as more than breads. Eat oatmeal, whole-grain rice, ground whole corn, popcorn, barley, and couscous. When baking, use whole-wheat flour instead of processed flour. If you do not like the flavor or texture, try mixing it half and half. Whole-wheat flour makes good breakfast muffins. Use oats for cookies, breads, and muffins, and to add texture to ground turkey, chicken, or beef meatloaf or meatballs.

## Beans

Beans come in a huge array of colors and sizes. If you are only familiar with two or three varieties, this is a good time to experiment. All beans are quite healthy and full of fiber. It is a good idea to eat beans at least twice a week. Beans can also be added to almost any vegetable dish. They go well in soups and stews. "Pork and beans" and baked beans are tasty with picnic foods, such as sandwiches or chicken.

Purchase a container of 16-bean soup with dried beans. Read the instructions while you are in the grocery store, as it may call for oil, canned tomatoes, or other ingredients you may not have. Eating this soup will familiarize you with many different types of beans, and you can begin to make your favorite beans on a regular basis. If you eat daily in the school cafeteria, and it rarely serves beans, ask the director to provide them more often.

Beans are frequently served with crackers or cornbread. Refried beans can be made from leftover pinto beans. Add one tablespoon of oil to a skillet and heat over medium heat. Remove excess liquid from two cups of pinto beans and mash with a masher. Add beans to skillet, and add salt and pepper to taste. Cook several minutes until beans are of desired consistency. This dish is excellent with Mexican dishes, such as tacos. They can be added to salads, burritos, or nachos.

To make basic pinto beans, rinse and sort the beans. You can presoak the beans using one of two methods:

1.  Place two cups of beans into a large saucepan filled with six to eight cups of water. Cover and allow to sit overnight or for eight hours. Discard the water.

2.  Place two cups of beans in a large saucepan filled with six to eight cups of water. Cover and heat at medium high until boiling. Allow to boil for one minute and turn off heat. Allow to sit for two hours. Discard the water.

Now that your beans are soaked, add six cups of water and bring them to a boil at medium high. Reduce heat to medium. Keep them covered, and check them every 30 minutes to make sure they are not sticking on the bottom. Add water as necessary to keep at least one inch of water above the beans. After three hours, check the beans for softness. If they are soft, cook with the lid off until they are as thick as you would like. Add salt during this period. If they are not soft enough, check every 15 minutes, removing the lid and cooking until desired thickness once they are soft. It makes six servings.

In reality, most people add other items to their beans. In the South, many people add a piece of salt pork or ham hock early in the cooking process. You can also add a raw slice of bacon or a tablespoon of bacon grease for flavor. Smoke seasoning can be added. Some cooks add a can of diced tomatoes in juice and a tablespoon of lemon juice. Tomatoes should be added in the last 30 minutes of cooking. A diced white or yellow onion can be added at any time during the cooking. Pepper can be added for flavor.

Another idea is to make the beans two-thirds pinto beans and one-third navy beans. This adds variety and a different flavor to the beans and is considered superior to many. As long as you let the meat get completely done, and you do not burn the beans or get them too salty, it is hard to go wrong. Enjoy your beans, and offer some to your friends.

Now that you can make pinto beans, experiment with some of the other beans you find. Follow their specific instructions carefully. Many do not require cooking for as long as pinto beans.

## Lentils

Lentils are delicious and easy to make. Rinse and sort one half-cup of lentils. Add to two cups of water in a medium saucepan, and heat to boiling on medium high heat. Cover and reduce heat to low. Cook for 20 minutes, checking every 5 minutes. Uncover, add salt to taste, and cook for five additional minutes. Lentils are a good source of fiber and an easy lunch.

## Oils

While you should focus on olive oil and canola oil for your cooking needs, a variety of oils can add life to your dishes. Peanut oil works well in Asian dishes and is used for deep frying turkeys. It can also be used for other deep frying. Corn oil is a healthy alternative, but does not work well when cooking eggs. Vegetable oil is actually soybean oil and should be an infrequent choice. It works well in baked goods that call for oil, such as cake. It also fries well, such as when one prepares French fries or fried chicken. Cottonseed oil and safflower oil have light, pleasant tastes and can be used anywhere canola oil is called for. Olive oil comes in many varieties, such as virgin and extra virgin. Read the label to find the best use of each type of olive oil. Some are best for drizzling on bread or salad, while others are intended for baking or sautéing. They have different flavors, so if you try one and do not like it, try another. The darker colored ones have the most flavor. Olive oil can add an unwelcome taste to cakes and similar items. Flavored oils are fun to try as an alternative to margarine on bread.

## Dark chocolate

Dark chocolate contains antioxidants known as flavonoids. You want to limit milk-chocolate offerings and look for dark chocolate that is greater than 70 percent cocoa. It is a good idea to consume one ounce per day of high-quality dark chocolate. Take into account the 135 calories found in the typical ounce of dark chocolate, and do not consume it with milk products. This may be the tastiest item you eat for your health.

## Healthy beverage options

You probably realize that sodas, milkshakes, and energy drinks are not the best beverage choices, but the following is a list of good ones.

- Water – Water is fantastic in all its forms. Lemon can be added if desired.

- Green tea – This cup of antioxidants is best consumed straight, but sweetener can be added.

- Black tea – Along with orange pekoe tea, this is what we think of as regular tea. It also contains antioxidants and can be drunk straight or with sugar, sweetener, or lemon.

- Soy milk – This beverage provides nutrition and good taste. It comes in several flavors.

- Skim milk – Milk helps you to meet your calcium/dairy needs.

- Coffee – One or two cups of black coffee consumed early in the day provides antioxidant effects and lowers the risk of type II diabetes, Parkinson's disease, and possibly other diseases. Watch your additives, or this can become a high-calorie drink. Drink half-caff or decaf if the caffeine bothers you.

- Vegetable juices – Choose low-sodium varieties of tomato or other juices. Other vegetable juices are healthy as well. They provide vitamins, other antioxidants, and some fiber to our diets.

- Fruit juices – If you do not eat enough whole fruit, small quantities of fruit juice can be a healthy addition to your diet. You can also find half-juice / half-water mixtures, or make your own. Some of the best juices include pomegranate, orange, grape, apple, mango nectar, and papaya nectar. Juices that are 100-percent juice are healthy. Avoid those with sugar, glucose, sucrose, corn syrup, or high-fructose corn syrup. Do not consume grapefruit juice at the same time you consume medication without medical approval, as it interferes with the absorption of many medicines. Fruit juices provide vitamins and other antioxidants.

- Smoothies – These drinks, when made with fat-free yo-gurt and fruit, can be a healthy beverage. Wheat germ or other fiber can be added. Monitor the number of calories, and limit them to 200 calories for a snack smoothie, or 450 calories for a meal smoothie.

- Cocoa – Some varieties of dark chocolate cocoa are healthy, in moderation. Cocoa provides antioxidants, but should not contain milk, as the milk counteracts the helpful effects. Watch the nutrition labels to find the healthiest cocoa.

- Low-fat buttermilk – This drink is another good way to meet your calcium/dairy requirements.

You may find other beverages that make positive health claims. Read the labels carefully, count the total calories, and use your common sense.

# CHAPTER 10

## Sophomore Year Recipes

## Chicken Noodle Soup

**Ingredients:**

3 cans chicken broth

8 ounces white meat chicken
— cooked and cubed

1 large carrot

1 rib celery

¼ medium onion

1 bay leaf

1 teaspoon parsley

½ teaspoon pepper

1 teaspoon margarine

1 ounce egg noodles

| Nutrition Facts | |
|---|---|
| per serving | |
| makes 4 servings | |
| **Amount per serving** | |
| **Calories** | 269 |
| Calories from fat | 104 |
| **% Daily Value \*** | |
| **Total Fat 11.7g** | 18% |
| Saturated Fat 3.1g | 15% |
| **Cholesterol 58mg** | 19% |
| **Sodium 1953mg** | 81% |
| **Total Carbohydrate 10.9g** | 4% |
| Dietary Fiber 2.2g | 9% |
| **Protein 30.3g** | |
| Percent values are based on a 2,000 calorie per day diet. Your daily values may differ. | |
| **Additional Information** | |
| 38.7% of calories from Fat 16.2% from Carbohydrates 45.1% from Protein | |

## Instructions:

Add the chicken broth to a large saucepan or Crock-Pot. Heat on medium until lightly boiling. Add chicken. Peel and cut carrot into small "wheels" and add. Cut celery into ¼-inch slices and add to broth. Cut onion into tiny pieces and add. Add bay leaf and pepper. Allow to return to a boil and then simmer on low for 1 hour. Keep covered at all times. Add egg noodles and margarine. Cook 30 minutes and add parsley. Cook another 10 minutes and taste. If the broth tastes weak, add up to 1 teaspoon of salt or ½ of a chicken bouillon cube. Simmer for 15 additional minutes, remove the bay leaf, and serve hot. Makes 4 servings.

## Accompaniments:

Serve alone or with oyster or saltine crackers. Add an orange or tangerine for dessert.

**Tips:**

*Chicken soup is soothing when you have a cold or the flu. You may wish to prepare this dish for a sick friend.*

# Grilled Veggies

**Ingredients:**

- 1 onion (can be red, white, or yellow)
- 1 squash
- 1 zucchini
- 1 portabello mushroom
- 1 tablespoon olive oil

**Instructions:**

Heat the Foreman-type grill. Slice the onion into ⅓-inch thick slices. Remove the cap and the bottom of the squash and the zucchini and slice them length-wise into four pieces each. Remove the stem of the mushroom (you will use both the cap and the stem). Coat some of the vegetables with olive oil and place on the grill. Watch closely and remove when the vegetables are soft and have nice grill marks. Some of the pieces may need to be removed sooner than others. Replace the done slices with more oil-coated ones until all the pieces are grilled.

| Nutrition Facts | |
|---|---|
| per serving | |
| makes 1 serving | |
| **Amount per serving** | |
| **Calories** | 308 |
| Calories from fat | 134 |
| **% Daily Value \*** | |
| **Total Fat 15g** | 23% |
| Saturated Fat 2.1g | 10% |
| **Cholesterol 0mg** | 0% |
| **Sodium 17mg** | 1% |
| **Total Carbohydrate 35.3g** | 12% |
| Dietary Fiber 10g | 40% |
| **Protein 8.1g** | |
| Percent values are based on a 2,000 calorie per day diet. Your daily values may differ. | |
| **Additional Information** | |
| 43.6% of calories from Fat | |
| 45.9% from Carbohydrates | |
| 10.5% from Protein | |

**Accompaniments:**

Grilled veggies naturally complement other grilled foods, such as grilled chicken, salmon, or steak. Add a whole-wheat roll, garlic breadstick, or slice of French bread if desired. For dessert, fat-free chocolate pudding or another pudding will be refreshing.

**Tips:**

*This is one of the easiest ways to eat your daily vegetables. The grill adds an immediate gourmet flavor.*

# Oven Baked Veggies

### Ingredients:

- 1 potato
- 1 sweet potato
- 1 large onion (red, white or yellow)
- 3 other vegetables of your choosing
- 2 tablespoons minced garlic
- 1 teaspoon salt
- ½ teaspoon pepper (optional)
- 1 tablespoon olive oil

| Nutrition Facts | |
|---|---|
| per serving | |
| makes 2 servings | |
| **Amount per serving** | |
| **Calories** | 257 |
| Calories from fat | 67 |
| | **% Daily Value \*** |
| **Total Fat 7.4g** | 11% |
| Saturated Fat 0.9g | 4% |
| **Cholesterol 0mg** | 0% |
| **Sodium 1210mg** | 50% |
| **Total Carbohydrate 42.5g** | 14% |
| Dietary Fiber 6.8g | 27% |
| **Protein 4.9g** | |
| Percent values are based on a 2,000 calorie per day diet. Your daily values may differ. | |
| **Additional Information** 26.1% of calories from Fat 66.3% from Carbohydrates 7.6% from Protein | |

### Instructions:

Preheat oven to 400 degrees. Dice the potato into 1-inch cubes with the peel left on. Dice the sweet potato the same way. Dice the onion into medium-size chunks. Place the diced vegetables in a baking dish. Add three other fresh vegetables, diced, if larger than 1 inch. Add olive oil, salt, pepper, and garlic and toss together. Place in oven on middle rack. Check after 15 minutes and move to the lowest rack if browning too quickly. Cook another 10 to 20 minutes until vegetables are lightly browned. Makes 2 servings.

### Accompaniments:

Serve this as a meatless meal. Add a breadstick if desired. If dessert is desired, choose a small peanut butter cookie or other cookie.

**Tips:**

*This dish can be made with your leftover fresh vegetables. It smells good while cooking and is frequently a favorite among people who normally are not fans of vegetables.*

# Broiled Tomato

## Ingredients:

1 large tomato
1 ounce grated Parmesan
   cheese
Sprinkle of oregano

## Instructions:

Preheat oven to 400 degrees. Choose a tomato that will stand on its own, and place it in an oven safe pan. Slice off the top ¼ of the tomato and place in the pan beside the tomato. Slightly shell out the tomato and sprinkle the oregano inside. Add the Parmesan cheese, leaving the top of the cheese parallel with the top of the tomato. Bake on the lowest rack for 15 minutes, and check to make sure the tomato has not turned over and that the tomato top is not getting over done. Continue to cook until the tomato looks soft but is maintaining its shape. Remove the top of the tomato from the pan. Turn the oven to broil, keeping the pan on the lowest rack. Watch the tomato closely, and remove when the cheese begins to brown slightly. Replace the top of the tomato, allow to set for 5 minutes, and enjoy.

| Nutrition Facts per serving makes 1 serving | |
|---|---|
| **Amount per serving** | |
| **Calories** | 186 |
| Calories from fat | 84 |
| % Daily Value * | |
| **Total Fat 9.2g** | 14% |
| Saturated Fat 5.5g | 28% |
| **Cholesterol 22mg** | 7% |
| **Sodium 548mg** | 23% |
| **Total Carbohydrate 11.7g** | 4% |
| Dietary Fiber 2.6g | 10% |
| **Protein 13.7g** | |
| Percent values are based on a 2,000 calorie per day diet. Your daily values may differ. | |
| **Additional Information** 45.3% of calories from Fat 25.2% from Carbohydrates 29.5% from Protein | |

## Accompaniments:

This dish goes well with hamburger steak and a vegetable, such as asparagus or lima beans. It can be eaten on its own for a light lunch. If you wish to serve dessert, consider a chocolate chip cookie or a small milkshake.

**Tips:**

*These do not hold up well, and you will not want to make them ahead or use them as leftovers. They are easy to prepare as you grill or fry a hamburger steak. As an alternative, replace half the Parmesan cheese with the same amount of cheddar cheese.*

# Crock-Pot Lima Beans

### Ingredients:

1 pound giant lima beans

2 slices bacon

2 teaspoon salt

1 teaspoon pepper

1 tablespoon margarine

### Instructions:

Soak lima beans in a bowl with 1 quart of water for 4 to 8 hours. Discard the water. Add 2 quarts of water to Crock-Pot and turn on highest setting. Add the lima beans. Keep covered. Cut each slice of bacon into four pieces and add to the water when it begins to boil lightly. Reduce the heat to low and allow to cook at least 4 hours. Check every half-hour by stirring to prevent sticking on the bottom. Add additional water if necessary, 1 cup at a time. After 4 hours from the time the water began to boil, take out a bean and see whether it is soft. If it is not, turn the heat to high and check every 20 minutes. When the beans are soft, remove the cover, add the salt, pepper, and margarine, and cook on high for 20 minutes. Stir every few minutes to prevent burning or sticking on the bottom. Serve as 4 large servings. Season to taste.

## Nutrition Facts

per serving
makes 4 servings

| Amount per serving | |
| --- | --- |
| **Calories** | 270 |
| Calories from fat | 154 |
| | **% Daily Value \*** |
| **Total Fat 17.1g** | 26% |
| Saturated Fat 5.5g | 28% |
| **Cholesterol 24mg** | 8% |
| **Sodium 1917mg** | 80% |
| **Total Carbohydrate 15.6g** | 5% |
| Dietary Fiber 4.2g | 17% |
| **Protein 13.3g** | |

Percent values are based on a 2,000 calorie per day diet. Your daily values may differ.

**Additional Information**
57.1% of calories from Fat
23.1% from Carbohydrates
19.7% from Protein

**Accompaniments:**

This dish goes well with cornbread, or cornbread muffins and a green onion. If you do not have cornbread, saltine crackers make an acceptable substitute. Offer milk or buttermilk with this meal. If dessert is desired, consider sugar-free fruited gelatin.

**Tips:**

*These beans, like all beans, contain a good deal of fiber and can create gas symptoms. If you decide not to add the bacon, add an additional tablespoon of margarine, olive oil, or canola oil when you add the margarine. Experiment with different flavors. Some add mayonnaise, ketchup, and hot sauce to their bowl of lima beans.*

# Beef and Broccoli Stir Fry

**Ingredients:**

4 ounces beef round steak, thinly sliced into strips

2 cups of broccoli florets

½ onion — white or yellow, chopped

2 tablespoons soy sauce

1 teaspoon sugar or brown sugar

¼ teaspoon ginger, or ½ teaspoon gingerroot

½ teaspoon garlic salt

2 tablespoons peanut oil or canola oil

| Nutrition Facts | |
|---|---|
| per serving | |
| makes 1 serving | |
| **Amount per serving** | |
| **Calories** | 563 |
| Calories from fat | 303 |
| **% Daily Value \*** | |
| **Total Fat 33.6g** | 52% |
| Saturated Fat 6.8g | 34% |
| **Cholesterol 88mg** | 29% |
| **Sodium 2136mg** | 89% |
| **Total Carbohydrate 21.9g** | 7% |
| Dietary Fiber 6.8g | 27% |
| **Protein 43.1g** | |
| Percent values are based on a 2,000 calorie per day diet. Your daily values may differ. | |
| **Additional Information** | |
| 53.8% of calories from Fat | |
| 15.6% from Carbohydrates | |
| 30.6% from Protein | |

## Instructions:

In a medium-size bowl, combine 1 tablespoon of the soy sauce, sugar, ginger, garlic salt, and 1 tablespoon of the oil. Add the beef to the mixture, covering the beef. Add 1 tablespoon of oil to a wok or large skillet and turn on medium-high. When the oil is hot, add the beef and stir frequently. Cook 3 minutes, and add the onion and broccoli. When the beef is cooked, add the remaining tablespoon of soy sauce and cook 1 additional minute. Remove from heat and serve immediately.

## Accompaniments:

This dish makes a large dinner meal. Accompany with a small side dish of white or whole-grain rice if desired. Have hot or iced tea as a beverage and fresh orange slices for dessert.

### Tips:

When you master this dish, you can begin to experiment with different vegetables. Carrots, bell peppers, and mushrooms can be substituted or added. Professional chefs add cornstarch to the marinade and to the soy sauce near the end of the cooking. It can be tricky to work with, and I do not recommend it to new cooks. When serving this meal to a guest, consider placing the rice on the plate first, scattered thinly all over the plate. Add the beef and broccoli on top of the rice. Serve with chopsticks for a gourmet flair.

# Kabobs

### Ingredients:

8 one-inch chunks beef,
   pork, chicken, or turkey
1 teaspoon salt

Choose 2 or 3:

Cherry tomatoes
Small mushrooms
Baby onions or white,
   yellow, or red onions
   sliced into quarters
Thick bell pepper slices
Fresh pineapple cubes
Squash rounds
Zucchini rounds

| Nutrition Facts | |
|---|---|
| per serving | |
| makes 1 serving | |
| **Amount per serving** | |
| **Calories** | 549 |
| Calories from fat | 170 |
| | **% Daily Value \*** |
| **Total Fat 18.9g** | 29% |
| Saturated Fat 7.2g | 36% |
| **Cholesterol 202mg** | 67% |
| **Sodium 165mg** | 7% |
| **Total Carbohydrate 22.5g** | 8% |
| Dietary Fiber 5.2g | 21% |
| **Protein 72.2g** | |
| Percent values are based on a 2,000 calorie per day diet. Your daily values may differ. | |
| **Additional Information** 31% of calories from Fat 16.4% from Carbohydrates 52.6% from Protein | |

### Instructions:

Use two metal skewers or wooden skewers that have soaked in water for 1 hour. Thread the meat and other ingredients onto the skewer, alternating the meat. These can be cooked on a traditional grill, a large Foreman-type grill, or in the oven. If cooking on any type of grill, add kabobs when hot and turn frequently. Salt occasionally while cooking. If you plan to use the oven, preheat it to 425 degrees. Spray a cookie sheet with spray oil and place the kabobs, not touching, on the sheet. Add salt. Place on the middle rack of the oven. Turn every 10 minutes, adding salt occasionally. Regardless of cooking method, make sure the meat is fully done before eating.

### Accompaniments:

These kabobs are a meal in themselves. Serve with a picnic-type beverage, such as lemonade. If dessert is desired, consider watermelon or homemade-style vanilla ice cream.

**Tips:**
*A dinner of kabobs is fun to make as well as eat. Experiment with basting sauces, such as orange juice, pineapple juice, or honey. You can add garlic or any other spices or herbs.*

# Mushroom Omelet

### Ingredients:

2 large eggs

1 teaspoon margarine or
   butter

½ teaspoon salt

3 ounces sliced mushrooms

### Instructions:

Add margarine or butter to a medium or large skillet over medium heat. Add mushrooms and sauté until some of the mushrooms begin to brown. Place the mushrooms in a small bowl and remove the skillet from the burner. Spray the skillet with spray oil, being careful not to breathe the fumes. Lower the heat to medium-low. Crack the eggs and place in a medium-size bowl. Add 1 teaspoon of water and beat thoroughly with a whip or blender on high for 1 minute. Alternatively, beat with a fork for 3 minutes. Pour eggs into the skillet and cover. Check after 4 minutes. As the egg begins to set, wiggle the skillet and move the unset part of the egg around to the edges of the skillet. When the egg can be turned over, carefully turn it with one or two spatulas. Cover for 1 minute. Wiggle pan to move the unset egg to the edges. When the egg is almost

| Nutrition Facts | |
|---|---|
| per serving | |
| makes 1 serving | |
| **Amount per serving** | |
| **Calories** | 205 |
| Calories from fat | 127 |
| | **% Daily Value \*** |
| **Total Fat 14.2g** | 22% |
| Saturated Fat 3.8g | 19% |
| **Cholesterol 425mg** | 142% |
| **Sodium 1308mg** | 54% |
| **Total Carbohydrate 5.2g** | 2% |
| Dietary Fiber 1g | 4% |
| **Protein 14.3g** | |
| Percent values are based on a 2,000 calorie per day diet. Your daily values may differ. | |
| **Additional Information** | |
| 62% of calories from Fat 10.1% from Carbohydrates 27.9% from Protein | |

completely set, add the mushrooms to one half of the egg. Avoid the very edges. Take the spatula and place the empty half of the egg over the other half. Turn the omelet over after 1 minute. Remove when done and add salt.

## Accompaniments:

This breakfast dish can be served with 1 slice of bacon if desired. Drink orange juice as a beverage.

### Tips:

*Ideally, an omelet is only very lightly browned, if at all. This can take practice. For variety, you can add 2 ounces of any variety of shredded cheese or a piece of American cheese, cut into cubes. Add the cheese when you add the mushrooms, and remove when the cheese is half melted. It will continue to melt inside the omelet. This meal can also be eaten for lunch or dinner, if you are low on groceries.*

# Pineapple Coleslaw

## Ingredients:

- ¼ cup diced pineapple (drained)
- 1 teaspoon sugar
- 1 teaspoon milk
- 1 cup of shredded cabbage
- ¼ carrot, shredded
- 1 tablespoon Miracle Whip®-type salad dressing or mayonnaise
- Dash of salt

| Nutrition Facts | |
|---|---|
| per serving makes 1 serving | |
| **Amount per serving** | |
| **Calories** | 130 |
| Calories from fat | 10 |
| % Daily Value * | |
| **Total Fat 1.2g** | 2% |
| Saturated Fat 0.5g | 2% |
| **Cholesterol 6mg** | 2% |
| **Sodium 405mg** | 17% |
| **Total Carbohydrate 28.3g** | 9% |
| Dietary Fiber 3.3g | 13% |
| **Protein 1.6g** | |
| Percent values are based on a 2,000 calorie per day diet. Your daily values may differ. | |
| **Additional Information** 7.7% of calories from Fat 87.3% from Carbohydrates 4.9% from Protein | |

## Instructions:

Add all ingredients to a large bowl and stir. Place in refrigerator for at least 1 hour. Stir just prior to serving.

## Accompaniments:

This dish can accompany baked or fried fish, barbecued chicken, pork, or fried chicken. Serve with a bland potato, such as mashed potatoes or fried potatoes.

**Tips:**

*Save any leftover pineapple juice for marinating, adding to a recipe, or drinking. For variety, add 1 ounce of raisins. If the slaw stays in the refrigerator over one day, you may have to add an additional ½ teaspoon of milk.*

# Breakfast Burrito

## Ingredients:

1 burrito

1 large egg

1 tablespoon milk

1 ounce of diced onion

1 ounce of diced bell
    pepper, any color

1 ounce of diced tomato

Dash of salt

Dash of pepper

1 sausage patty, cooked

2 teaspoons margarine

1 ounce shredded cheddar
    cheese

| Nutrition Facts | |
|---|---|
| per serving | |
| makes 1 serving | |
| **Amount per serving** | |
| **Calories** | 548 |
| Calories from fat | 300 |
| | **% Daily Value \*** |
| **Total Fat 33.4g** | 51% |
| Saturated Fat 12.5g | 62% |
| **Cholesterol 447mg** | 149% |
| **Sodium 1120mg** | 47% |
| **Total Carbohydrate 35.3g** | 12% |
| Dietary Fiber 2.8g | 11% |
| **Protein 26.8g** | |

Percent values are based on a 2,000 calorie per day diet. Your daily values may differ.

**Additional Information**
54.7% of calories from Fat
25.7% from Carbohydrates
19.5% from Protein

**Instructions:**

Place the margarine in a skillet and heat on medium. Add the vegetables and allow to cook 2 minutes, until the veggies begin to soften. Meanwhile, crack the egg and place it into a medium-size bowl. Add milk, salt, and pepper. Beat well and add to the veggies. Stir frequently, allowing the egg to set but not to turn brown. When the egg is just done, crumble the sausage patty and add. Cook for 30 seconds and remove from heat. Add the cheese and stir while the egg mixture is still in the skillet.

Heat the burrito in the microwave for 25 seconds on high. Alternatively, preheat the oven to 350 degrees and place the burrito on a cookie sheet. Place on the middle rack of the oven for 4 minutes or until hot. Place the burrito on a plate and add filling. Roll burrito closed, and enjoy.

**Accompaniments:**

This breakfast meal can be served with a glass of milk or orange juice.

**Tips:**

*For instructions on cooking the sausage, refer to Cooking Basics — Breakfast in Chapter 6. If desired, add a teaspoon of salsa to the burrito. You can prepare two or three at once by multiplying the recipe, refrigerating the extra ones, and heating in the microwave or oven the next morning. Wrap the burrito in a napkin or paper towel, and you are set to go. To make this dish healthier, use turkey or vegetarian sausage.*

# Apricot Pie

### Ingredients:

5 pack of refrigerated rising
   buttermilk biscuits

6 ounces of dried apricots

1 teaspoon margarine

2 tablespoons flour

### Instructions:

Place the apricots in a small saucepan and cover with water. Add margarine. Cover and heat on medium-high until boiling. Reduce heat to low and cook for 30 minutes or until apricots have softened. Add ¼ cup water if needed during cooking. Remove from heat and beat with mixer on medium until smooth.

Preheat oven to 375 degrees. Lightly flour a plate or board and place the first uncooked biscuit on it. Flour a rolling pin or a tall glass and roll the dough until it is twice its original diameter. Add ⅕ of the apricots to one half of the dough, avoiding the very edge. Fold the remaining dough over to enclose the apricots and pinch the edges closed. Place on a cookie sheet and make the other four pies. Place the cookie sheet in the oven on the middle rack for 9 minutes, checking after 7 minutes. Remove when pies are lightly brown. Makes 5 servings.

| Nutrition Facts | |
|---|---|
| per serving | |
| makes 5 servings | |
| **Amount per serving** | |
| **Calories** | 490 |
| Calories from fat | 250 |
| | **% Daily Value \*** |
| **Total Fat 12g** | 17% |
| Saturated Fat 3g | 15% |
| **Cholesterol 0mg** | 0% |
| **Sodium 690mg** | 27% |
| **Total Carbohydrate 101.5g** | 38% |
| Dietary Fiber 10g | 42% |
| **Protein 8g** | |
| Percent values are based on a 2,000 calorie per day diet. Your daily values may differ. | |
| **Additional Information** | |
| 38.4% of calories from Fat 55.1% from Carbohydrates 6.5% from Protein | |

## Accompaniments:

This pie can be eaten alone or with a glass of milk. If it is to be eaten as dessert, serve it with a light meal that does not have bread or sweets. A light salad with grilled chicken would be ideal.

**Tips:**

*Baking can be fun and simple. Creating this delicious treat may cause you to develop a lifelong love of baking. Share the extra pies with friends.*

# Easy Garlic Rolls

## Ingredients:

> ½ cup self-rising flour
> 1 tablespoon Miracle-Whip-type salad dressing or mayonnaise
> ¼ cup milk
> ½ teaspoon garlic powder or garlic salt

## Instructions:

Preheat oven to 375 degrees. Place all ingredients in a small bowl and blend well with a fork. Spray four cups of a muffin pan and distribute the dough evenly into the four cups. Place the muffin pan on the middle rack of the oven. Check after 10 minutes and remove when rolls begin to lightly brown. Serve warm. Makes 4 servings.

| Nutrition Facts | |
|---|---|
| per serving | |
| makes 4 servings | |
| **Amount per serving** | |
| **Calories** | 67 |
| Calories from fat | 6 |
| **% Daily Value \*** | |
| **Total Fat 0.7g** | 1% |
| Saturated Fat 0.3g | 2% |
| **Cholesterol 3mg** | 1% |
| **Sodium 225mg** | 9% |
| **Total Carbohydrate 13g** | 4% |
| Dietary Fiber 0.4g | 2% |
| **Protein 2.2g** | |
| Percent values are based on a 2,000 calorie per day diet. Your daily values may differ. | |
| **Additional Information** 9% of calories from Fat 77.8% from Carbohydrates 13.2% from Protein | |

## Accompaniments:

Garlic rolls are appropriate with Italian dishes, such as spaghetti or lasagna. They can also accompany any beef dish, whether steak or meatloaf and veggies. Serve with milk or iced tea and a bland dessert, such as a bowl of vanilla low-fat frozen yogurt, if desired.

> **Tips:**
> *This is a simple recipe to make when you desire bread with a meal. Handle the rolls carefully, as they crumble easier than most rolls. Add a sprinkle of parsley to the batter if you have it. For extra decadence, serve with margarine, butter, or honey butter.*

# Orange Chicken and Veggie Stir Fry

**Ingredients:**

   4 ounce boneless, skinless chicken breast

   ¼ cup orange marmalade

   ½ cup chicken broth

   2 teaspoons minced garlic

   1 tablespoon soy sauce

   1 tablespoon peanut oil or canola oil

Pick 3 of the following vegetables:

   ½ cup broccoli florets

   ½ chopped large onion — white, yellow, or red

   ½ bell pepper, any color

   ½ cup of snow peas

   ½ cup cauliflower

| Nutrition Facts |  |  |
|---|---|---|
| per serving |  |  |
| makes 1 serving |  |  |
| **Amount per serving** |  |  |
| **Calories** |  | 718 |
| Calories from fat |  | 271 |
|  |  | **% Daily Value \*** |
| **Total Fat 30.1g** |  | 46% |
| Saturated Fat 6.8g |  | 34% |
| **Cholesterol 106mg** |  | 35% |
| **Sodium 1975mg** |  | 82% |
| **Total Carbohydrate 68.6g** |  | 23% |
| Dietary Fiber 4.4g |  | 18% |
| **Protein 43.2g** |  |  |
| Percent values are based on a 2,000 calorie per day diet. Your daily values may differ. |  |  |
| **Additional Information** 37.7% of calories from Fat 38.2% from Carbohydrates 24.1% from Protein |  |  |

**Instructions:**

Pour oil into a wok or large skillet. Heat to medium. Add chicken broth, marmalade, and soy sauce to a medium-size bowl. Slice the chicken into 2-inch by ½-inch strips and place in the hot oil. Cook until lightly brown. Add the vegetables and garlic, and continue to heat for 5 minutes. Add the sauce, stir well, and continue to heat for 2 more minutes.

## Accompaniments:

This dish can be served on a bed of white or whole-grain rice. Serve with iced or hot tea. If dessert is desired, serve a cookie or miniature cake. A ginger or almond cookie is ideal.

**Tips:**

*Sesame seeds can be added for the last 5 minutes of cooking. You can offer chopsticks if you create this meal for guests. If you purchased marmalade to make this recipe, use the rest of it for breakfast toast or another morning bread.*

# Easy Egg Drop Soup

## Ingredients:

1 can of chicken broth

1 large egg

1 small gingerroot or ¼ teaspoon ginger

½ teaspoon chicken bullion

2 tablespoons green onion, optional

1 teaspoon parsley, optional

| Nutrition Facts | |
|---|---|
| per serving | |
| makes 2 servings | |
| **Amount per serving** | |
| **Calories** | 86 |
| Calories from fat | 37 |
| **% Daily Value \*** | |
| **Total Fat 4g** | 6% |
| Saturated Fat 1.3g | 6% |
| **Cholesterol 108mg** | 36% |
| **Sodium 971mg** | 40% |
| **Total Carbohydrate 2.5g** | 1% |
| Dietary Fiber 0.2g | 1% |
| **Protein 9.8g** | |
| Percent values are based on a 2,000 calorie per day diet. Your daily values may differ. | |
| **Additional Information** | |
| 42.9% of calories from Fat 11.6% from Carbohydrates 45.5% from Protein | |

## Instructions:

Add the chicken broth to a medium-size saucepan and heat on medium-high. Add the washed, peeled, whole piece of gingerroot to the broth. When the broth begins to boil, cover the pan and reduce the heat to low. Simmer 5 minutes and add bullion. Cook an additional 10 minutes, and carefully remove the gingerroot. Crack the egg into a small bowl and beat it with a fork or mixer. Turn the heat to medium high, and when the broth is boiling rapidly, slowly add the egg with a swirling motion. Cook for one to two minutes, until the egg is set. Add parsley if desired, and remove from heat. Pour into two serving bowls and add green onion to the center of the bowl if desired. If you do not have gingerroot, add the ginger when you add the chicken bouillon.

## Accompaniments:

This soup is traditionally served with crispy noodles as a first course of a Chinese meal. Serve with hot or iced tea, and fresh orange slices for dessert.

### Tips:

This dish is high in sodium and should be regarded as an occasional treat. Try adding 2 eggs instead of one, which makes a unique creation that you may also enjoy. Professional chefs add cornstarch to this dish, which is not recommended for beginner cooks.

# Crock-Pot Roast

## Ingredients:

- 1 2- to 3-pound beef or pork pot roast
- 1 tablespoon oil
- 1 package pot roast seasoning mix
- 4 carrots
- 6 ounces frozen peas
- 4 white or yellow onions
- 4 stalks celery
- 4 medium potatoes or 12 whole new potatoes

| Nutrition Facts | |
|---|---|
| per serving | |
| makes 8 servings | |
| **Amount per serving** | |
| **Calories** | 368 |
| Calories from fat | 97 |
| | **% Daily Value \*** |
| **Total Fat 10.8g** | 17% |
| Saturated Fat 3.3g | 16% |
| **Cholesterol 102mg** | 34% |
| **Sodium 188mg** | 8% |
| **Total Carbohydrate 27.4g** | 9% |
| Dietary Fiber 4.8g | 19% |
| **Protein 40.3g** | |
| Percent values are based on a 2,000 calorie per day diet. Your daily values may differ. | |
| **Additional Information** 26.4% of calories from Fat 29.8% from Carbohydrates 43.8% from Protein | |

## Instructions:

Take roast and pierce with fork several times on each side. Turn Crock-Pot to medium and add oil. After 5 minutes, add roast and lightly brown on each side. Add enough water to cover roast with 3 inches of water. Add pot roast seasoning mix. Note the time, and cook at medium for 1 hour. If the broth is not bubbling after 30 minutes, turn heat to high if desired. After the 1-hour mark, peel the carrots and slice into 1½ inch portions. Add to the broth. At the 1½-hour mark, slice the celery into 1-inch portions and add to the broth.

Peel the onions and cut each one into quarters and add.

At the 2-hour mark, add the whole new potatoes, or cut medium potatoes into ⅛ portions and add. If needed, add enough water to cover the roast and vegetables. At the 2½-hour mark, add the peas. At the 4-hour mark, check the roast for doneness and turn the heat up or down, depending on when you wish to serve the meal. When you are ready, remove the roast, pour broth over it and allow it to set for 10 minutes. Carve only the amount you need, and serve with a bowl of broth and vegetables. Makes around 8 servings.

## Accompaniments:

This meal is ideally served with warm biscuits. Alternatively, cornbread, French bread, Italian bread, or sourdough bread can be served. Offer fresh, whole fruit, such as an apple or pear for dessert. If a side vegetable is desired, try corn on the cob or fresh tomato slices.

### Tips:

*For variety, add 1 cup of mushrooms (any type) at the 3-hour mark. If you wish to make your own pot roast seasoning mix, combine 1 tablespoon salt, 1 teaspoon pepper, 1 tablespoon garlic salt or powder or minced garlic, and ½ teaspoon onion powder. Add 1 teaspoon seasoning salt or no-sodium seasoning, if desired.*

*When you put the roast in the refrigerator, return it to the broth and vegetables. For leftovers, take a medium-sized microwaveable bowl and add the amount of roast desired. Cut into small pieces. Add the broth and vegetables, and heat on high in the microwave for 90 seconds. Heat until hot and serve with bread.*

# JUNIOR SECTION

# CHAPTER 11

## More Cooking Methods

This chapter continues the primer begun in Chapter 6.

## Cooking Methods

### Frying

You can fry foods in several different ways, depending on the amount of oil used.

#### Frying with a non-stick pan or spray oil

This method is the healthiest of the frying alternatives.

- Boneless chicken – Place cold chicken in skillet. Cook at medium-low, turning every few minutes, until the inside is fully done. You can cook it with the lid on or off; the lid left on will leave the chicken moist and less crispy. Season as desired while cooking by adding your favorite herbs and spices.

- Fish – Place cold fish in skillet. Cook at medium low, turning often to ensure the fish does not stick to the skillet. Do not use the skillet lid unless the recipe calls for it. Add your favorite herbs and spices while cooking. Make sure the fish is completely done by checking that the thickest part flakes easily with a fork.

- Pork – Place cold pork in skillet. Cook at medium, turning several times until fully done. Pork is generally served slightly crispy, so you may wish to cook it with the lid off. Season while cooking.

- Steak – Place cold steak in skillet. Cook at medium, turning at least three times. Begin cooking with the skillet lid on, and consider removing it for the last few minutes to make it somewhat crispy. Cook to desired doneness. Make sure that steak juices are clear. You can experiment with frying the steak in a tablespoon of butter or margarine and/or two tablespoons of Worcestershire sauce.

**Frying with ¼ inch of oil in the skillet**

Heat oil to medium and add food slowly. This method works well for chicken, with or without the bone; breaded meats such as veal; cubed steak; and pork chops. When preparing fried chicken on the bone, you may need to reduce the heat to medium low and cook with the skillet lid on for most of the cooking. Fried chicken can take as long as 45 minutes to cook. Meatballs can be prepared this way as well. Try breaded vegetables with this method. Turn food occasionally and remove when done. Allow to drain on a dish with paper towels, and season as desired. This method of frying adds significant calories to your food, as a good deal of the oil is absorbed during the cooking.

## Deep frying

Deep frying must be done with caution. If you have a fryer, follow the instructions carefully. If you use a saucepan, fill it no more than halfway with oil, leaving two inches of empty pan even after the food is added. Heat the oil to medium and add one piece of the food you are preparing. If the oil is bubbling when the food is added, slowly add the rest of the food. If the oil does not bubble when the food is added, the oil is not hot enough. If the food begins to brown much too quickly, the oil is too hot. It is difficult to salvage the meal at this point, but you can attempt to remove the pan from the burner for a few minutes, and then replace it with the burner turned slightly lower. Your food may cook quickly with deep frying. Do not allow the oil to bubble up anywhere near the top of the pan, and do not leave unattended.

Deep frying is appropriate for French fries; tater tots; breaded vegetables, including onion rings; fish; chicken; hushpuppies; doughnuts; and corn dogs. It adds many calories to the foods you are cooking, most of which could be baked in the oven instead.

## Microwaving

Many foods can be prepared in the microwave. If it is your only cooking source, do not despair. For many items, prepare just as one does on a stovetop. Follow package directions, if you have them, for items such as oatmeal. Do not make a habit of microwaving using plastic or foam. Choose paper plates (for dry items), Chinet® -type plates, or durable, microwave-approved containers instead.

### Water and other liquids

Place in a microwave-safe bowl or glass (such as a glass measuring cup) and heat on high until warm or boiling, whichever is desired. Keep liquid items one inch from the top of the bowl or glass so that they will have room to boil without boiling over.

### Vegetables and fruits

Whole vegetables and fruits should be pierced in several places before cooking, or they could burst. To cook raw vegetables, such as broccoli or cauliflower, place them in a microwave-safe bowl and add two tablespoons of water. Heat on high for four minutes, and check for doneness.

### Fish

Cook fish fillets on high, and check for doneness after four minutes.

### Poultry

Prick poultry pieces with a fork in several places and cook on high, checking after eight minutes.

### Steak

Cook on high and check for doneness after four minutes.

### Ground beef

Heat a raw ground beef patty on high for three minutes and check. Cook a pound of ground beef on high for three minutes and stir. Continue to cook for three more minutes and stir. Heat for three more minutes and check for doneness.

### Pork chops

Heat on high and check after four minutes.

## Bacon

Cover raw bacon slices with a safe paper towel and check after cooking for three minutes on high.

## Sausage

Prick sausage links with a fork in several places, and check after two and a half minutes on high.

## Raw beans

To cook raw beans in the microwave, pre-soak according to the instructions in the Variety — Beans section in Chapter 9. Place the pre-soaked beans in a large, microwave-safe bowl with an equal amount of water to the beans. Cover with a loose-fitting lid, and cook on high for ten minutes. Stir and cook on medium for ten more minutes. Stir and check for doneness. Continue to cook at five-minute intervals until beans are soft. Add extra hot water if needed while cooking. Season to taste with salt, pepper, oil, or margarine.

## Pasta

To make pasta in the microwave, bring one and a half cups of water to a boil in a large bowl by heating on high. Add one or two servings of pasta and heat on high while covered loosely with a lid. Check after five minutes. Continue to cook at two-minute intervals until pasta is at desired tenderness.

## Wild rice

To prepare wild rice in the microwave, place one cup of water in a large bowl, and heat on high until boiling. Add ⅓ cup of rice and cover loosely with a lid. Heat on high for three minutes. Cook at medium for ten minutes and stir. Add ¼ cup of water if needed. Continue to cook at four-minute intervals until the rice has absorbed the water and has softened. For extra flavor, use chicken broth instead of the water.

# Beyond the Basics: Creating Traditional Favorites and Finding New Ones

To prepare your favorite foods from home, the best advice is to ask your relatives to provide the recipes for you. Ask plenty of questions, and be sure you know whether the ingredients are fresh, canned, or frozen. Ideally, you can watch the food being prepared while you take notes.

You are quite likely to find new dishes you love during your college career. If the food is from a restaurant or the cafeteria, ask for the recipe, or see whether an ingredient list is available online. If a friend created the dish, that is even easier — just watch them prepare it next time. If you come across dishes you enjoy, but that are quite complex to make, keep the recipe for the future. You can begin your post-college life with a nice supply of good cooking ideas.

## Preparing ethnic foods

### Italian cooking

Cooking Italian foods lends itself to considerable experimentation with herbs and spices. Use plenty of tomato-based sauces, garlic, onion, mushrooms, and fresh or dried herbs and spices. Explore the new pastas that contain whole grains or other healthy ingredients. Add a tablespoon of olive oil to your sauces for extra nutrition.

### Mexican cooking

Learn to make dishes that are heavy on vegetables and light on sauces. Add black beans to dishes, and learn how to make refried beans with a tablespoon of margarine instead of animal fat. Use plenty of hot spices; they are filled with antioxidants.

### Asian cooking

Prepare large cuts of vegetables, like those you find at Asian restaurants. Stir fry in a small amount of peanut oil or healthier oil. Learn how to steam vegetables. Use plenty of seafood, chicken, and tofu in your dishes. Experiment with curry, and substitute white rice with whole grain rice.

# Make Existing Recipes Healthier

There are many ways to make existing recipes healthier and lighter.

## Lower the fat and cholesterol

If your grandmother gives you a recipe that calls for ½ cup of lard, what can you do? Here are a few alternatives:

- Purchase a small can of lard and use ¼ lard and ¾ shortening (with no trans fat) to replace the lard.

- Save your bacon grease from frying bacon and add a tablespoon of it, replacing the rest with shortening.

- If the recipe calls for frying in lard or shortening, try cooking it in corn oil to see whether the food tastes just as good.

Other ways to reduce fat and cholesterol:

- Fry with a non-stick skillet or grill with a Foreman-type grill.

- Fry with spray oil instead of vegetable oil.

- Cook chicken with the skin on, but remove it prior to serving.

- Try making biscuits with tub margarine instead of lard or shortening.

- When seasoning with fat, add ⅓ of what the recipe calls for.

- Eat a smaller portion of high-fat foods, and add a large side of grilled or steamed vegetables.

- Experiment with herbs, spices, and marinades instead of greasy flavorings.

- Try spray margarine instead of adding two tablespoons of margarine or butter.

- Bake instead of fry.

## Lower the sodium

- Do not add salt to the water you are boiling foods in.

- Do not add table salt to your food. Experiment with herbs, spices, and no-salt mixtures instead.

- Purchase the low-sodium varieties of soup, broth, bacon, canned vegetables, frozen dinners, and other foods.

# Advanced Appliance Use

## Cooking with a wok

With a wok, you can create authentic Oriental dishes and many other favorites. Foods tend to be cooked at a fairly high temperature with a wok. This helps to retain the foods look, flavor, and nutrients. For basic cooking, you may add one or two tablespoons of peanut oil or your favorite oil to the wok and heat to medium high. Add strips of meat (usually beef, pork, or chicken) or whole shrimp, if desired, and cook until no longer pink. This can take just three to four minutes. Stir with wooden utensils or the utensils that came with your wok. Add desired vegetables and stir frequently.

Vegetables are often cut fairly large for wok cooking. Using the lid is optional and will make the food soft instead of crispy. Cook just until vegetables are slightly softened, usually two to five minutes. You may wish to add soy sauce or teriyaki sauce. Most meals have a nice flavor without sauce. Serve with a bed of whole-wheat noodles or rice. Many chefs simply wipe out their wok with a damp towel, followed by a dry towel, when cooking is complete. The wok gets tempered in time and becomes a better cooking tool over the years.

Some typical vegetables to cook in a wok include broccoli, squash, zucchini, onions, bell peppers, carrots, mushrooms, cabbage, baby corn, cauliflower, and green beans. You can also add bamboo shoots, tofu, and chestnuts.

# Food Substitutions

What you can do if you are lacking a part of a recipe:

- If it is a minor spice or herb, you can usually make the recipe without it.

- Many times, a vegetable can be substituted with another one.

- Sugar can often be replaced by sweetener.

- Spray oil can be substituted by taking canola oil or vegetable oil and pouring a teaspoon on the surface and wiping with a clean paper towel.

- A cup of self-rising flour can be substituted by 7 ounces of plain flour, 1½ tablespoons of baking powder, and ½ tablespoon of salt, mixed well.

- A teaspoon of baking powder can be replaced by ⅓ teaspoon of baking soda.

- A teaspoon of baking soda can be replaced by a tablespoon of baking powder and a teaspoon of salt.

- Margarine and butter are generally interchangeable. Butter is superior in baking.

# CHAPTER 12

## Exercise

## Athletes – Eating for Optimum Performance

Athletes must learn the proper way to use nutrition to increase their performance. This will vary according to the length of the events you participate in.

### Needs depend on length of event

As you begin to move, carbohydrates provide 40 to 50 percent of your energy requirements. Begin the event well-hydrated and drink cold water during the event, if possible.

Athletes who compete in events of more than 90 minutes should consume a high-carbohydrate diet for three days before the event. Stay hydrated with pure water. Fats contribute half of your energy requirements during events of this length.

Those who compete in events of more than three hours should also consume a high-carbohydrate diet for three days before the event. Drink plenty of cool water. Endurance athletes should also consume a solution containing sugar and salt during the event. Fats contribute a large amount of energy during especially long events.

## Nutrition tips for all athletes

- Athletes need more protein than non-athletes, but most Americans' needs are met by our normal diets, and extra effort is not required.

- Female athletes need to make sure they get enough calcium from their diet.

- All athletes should eat potassium-rich foods, such as bananas.

- Eat a moderate-size meal three or four hours before your competitive event. Drink two glasses of water with this meal. Make the meal high in complex carbohydrates, such as breads, fruits, and vegetables, and high in fiber and low fat.

- A small, balanced meal should be eaten after a competitive event.

## Practices to avoid

- Do not continuously eat a high-carbohydrate diet. It keeps your body from using the fats that it needs to use.

- Do not eat simple carbohydrates, such as a candy bar, immediately before performing. Your blood sugar can crash soon after.

- Do not take protein supplements. They are unnecessary and increase your need for water and oxygen.

- Do not take caffeine right before an event if you cannot stop to void during the event.

- Do not take salt tablets; they only weaken your muscles.

# Non-Athletes

## How much exercise do you need?

Write down your weekly physical activity. Do you get at least 30 minutes on most days? How about two sustained hours at least once a week? If you have difficulty getting the amount of exercise you should, evaluate the reason why. If you feel that you do not have enough time, you need to look closely at your schedule. How much of your free time is wasted? Place 30-minute blocks for exercise into your schedule for the next two weeks. Five days a week is ideal, plus a two-hour block one day. Try exercising early in the morning, before classes, and see whether it revs you up for the day. If you do not like that, try right after classes. It is best to not exercise for the last two hours you are awake each day, as it can interfere with your sleep.

If your reason for not exercising is that you just do not like it, then you need to try a variety of different activities.

## Your exercise personality

Are you competitive? Do you prefer to work in a group or alone? Does traditional exercise or walking bore you? Do you love to beat your "personal best?" Once you understand your own motives, it becomes easier to encourage yourself to get the exercise your body needs.

## Three types of exercise

### The workout

There are many types of exercise routines available today. Kick-boxing, weight lifting, Pilates, yoga, aerobics, martial arts, jogging, power walking, and calisthenics are just a few of your choices.

### Games and sports

Numerous games exist, both organized and freestyle. For group activities, do you like basketball, baseball, softball, Frisbee, football, soccer, bowling, archery, competitive running, or swimming? You can easily get two hours of sustained activity by engaging in any of these sports. For solo activities, you can swim, skate, skateboard, shoot hoops, bicycle, or dance.

### Productive activities

If your personality just does not allow you to engage in "unproductive activities," try pet walking for the local shelter, washing a car, assisting with repairs, building a fence, playing catch with a child, painting, or anything else that gets you moving.

## Why exercise?

Good physical activity helps to prevent a wide variety of diseases, including heart disease, cancer, Alzheimer's disease, and diabetes. It helps to ward off depression and alleviate anxiety. Exercising outdoors has even greater benefits. You can see nature, get vitamin D from the sunlight, and interact with others. Exercise helps keep your weight under control and aids in sleeping well. You feel emotionally better when you are in good physical shape and do not tire from simple tasks.

## How hard should you exercise?

You need to develop a good sweat most days to get maximum benefits. Some people like to track their heart rate and elevate it to certain points, but if you work hard enough that you are sweating, you will likely get substantial benefits. It is important to warm up before and cool down after exercise. Try for five minutes of a warm-up, slowly stretching and walking as you prepare for your activity. After your workout, cool down for five minutes by moving slowly in light stretches or a slow walk.

Another popular routine is to walk 10,000 steps per day. While this is a healthy concept, you will not work up the needed sweat. The best advice is to walk all you can, and get moderate to vigorous exercise most days of the week.

Another way to look at exercise is to strive to get a balance of cardiovascular aerobic activity plus strength training. As it sounds, cardio activities work your heart and lungs. This is important to keep your body in good physical shape and not lose energy too quickly. Your stamina should increase from a good cardio routine. Strength training involves moving your muscles in ways that force them to work, such as weight lifting. You do not need to lift heavy weights to obtain benefits. Hand weights of 5 pounds or so used for 15 minutes is an example of a good strength-training activity; combine this with an exercise that works your leg muscles against resistance for 15 minutes. Remember to vary your routine so that you work all your muscle groups. Strength training keeps your muscles in shape and also helps your bones on a long-term basis.

# CHAPTER 13

## Sleep

## How Much Sleep Do You Need?

A simple answer is eight hours. Some people find that they need nine. But eight hours of sleep is a lofty goal when you have a hectic schedule. As we discussed in the section about time management, it is important to add your sleep time to your daily schedule.

## Things that Interfere with Sleep

- Light
- Noise — constant or sporadic
- Eating right before bed
- Caffeine after 3 p.m.
- Stress
- Television
- Not relaxing before bed
- Drugs
- Pain or discomfort
- Not getting enough daily exercise

- Taking a nap after 4 p.m.
- Anticipation of the coming day — negative or positive
- A snoring roommate
- A room that is too warm or cold
- Uncomfortable night clothing

# Sleep Disorders and What to Do

## Insomnia

Insomnia is rampant in the United States. It is classified according to whether you have difficulty falling asleep, or whether you awaken during the night and cannot go back to sleep. For most people, medications for sleep can lead to habituation and are not a good long-term solution. If you suffer insomnia more than one night a week, you need to evaluate your sleep hygiene.

- Do you sleep in quiet surroundings and darkness?
- Do you allow yourself quiet, relaxing time before bed?
- Are you able to "shut down your mind" and fully relax?
- Do you refrain from stimulants, including caffeine?
- Do you awaken at a reasonable hour and stay awake all day?

If you answered "no" to any of these questions, try making these lifestyle changes. If you answered yes to all the questions, and still have difficulty sleeping, you may want to consult with your primary care provider for advice. Poor sleep interferes with your concentration and can make you an unsafe driver. Your performance can fall in many areas from sleep deprivation.

## Snoring and sleep apnea

While occasional light snoring can be harmless, a regular snorer can suffer health consequences. Snoring interferes with the quality of your sleep and frequently awakens the snorer. Snoring can be accompanied by sleep apnea, which means the snorer stops breathing for periods of time. This leads to daily fatigue and difficulty concentrating. It can also lead to high blood pressure and other serious medical problems. If you have been told that you snore on a regular basis, or you wake yourself up snoring, you may wish to seek medical help. Over-the-counter remedies include breathing strips that keep the nasal passages open and spray that moisturizes the throat. Some self-help tips include:

- Sleeping on your side and not your back
- Not waiting until you are exhausted before going to sleep
- Abstaining from alcohol and drugs
- If you are overweight, losing weight

If these do not help, or you have been told that you have sleep apnea, ask your primary health care provider for advice. You may need to undergo a sleep study, where you are monitored while you sleep in a laboratory. One treatment that may be ordered involves a mask worn over your nose and mouth at night to assist your breathing. Less invasive methods of controlling sleep apnea are usually tried first.

## Sleepwalking and its cousins

Sleepwalking, also called somnambulism, is characterized by walking during sleep. Some people also do other things while asleep, such as eating or talking nonsensically. Needless to say, there is an element of danger to most of these practices. Sleepwalking frequently begins in childhood and flares up during times of stress. Drugs, sleep deprivation, fever, asthma, seizures, and heartburn can also cause sleepwalking. There is a strong genetic component. Get adequate sleep, avoid stimulation before bedtime, and keep your environment as safe as possible, with sharp objects put away and pathways clear. Medical treatment is aimed at relieving the underlying cause. You may need to learn relaxation techniques or undergo anticipatory waking. In this treatment, someone awakens you prior to the time you normally sleepwalk, thus breaking the cycle. Some people will require medication to treat their sleepwalking, which is often given for a short period of time.

## Practical Ways to Get More Rest

Getting more rest takes a concerted effort. Do you spend mindless time on the computer, when you could be resting or sleeping? Do you organize your study time efficiently? Do you spend time watching television shows that you do not even enjoy? Learn what your time-wasters are and make appropriate changes.

## The Link Between Healthy Eating and Good Sleep

Healthy eating and a good night's sleep go hand-in-hand. Medical research is finding that getting too few hours of sleep leads to a higher risk of obesity. A poor night's sleep frequently leads to oversleeping in the morning. This can cause people to skip breakfast and overeat later in the day.

Eating also has a large effect on your night's sleep. Consuming calories late at night can cause insomnia or excessive dreaming for some. Of course, trying to go to sleep while you are hungry can be problematic as well. Aim for a healthy snack around two hours before bedtime. Some good ideas include:

- Apple wedges with a tablespoon of peanut butter and a cup of skim milk
- Fat-free cottage cheese with blueberries

- Air-popped popcorn
- Whole-grain cereal with skim milk
- A piece of cheese toast
- Yogurt with granola
- A cup of soup

Avoid caffeinated beverages before bedtime. Those prone to indigestion or other gastrointestinal problems will need to avoid their triggering foods.

# CHAPTER 14

## Maintaining a Healthy Weight

## To Diet or Not to Diet

One of the most hotly debated topics in medicine today simply involves whether one should diet. Many different diets exist, and some medical experts caution you to avoid all of them. Let us try to separate the sense from the nonsense.

- If you weigh within 5 percent of what you should weigh, you do not need to diet. Eat a balanced diet based on the food pyramid and exercise regularly.

- If your body weight is 10 percent or more above what it should be, you would be healthier at your normal body weight. To lose the weight, you must either take in fewer calories than your body needs, or you must exercise and use more calories than you take in. This will burn the calories stored in fat.

Where people seem to go wrong is with following fad diets or diets that are too low in calories. This is unhealthy, and it sets you up for failure. A reasonable diet, coupled with increased physical activity, will produce desired, long-lasting results.

One of the main objections of the anti-dieters is that, once you are told not to eat certain foods, you will only want them more. Deprivation does not tend to work in the long-term. In a sense, moderation is key. However, some foods are so bad for our health that it is best for us all to avoid them. They include trans fat and high-fructose corn syrup. These abnormal substances are not intended to be foods, and our bodies do not process them properly. Just as someone allergic to nuts should avoid them, we should avoid the foods clearly bad for our health. Thousands of healthy foods exist, and they can easily replace any bad ones you used to consume. View unhealthy food products as poison, and you should be less tempted.

Diet when you feel sufficiently motivated to do so. Yo-yo dieting creates more problems than it solves, and it is hard on your organs.

## Mindful Eating

Are you familiar with mindful eating? It simply involves being in tune with your body and allowing your body to dictate its own needs. Our distant ancestors were much better at this than we are today. Try this exercise:

Sit down for a meal with no television, book, or computer to distract you. Smell the aroma of your food as you anticipate how good it is going to taste. Take one small bite and slowly savor the flavor as you chew it at least ten times. Take another bite and feel the texture of your food. Enjoy the crunchiness or smoothness. Drink water or a low-calorie beverage every few bites. Take at least 30 minutes to complete your meal, remembering to take small bites and chew at least ten times for each bite. Think about each flavor and what it reminds you of.

While you cannot always spend 30 minutes eating each meal, re-membering to slow down and use all your senses to truly enjoy your food can have many bonuses. If you do this most of the time, you will begin to get in tune with your body about when you are truly hungry, versus bored or stressed. Eating slowly allows the body to send its message of fullness, which can take 20 minutes to reach our brain. By that time, most of us have eaten much more than we needed for proper nutrition. Eating in this manner will encourage us to consume healthy portions of food. Restaurants, in particular, have given us ever-increasing amounts of food to eat as one meal. If you eat two sandwiches or hamburgers at a meal, slow down and eat one, taking the same amount of time that you did for two.

At mealtime, ask yourself how hungry you truly are. Do you want a full meal, or a light one? Would half a sandwich give you the nutrition you need? How about a cup of soup instead of a large bowl? It is helpful to have small bowls, plates, and cups to remind you of what a serving should be. Use a measuring cup to get yourself one serving of morning cereal. Then, add ½ cup of milk. Eaten slowly, it will satisfy you just as well as the two or three servings you might be accustomed to. Count out potato chips, if you must have them. Try for one serving at first; then, grow accustomed to eating a half-serving with your sandwich. Share with a friend, or save the rest for later. Monitoring portion size is possibly the single most important part of a weight-loss diet, and it is a good idea for all of us.

If you diligently follow mindful eating practices, your body will begin to tell you its needs. If you need protein, you will crave meat or your favorite meatless alternative. You will crave milk when your body needs calcium. The proper foods will be what you desire, and junk foods with empty calories will seem unimportant and easy to pass up. When you are offered an unhealthy but tempting dessert, you may be able to satisfy yourself with one small bite.

A large part of mindful eating involves avoiding mindless eating. Do you munch on a bag of chips or popcorn as you watch a movie, or eat candy until the entire box is empty? Mindless eating adds large amounts of unneeded calories and causes our bodies to process food we do not use for nutrition.

## An Evaluation of Your Progress

How is your healthy eating and cooking coming along? How many foods have you eaten in the last week that you regret? How many are you proud of? Are you following the USDA Food Pyramid guidelines for you? Ask yourself the following questions:

- Did I eat any whole grains yesterday?
- How many servings of vegetables did I eat?
- How many servings of fruits did I eat?
- Do I eat a variety of vegetables and fruits?
- Do I vary my protein, limiting red meat and eating plenty of fish and beans?
- Did I get enough dairy products yesterday?
- Is my weight appropriate or headed in the direction I wish it to?
- Do I work out like I planned to?
- Do I get eight hours of sleep each night?
- Do I prepare as many meals for myself as I mean to?

Give yourself credit for all your dietary improvements. These have been big accomplishments during a time when most people are heading backward with their nutrition. Write down a list of the areas you still need to work on. Create a plan for improvement based on the ideas in the earlier chapters. Remember that each day is a new opportunity.

# Pitfalls to Avoid

## Alcohol misuse

Many students begin to consume alcohol during their college years. It tends to be for one of two reasons. The first reason is the desire to party — to be in an altered state of mind — frequently to fit in with other fellow students. The second is to deal with the stress of adult life and college studies. You have to decide for yourself whether these are good reasons to consume alcohol. Consider these facts:

- Some people are inherently more at risk of consuming alcohol on a regular basis and becoming addicted. With genetic predisposition to alcoholism, you may spend a good part of your lives as alcoholic — a bad scenario physically, financially, and socially.
- People often do activities they regret while under the influence of alcohol; think of driving under the influence, getting drunk and being in a bad social situation (such as date rape), or being in a video that forever haunts you.

If you are of legal age and do consume alcohol, it is best not to over-consume. For women, that often means stopping after one drink of alcohol. For men, that may mean stopping after two drinks. Alcohol contains empty calories and can cause you to rob your body of essential nutrients, leaving you fatigued, stressed, and with a weakened immune system. If you feel you need help with alcohol or other drugs, contact a school counselor, a mental health professional, or Alcoholics Anonymous or another support group.

## Habit eating

As we mentioned in the section on mindful eating in this chapter, habit eating can create inches around your waistline. This involves not only the munchies that may happen during a movie, but eating because everyone else is, or because you always do while you study. Here are some suggestions for avoiding habit eating when you are not truly hungry.

- Try drinking cold water.
- Try sugarless mints or gum.
- Brush your teeth or use mouthwash. You will be less inclined to mess up the fresh feeling in your mouth.
- Find something to do with your hands while watching television. Work out with light weights, or squeeze a stress ball.
- Keep a picture of how you wish to look nearby. Look at it each time you start to head toward the kitchen.
- If you must eat something, try something healthfully sweet, such as grapes, or naturally crunchy, such as carrot sticks.

# What to Do if You are Off Track

If you are gaining more than three unwanted pounds a year, or not losing weight when you intend to, you need to reevaluate your dietary plan. You probably know the foods you have been eating that you should have avoided. Instead of denying yourself foods, remember that you can eat most items in moderation. Starting immediately, cut in half servings of high calorie foods. Instead of two rolls, eat one. If you normally eat one roll, eat half and save the rest. Cut the steak or other meat in half. Eat one slice of loaded pizza or two slices of one topping pizza, and have water as your only accompaniment.

Quit snacking entirely for a week and see how you feel. Do not add dressings of any kind to your salad. Make sure that you stop eating before you are overly full. Do not buy any unhealthy foods at the grocery store. Increase your activity level, and have a five-minute workout when you feel hungry between meals. See whether the pounds begin to drop off from these actions. If they do, then you have a good idea of what changes you need to incorporate. If they do not, you may need to begin writing down each food you eat, along with a calorie count, to see whether you are consuming more calories than you realize. Follow the USDA Food Pyramid guidelines diligently, and do not over-consume meats, breads, and oils.

It is important to remember that each morning begins a new day and a new opportunity. Find a pace that works for you, and stick with it, as yo-yo dieting is hard on your body. Do not go on a strict diet that you cannot possibly continue indefinitely. Look at your eating habits. Do you frequently skip breakfast? Avoid dairy products? Forget to get enough fiber? Eat because everyone else is? Eat before bedtime out of habit? Snack during television viewing? If any of these sound familiar, you know what you need to work on. Reread the sections on healthy eating principles that apply, and begin afresh. Find peers who eat healthfully and support each other's efforts.

# CHAPTER 15

## Junior Year Recipes

## Broccoli Salad

**Ingredients:**

2 cups fresh broccoli

¼ cup raisins

¼ cup chopped walnuts or pecans

1/8 cup chopped red onion

4 slices bacon (or turkey bacon)

1 ½ ounces Miracle-Whip-type dressing

2 teaspoons sugar or your favorite sweetener

**Instructions:**

Fry or bake the bacon slices until crisp, following the instructions in Chapter 6. Remove from grease and allow to cool. Crumble into various-size pieces. Place broccoli florets in large bowl. Cut

| Nutrition Facts | |
|---|---|
| per serving | |
| makes 4 servings | |
| **Amount per serving** | |
| **Calories** | 284 |
| Calories from fat | 174 |
| **% Daily Value \*** | |
| **Total Fat 19.3g** | 30% |
| Saturated Fat 5.6g | 28% |
| **Cholesterol 29mg** | 10% |
| **Sodium 520mg** | 22% |
| **Total Carbohydrate 15.8g** | 5% |
| Dietary Fiber 2.2g | 9% |
| **Protein 11.6g** | |

Percent values are based on a 2,000 calorie per day diet. Your daily values may differ.

**Additional Information**
61.4% of calories from Fat
22.3% from Carbohydrates
16.4% from Protein

extra-large florets into two pieces. Add raisins, nuts, and onion. Add bacon. Add dressing and stir. Add sugar or sweetener to desired taste. Place in refrigerator for at least one hour. Divide into 4 servings.

## Accompaniments:

Broccoli salad makes an excellent light lunch. It can accompany a poultry dish or be part of a vegetable plate. Add a slice of whole-grain bread or a roll. Do not have dessert with this meal.

**Tips:**

Broccoli salad is fun to serve to guests. Many people have never heard of it, but most enjoy the taste. Be sure to tell them it contains nuts.

# Stuffed Bell Peppers

## Ingredients:

2 large green bell peppers

8 ounces lean ground beef

¼ cup uncooked rice

½ small onion

6 ounces tomato sauce

2 tablespoons ketchup

1 teaspoon salt

Dash pepper

1 teaspoon minced garlic

Dash of oregano, thyme,
    or any Italian spice
    (optional)

| Nutrition Facts per serving makes 2 servings | |
|---|---|
| **Amount per serving** | |
| **Calories** | 481 |
| Calories from fat | 191 |
| % Daily Value * | |
| **Total Fat 21.3g** | 33% |
| Saturated Fat 8.2g | 41% |
| **Cholesterol 88mg** | 29% |
| **Sodium 1939mg** | 81% |
| **Total Carbohydrate 40.9g** | 14% |
| Dietary Fiber 4.7g | 19% |
| **Protein 31.5g** | |
| Percent values are based on a 2,000 calorie per day diet. Your daily values may differ. | |
| **Additional Information** 39.7% of calories from Fat 34% from Carbohydrates 26.2% from Protein | |

## Instructions:

Bring 2 cups of water to a boil in a small, covered saucepan over medium-high heat. Add rice and ½ teaspoon salt and recover pan. When boiling, lower the heat to low and allow to cook until rice is soft. Drain and remove the rice, and place in a medium-size mixing bowl.

Place ground beef in a large skillet over medium heat. Dice onion into small pieces and add. Cut off the top ⅛ of the peppers. Cut around the center of the top and remove. Dice the rest of the top of the peppers and add to the beef. Add the garlic, ½ teaspoon of salt, pepper, and Italian spice. Break the beef into small pieces while it is cooking. When the beef is done, drain the grease off and add the beef mixture to the rice in the mixing bowl. Add the tomato sauce and ketchup and stir.

Preheat the oven to 350 degrees. Carefully remove the seeds and some of the spines of the peppers. Place the peppers in a baking dish, standing upright. Add the mixture to the peppers. Carefully pour 1 cup of water into the bottom of the baking dish and place the dish in the oven on the middle rack. Check after 15 minutes; if the peppers are browning too quickly, place aluminum foil over them. Cook 15 to 20 more minutes and remove from oven. Wait 5 minutes and serve. Makes 2 servings.

## Accompaniments:

Serve this dish with two vegetables that are not green, such as mashed potatoes, carrots, sweet potatoes, corn, cauliflower, boiled squash, or baked potatoes. Do not serve bread, due to the rice. Serve with iced tea and a small serving of vanilla ice cream or fat-free frozen yogurt if desired.

**Tips:**

After you perfect this dish, you may wish to experiment with using orange, yellow, or red bell peppers. Be aware that some varieties can be quite hot. For variety, add 1 ounce of shredded cheddar cheese to the top of each pepper during the last 5 minutes.

# Baked Salmon

### Ingredients:

4 ounces fresh or frozen
    salmon fillet (thawed)
2 tablespoons honey
1 tablespoon mustard,
    yellow or brown
Dash of parsley, optional

### Instructions:

In a small bowl, mix the honey, mustard, and parsley. Add the salmon fillet and coat the entire fillet with the mixture. Refrigerate for at least 2 hours. Preheat the oven to 400 degrees. Spray the bottom of a baking dish with spray oil. Add the fillet and re-coat with the marinade. Place the dish in the oven on the low rack for 15 minutes. Move to the middle rack and cook an additional 10 minutes. Continue to cook until salmon is done. Make sure it flakes easily with a fork.

| Nutrition Facts | |
|---|---|
| per serving | |
| makes 1 serving | |
| **Amount per serving** | |
| **Calories** | 321 |
| Calories from fat | 64 |
| | **% Daily Value \*** |
| **Total Fat 10.8g** | 11% |
| Saturated Fat 3.3g | 4% |
| **Cholesterol 102mg** | 20% |
| **Sodium 188mg** | 3% |
| **Total Carbohydrate 27.4g** | 13% |
| Dietary Fiber 4.8g | 7% |
| **Protein 40.3g** | |
| Percent values are based on a 2,000 calorie per day diet. Your daily values may differ. | |
| **Additional Information** 19.9% of calories from Fat 48.3% from Carbohydrates 31.8% from Protein | |

### Accompaniments:

The perfect accompaniment for salmon is wild or whole-grain rice. Have a serving of vegetables, such as baked Italian mixed veggies or creamed spinach. It is a growing trend to serve a baked salmon as one would grilled chicken — with a salad, baked potato, and garlic breadstick. This is a nutritious option, should you wish to try it. If you desire dessert with salmon, consider fresh or baked fruit. Offer iced tea or some type of water.

**Tips:**
You will learn whether you prefer your salmon soft and moist, slightly browned, or crunchy on the edges. You may wish to serve with a wedge of fresh lemon that can be squeezed on the filet. When thawing salmon or any fish thaw it only in the refrigerator, or in the microwave on a "defrost" setting.

# Oven Fried Fish

**Ingredients:**

4 ounce fish fillet, any type
½ cup corn flakes
¼ teaspoon paprika
¼ teaspoon onion powder
½ teaspoon lemon pepper
½ teaspoon salt
Dash of Italian seasoning
1 tablespoon milk

**Instructions:**

Preheat the oven to 350 degrees. In a shallow bowl, crush the corn flakes and add paprika, onion powder, lemon pepper, salt, and Italian seasoning. Mix well. Place the fillet on a plate or in a shallow bowl, and pour the milk over it. Pick up the fillet and dip the bottom of the fillet in the milk as well. When the fillet is covered with milk, dip it into the corn flake mixture. Use your hands to place the mixture all over the filet, and place the fillet

| Nutrition Facts | |
|---|---|
| per serving | |
| makes 1 serving | |
| **Amount per serving** | |
| **Calories** | 228 |
| Calories from fat | 81 |
| | **% Daily Value \*** |
| **Total Fat 8.9g** | 14% |
| Saturated Fat 1.5g | 8% |
| **Cholesterol 89mg** | 30% |
| **Sodium 1321mg** | 55% |
| **Total Carbohydrate 7.7g** | 3% |
| Dietary Fiber 0.6g | 2% |
| **Protein 29g** | |
| Percent values are based on a 2,000 calorie per day diet. Your daily values may differ. | |
| **Additional Information** 35.6% of calories from Fat 13.5% from Carbohydrates 50.9% from Protein | |

into a baking dish you have sprayed with spray oil. Lightly spray the top of the fillet with the spray oil. Place the baking dish into the oven on the lowest rack and bake for 15 minutes. Move the dish to the middle rack and cook for 10 additional minutes. Cook until the fish is done. It should flake easily with a fork.

## Accompaniments:

Accompany this dish with oven-baked potato logs and coleslaw, green beans, or mixed vegetables. Offer a breadstick if desired. Drink iced tea and have a dry dessert, such as a hard cookie or a chocolate-covered pretzel.

### Tips:
You may wish to eat fish with ketchup, cocktail sauce, or a wedge of fresh lemon. If you notice that the fish is cooking unevenly, turn with a spatula at any point during the cooking process. School cafeterias used to serve fish on Fridays, and planning fish for yourself on Fridays can be a fun way to remember to get one of your fish servings each week.

# Tuna Noodle Casserole

## Ingredients:

10 Ritz-type crackers

½ cup giant elbow
    macaroni, uncooked

1 can tuna in water, drained

¼ cup frozen peas, thawed

1 box macaroni and
    cheese's cheese packet

½ cup milk

½ cup shredded, low-fat,
    sharp cheddar cheese

½ teaspoon pepper

1 teaspoon margarine

| Nutrition Facts | |
|---|---|
| per serving | |
| makes 2 servings | |
| **Amount per serving** | |
| **Calories** | 581 |
| Calories from fat | 219 |
| | **% Daily Value \*** |
| **Total Fat 24.4g** | 38% |
| Saturated Fat 10g | 50% |
| **Cholesterol 63mg** | 21% |
| **Sodium 854mg** | 36% |
| **Total Carbohydrate 51.4g** | 17% |
| Dietary Fiber 2.3g | 9% |
| **Protein 39.2g** | |
| Percent values are based on a 2,000 calorie per day diet. Your daily values may differ. | |
| **Additional Information** | |
| 37.7% of calories from Fat | |
| 35.4% from Carbohydrates | |
| 27% from Protein | |

## Instructions:

Pour 2 cups of water into a medium skillet and cover. Heat on medium-high until boiling, and add the giant elbow macaroni. Allow to return to a boil and lower the heat to low. Keep at a low boil for 8 minutes and drain.

Preheat the oven to 375 degrees. Put the dry cheese mix from the macaroni and cheese box into a baking dish and add the milk. Stir well. Add the cooked giant elbow macaroni and margarine and stir. Add the pepper, peas, and drained tuna. Stir lightly. Place the baking dish on the middle rack of the oven and cook for 25 minutes. Crush the Ritz-type crackers in a small bowl and add sharp cheddar cheese. Mix and place on top of the casserole. Place the dish on the bottom rack of the oven and cook for 5 minutes or until the cheese is melting and the topping is beginning to brown. Makes 2 servings.

## Accompaniments:

Serve this dish with 1 or 2 side vegetables, such as carrots, green beans, corn on the cob, or broccoli. Do not serve bread. Add tea or lemonade and fresh fruit for dessert, such as a small bunch of purple grapes.

**Tips:**

When reheating the casserole, you may need to add 1 tablespoon of milk. Save the raw macaroni from the macaroni and cheese box to boil and add to diced tomatoes and juice at a later time. Once you try giant elbow macaroni, you will probably be hooked on it for casseroles and soups.

# Banana Walnut Muffins

## Ingredients:

1 large, ripe banana

1 cup all purpose flour or
   ½ cup all purpose flour
   and ½ cup whole-grain
   flour

½ tablespoon baking
   powder

½ teaspoon salt

¼ cup packed brown sugar

⅓ cup milk

1 egg

3 tablespoons margarine

½ cup chopped walnuts

1 teaspoon cinnamon

| Nutrition Facts | |
|---|---|
| per serving | |
| makes 6 servings | |
| **Amount per serving** | |
| **Calories** | **280** |
| Calories from fat | 120 |
| **% Daily Value *** | |
| **Total Fat 13.3g** | 20% |
| Saturated Fat 2.3g | 11% |
| **Cholesterol 36mg** | 12% |
| **Sodium 218mg** | 9% |
| **Total Carbohydrate 34.5g** | 12% |
| Dietary Fiber 2g | 8% |
| **Protein 5.4g** | |
| Percent values are based on a 2,000 calorie per day diet. Your daily values may differ. | |
| **Additional Information** | |
| 42.9% of calories from Fat 49.4% from Carbohydrates 7.7% from Protein | |

## Instructions:

Preheat oven to 375 degrees. Spray six muffin cups with spray oil. Cut the banana into four pieces and place in a small bowl. Sprinkle with cinnamon. Mash with a fork until well mashed. Place the margarine into a small, microwave-safe bowl, and heat on high for 25 seconds. Place the flour in a medium-size bowl and add the baking powder and salt. Mix well. Add brown sugar, milk, banana, egg, margarine, and walnuts. Stir just until blended. Pour batter evenly into the six muffin cups. Place muffin tin on the middle rack of the oven for 15 minutes. Check for doneness. Return to the oven for 3-minute intervals until muffins are done. Move the muffins to the bottom rack of the oven if the tops are browning too quickly. Makes 6 servings.

## Accompaniments:

Eat with a small pat of margarine or butter if desired. These muffins make a good occasional breakfast with a glass of milk or fruit juice.

### Tips:

Muffins are generally not as sweet as cupcakes. They can be reheated in the microwave by wrapping in a safe paper towel and heating on high for 20 seconds. They make a thoughtful gift for a sick friend. Be sure to tell them that they contain nuts.

# Carrot Cake Muffins

## Ingredients:

1 carrot

½ cup chopped walnuts

1 cup self-rising flour

½ cup packed brown sugar

3 tablespoons margarine

1 egg

½ teaspoon cinnamon

Dash of allspice

Dash of ginger, optional

⅓ cup milk

½ teaspoon salt

| Nutrition Facts | |
|---|---|
| per serving | |
| makes 6 servings | |
| **Amount per serving** | |
| **Calories** | 291 |
| Calories from fat | 119 |
| | **% Daily Value \*** |
| **Total Fat 13.2g** | 20% |
| Saturated Fat 2.2g | 11% |
| **Cholesterol 36mg** | 12% |
| **Sodium 491mg** | 20% |
| **Total Carbohydrate 37.7g** | 13% |
| Dietary Fiber 1.7g | 7% |
| **Protein 5.2g** | |
| Percent values are based on a 2,000 calorie per day diet. Your daily values may differ. | |
| **Additional Information** | |
| 40.9% of calories from Fat 51.9% from Carbohydrates 7.2% from Protein | |

## Instructions:

Preheat the oven the 375 degrees. Spray six muffin cups with spray oil. Peel and shred the carrot into a medium bowl. Place the margarine in a small, microwave-safe bowl and heat on high for 25 seconds. Add all ingredients to the carrot and stir until blended. Pour batter evenly into the six muffin cups. Place the muffin tin on the middle rack of the oven and cook for 20 minutes. Check for doneness. Continue to cook until done, checking at 3-minute intervals. If the tops begin to brown too quickly, move the tin to the bottom rack of the oven. Makes 6 servings.

## Accompaniments:

Have these delicious muffins as a snack or as dessert to a light meal, such as grilled chicken. Serve with milk.

> **Tips:**
>
> For an indulgent treat, create a topping by mixing 4 ounces of low-fat cream cheese with 2 tablespoons of confectioner's sugar and ½ teaspoon of vanilla extract. Soften the cream cheese ahead of time by leaving it out of the refrigerator 1 hour ahead of time. Do not top muffins until they are completely cool. Share these muffins with friends. Be sure to tell them that the muffins contain nuts.

# Tacos

## Ingredients:

8 standable taco shells

1 pound extra lean ground beef or turkey

1 package taco seasoning mix

8 ounces shredded cheddar cheese

½ cup sour cream

½ cup shredded lettuce

1 large, chopped tomato

Optional items:

¼ cup diced onion, any type

¼ cup black olives, sliced

½ cup salsa

| Nutrition Facts | |
|---|---|
| per serving | |
| makes 8 servings | |
| **Amount per serving** | |
| **Calories** | 290 |
| Calories from fat | 202 |
| | **% Daily Value \*** |
| **Total Fat 22.4g** | 34% |
| Saturated Fat 12.6g | 63% |
| **Cholesterol 70mg** | 23% |
| **Sodium 237mg** | 10% |
| **Total Carbohydrate 3.8g** | 1% |
| Dietary Fiber 0.4g | 2% |
| **Protein 18.3g** | |
| Percent values are based on a 2,000 calorie per day diet. Your daily values may differ. | |
| **Additional Information** 69.6% of calories from Fat 5.2% from Carbohydrates 25.2% from Protein | |

## Instructions:

Place the ground beef or turkey in a large skillet and heat on medium. Break with a fork into very small pieces while cooking. Cook until the meat is no longer pink. Completely drain the grease. Do not pour the grease into the sink. Preheat the oven to 300 degrees. Add ¾ cup of water and the seasoning mix to the skillet. Bring to a boil over medium heat with the lid on. Reduce heat to low and simmer with the lid on for 10 minutes, stirring occasionally. Meanwhile, place the taco shells on a cookie sheet and place on the middle rack of the oven for 4 minutes. Remove when shells are hot. You do not want them to brown at all. Remove the taco meat from heat and divide among the taco shells. Add cheese, then lettuce, tomato, and sour cream. Add optional items, if desired.

## Accompaniments:

Serve these tacos with any Mexican dish you wish. A few options include refried beans, chips with salsa, or salad. Offer milk as a beverage and a small serving of fat-free frozen yogurt, if desired.

### Tips:

When you drain grease from meat, drain it into a safe bowl or cup. Allow it to solidify and place it in the trash. To reduce even more calories, drain cooked meat and add 3 cups of hot water and drain again. This will reduce the fat, but will also alter the flavor somewhat. Do the math on creating tacos, and decide whether it is more economical to make them or to purchase them from a restaurant.

# Oven Fried Chicken

**Ingredients:**

2 pieces chicken, any cut,
   skin removed

¼ cup milk

1 cup flour

1 tablespoon poultry
   seasoning or
   seasoned salt

1 teaspoon paprika

| Nutrition Facts | |
|---|---|
| per serving | |
| makes 2 servings | |
| **Amount per serving** | |
| **Calories** | 351 |
| Calories from fat | 24 |
| | **% Daily Value \*** |
| **Total Fat 2.6g** | 4% |
| Saturated Fat 0.9g | 4% |
| **Cholesterol 59mg** | 20% |
| **Sodium 80mg** | 3% |
| **Total Carbohydrate 51g** | 17% |
| Dietary Fiber 2.1g | 8% |
| **Protein 30.8g** | |
| Percent values are based on a 2,000 calorie per day diet. Your daily values may differ. | |
| **Additional Information** 6.8% of calories from Fat 58.1% from Carbohydrates 35.1% from Protein | |

**Instructions:**

Preheat oven to 375 degrees. Spray a baking dish with spray oil. Place the flour, seasoning, and paprika in a large baggie and mix thoroughly. Pour the milk into a shallow bowl. Dry the chicken pieces with a paper towel and dip one piece into the milk. Shake off the excess milk and place the chicken piece into the baggie and shake. Remove the chicken from the bag and place in the baking dish. Repeat with the second piece of chicken. Make sure the pieces of chicken are not touching in the baking dish, and place the dish on the middle rack of the oven. Turn the pieces over after 20 minutes and return to the middle rack. Oven times will vary, depending on the cut used. Begin checking for doneness after 30 full minutes in the oven and every 10 minutes thereafter. Remove from oven when done and serve immediately. Makes 2 servings.

**Accompaniments:**

This dish is traditionally served with mashed potatoes and chicken or brown gravy, a vegetable, and a roll. To lighten this meal, serve with a small serving of plain mashed potatoes and a non-starchy vegetable, such as steamed broccoli, and skip the bread. Serve with milk or iced tea.

**Tips:**

White meat is lower in fat and calories than dark meat. Chicken with bones takes considerably longer to cook than boneless chicken. To see whether chicken is done, cut into the thickest part and continue to the bone, if it has one. Make sure the innermost part is cooked and not raw.

# Pumpkin Babies

### Ingredients:

4 ounces canned pumpkin

1 egg

1 tablespoon canola oil

1 tablespoon margarine

1 tablespoon self-rising
  flour

4 tablespoons sugar or
  sweetener

¼ teaspoon salt

½ teaspoon cinnamon

¼ teaspoon allspice or
  pumpkin pie spice

| Nutrition Facts | |
|---|---|
| per serving | |
| makes 2 servings | |
| **Amount per serving** | |
| **Calories** | 286 |
| Calories from fat | 136 |
| | **% Daily Value \*** |
| **Total Fat 15.2g** | 23% |
| Saturated Fat 2.9g | 15% |
| **Cholesterol 106mg** | 35% |
| **Sodium 379mg** | 16% |
| **Total Carbohydrate 33.5g** | 11% |
| Dietary Fiber 2g | 8% |
| **Protein 4.1g** | |
| Percent values are based on a 2,000 calorie per day diet. Your daily values may differ. | |
| **Additional Information** 47.5% of calories from Fat 46.8% from Carbohydrates 5.7% from Protein | |

### Instructions:

Pour the oil into a medium-size skillet and heat on medium. Place all the other ingredients into a medium-size bowl and mix well. Take the batter out with a large spoon and drop, by spoons, into the hot oil, forming four evenly shaped patties. Turn with a spatula every 2 minutes, until browned on both sides. Makes 2 servings of two patties each.

## Accompaniments:

This dish is relatively high in calories and should be served with low-calorie items, such as thin-sliced, low-fat ham and Brussels sprouts. It can also accompany grilled chicken. Do not serve dessert with this sweet dish. Have milk, coffee, or a vegetable juice as a beverage.

**Tips:**

This delicious side dish is packed with vitamin A and fiber. It tastes more like a vegetable than a fruit. You may want to freeze the rest of the canned pumpkin to make this recipe again at a later date.

# Strawberry Shortcake

## Ingredients:

8 fresh, large strawberries

2 teaspoons sugar

2 tablespoons dairy
    whipped cream

1 small sponge cake,
    individual size

1 teaspoon chopped
    peanuts, mixed nuts, or
    walnuts — optional

| Nutrition Facts | |
|---|---|
| per serving | |
| makes 1 servings | |
| **Amount per serving** | |
| **Calories** | 467 |
| Calories from fat | 64 |
| | **% Daily Value \*** |
| **Total Fat 7g** | 11% |
| Saturated Fat 2g | 10% |
| **Cholesterol 122mg** | 41% |
| **Sodium 289mg** | 12% |
| **Total Carbohydrate 92.9g** | 31% |
| Dietary Fiber 5.3g | 21% |
| **Protein 7.9g** | |
| Percent values are based on a 2,000 calorie per day diet. Your daily values may differ. | |
| **Additional Information** | |
| 13.7% of calories from Fat 79.5% from Carbohydrates 6.8% from Protein | |

## Instructions:

Remove the green tops from the strawberries and slice them, creating thick slices and some thin slices. Place the slices into a shallow bowl and add 1 tablespoon of water and the sugar. Mash with a potato masher or fork until some of the slices are pulverized while others remain whole. Pour over the sponge cake. Add whipped cream and nuts if desired.

## Accompaniments:

Strawberry shortcake is well-complemented with a tall glass of milk. It can also accompany a light beef, pork, chicken, or turkey meal that does not contain bread.

> **Tips:**
> Try to buy real dairy whipped cream instead of non-dairy topping for this recipe. The taste is superior. To serve company an extravagant dessert, add a small serving of vanilla ice cream. This dish is much lighter in fat and calories than a traditional shortcake.

# Brown Rice

### Ingredients:

½ cup brown rice, uncooked

1 teaspoon margarine

¼ white onion, diced

¼ cup mushroom, canned or fresh

1 teaspoon minced garlic

1 can low-sodium chicken broth

Dash of salt, optional

### Instructions:

| Nutrition Facts | |
|---|---|
| per serving | |
| makes 2 servings | |
| **Amount per serving** | |
| **Calories** | 249 |
| Calories from fat | 43 |
| | **% Daily Value \*** |
| **Total Fat 4.8g** | 7% |
| Saturated Fat 1.2g | 6% |
| **Cholesterol 2mg** | 1% |
| **Sodium 1046mg** | 44% |
| **Total Carbohydrate 40.5g** | 14% |
| Dietary Fiber 2.5g | 10% |
| **Protein 11g** | |
| Percent values are based on a 2,000 calorie per day diet. Your daily values may differ. | |
| **Additional Information** | |
| 17.3% of calories from Fat | |
| 65.1% from Carbohydrates | |
| 17.7% from Protein | |

Pour chicken broth into a small saucepan and cover. Heat on medium-high until boiling. Add all the other ingredients and return to a boil. Keep covered and reduce heat to medium-low. Cook for 25 minutes, stirring occasionally. Remove a teaspoon of rice to see if soft and cook an additional 5 minutes, if necessary. Remove from heat and leave covered 5 minutes. Salt if desired. Makes 2 servings.

**Accompaniments:**

This dish can be served with baked chicken or fish or as part of a vegetable plate. Add a green vegetable on the side. Do not serve bread or potatoes. If eating this dish alone, eat as one large serving in a bowl. If dessert is desired, consider a soft fruit, such as canned peaches in juice.

**Tips:**

If your rice becomes dry before it softens, add 2 ounces and increase the cooking time slightly.

# Chicken and Rice

**Ingredients:**

1 large chicken breast —
    skin left on, bone in
1 can chicken broth
1 teaspoon parsley
1 cup frozen broccoli,
    cauliflower,
    and carrots
    mixture, thawed
⅔ cup rice — any type,
    except instant

| Nutrition Facts | |
|---|---|
| per serving | |
| makes 2 servings | |
| **Amount per serving** | |
| **Calories** | 361 |
| Calories from fat | 12 |
| % Daily Value * | |
| **Total Fat 1.4g** | 2% |
| Saturated Fat 0.3g | 2% |
| **Cholesterol 33mg** | 11% |
| **Sodium 380mg** | 16% |
| **Total Carbohydrate 66.5g** | 22% |
| Dietary Fiber 6g | 24% |
| **Protein 20.8g** | |
| Percent values are based on a 2,000 calorie per day diet. Your daily values may differ. | |
| **Additional Information** | |
| 3.3% of calories from Fat | |
| 73.6% from Carbohydrates | |
| 23% from Protein | |

**Instructions:**

Place 8 cups of water in a large saucepan. Cover and heat on medium-high until boiling. Carefully add the chicken breast, making sure it is well covered with water. Heat until boiling again and reduce heat to medium. Cook with the lid on for 35 minutes, turning chicken every 15 minutes. Remove from heat and cut into the thick part of the chicken with a knife to make sure it is completely done. Boil until done, and remove from heat. Place chicken on a plate to cool. Keep 1 cup of the water and dispose of the rest. Add the canned chicken broth to the cup of water you have reserved in the saucepan, cover, and heat on medium-high until boiling. Add the rice and re-cover. Heat until boiling again and reduce heat to medium. Tear the chicken from the bone. After the rice has been boiling for 10 minutes, add the chicken, vegetables, and parsley. With the lid on, keep the heat on medium for 10 minutes and then reduce the heat to low. Stir occasionally. When the heat has been at low for 5 minutes, test the rice for softness. Continue to cook until soft. Remove the lid and cook at medium until most of the liquid is absorbed. Remove from heat and serve. Makes 2 servings.

**Accompaniments:**

This dish is generally served solo with iced tea. If dessert is desired, consider a small cookie or low-fat fruit yogurt with granola.

**Tips:**
The veggies in this dish can be substituted with onions, squash, zucchini, green onion, or snow peas.

# Waldorf Salad

## Ingredients:

1 red apple, diced
with peel
1 green apple, diced
with peel
½ cup chopped celery
¼ cup raisins
⅓ cup low-fat mayonnaise
2 teaspoons lemon juice
1 tablespoon sugar
1/3 cup chopped walnuts

## Instructions:

Mix all ingredients in a large bowl and refrigerate for 1 hour. Makes 3 servings.

## Accompaniments:

This dish is a meal by itself with water or unsweetened tea.

| Nutrition Facts | |
|---|---|
| per serving<br>makes 3 servings | |
| **Amount per serving** | |
| **Calories** | 380 |
| Calories from fat | 252 |
| | **% Daily Value \*** |
| **Total Fat 27.9g** | 43% |
| Saturated Fat 3.6g | 18% |
| **Cholesterol 14mg** | 5% |
| **Sodium 27mg** | 1% |
| **Total Carbohydrate 29.2g** | 10% |
| Dietary Fiber 3.2g | 13% |
| **Protein 2.9g** | |
| Percent values are based on a 2,000 calorie per day diet. Your daily values may differ. | |
| **Additional Information**<br>66.2% of calories from Fat<br>30.7% from Carbohydrates<br>3% from Protein | |

**Tips:**

Make this dish dressy by serving on a large lettuce leaf. Waldorf salad was invented in the late 1800s and remains popular today. Feel free to experiment with changing the ingredients.

# Wilted Greens

## Ingredients:

5 cups chopped turnip
    greens or spinach
1 tablespoon olive oil or
    vegetable oil
1 small onion, white or
    yellow
1 tablespoon minced
    garlic
½ teaspoon salt
1 tablespoon sugar
¼ cup chicken broth
Vinegar, any kind

| Nutrition Facts | |
|---|---|
| per serving | |
| makes 2 servings | |
| **Amount per serving** | |
| **Calories** | 179 |
| Calories from fat | 70 |
| **% Daily Value \*** | |
| **Total Fat 7.7g** | 12% |
| Saturated Fat 1.1g | 6% |
| **Cholesterol 0mg** | 0% |
| **Sodium 843mg** | 35% |
| **Total Carbohydrate 22.3g** | 7% |
| Dietary Fiber 5.8g | 23% |
| **Protein 4.9g** | |
| Percent values are based on a 2,000 calorie per day diet. Your daily values may differ. | |
| **Additional Information** | |
| 39.1% of calories from Fat | |
| 49.9% from Carbohydrates | |
| 11% from Protein | |

## Instructions:

Place oil in a large skillet and heat on medium. Dice the onion and add when the oil is hot. Cook for 3 minutes and add the greens. Toss them carefully to disperse the oil to all the greens. Stir frequently and cook for 4 minutes. Add the sugar and chicken broth, being careful not to let the oil splash. Sir and cover the skillet. Cook for 7 minutes. Remove the cover and cook for 5 minutes, or until the liquid is absorbed. Remove from heat, sprinkle with salt, and serve with a bottle of vinegar. Makes 2 servings.

## Accompaniments:

Serve this dish with a simple country meat, such as hamburger steak, cubed steak, or chicken and potatoes. The potatoes can be mashed or fried. Southern purists will add a side dish of pinto beans and cornbread. Offer milk, buttermilk, or iced tea as a beverage. Dessert should be fruit-based, such as canned pears or spiced apples.

**Tips:**

To "countrify" this dish, first cook three slices of bacon in the skillet on medium. Turn frequently, and remove the bacon when done. Add the onion to the grease and follow the original recipe from that point, eliminating the oil. Crumble the bacon and add when the salt is added.

# SENIOR
# SECTION

# CHAPTER 16

## Eating Disorders

**E** ating disorders are quite prevalent on college campuses. Learn the warning signs, both for yourself and your friends. Stick to healthy eating principles and reap the many benefits.

## Healthy Eating Principles

Healthy adults consume three or four meals a day. This begins with a breakfast to fuel their bodies for the day. An ideal breakfast consists of:

- Protein
- Dairy
- Fruit
- Grain

While you can miss one of these occasionally, skipping breakfast entirely will leave you sluggish and unable to fully concentrate by lunchtime. You may be ravenous and overeat by then as well.

Lunch and dinner can vary, but they should contribute protein, dairy, fruits, vegetables, and grains to your diet. You should spread your calories throughout the day, eating a similar amount for each meal. Bingeing is hard on your body and can eventually contribute to type II diabetes. Fasting is difficult for your body as well. It must try to maintain equilibrium with a roller coaster of blood sugar levels. Most Americans snack, although you could be considered healthy just eating your three to four meals a day. Small, healthy snacks can keep us satisfied throughout the day and help to avoid binge eating.

A healthy adult plans their meals but does not spend an inordinate amount of time focused on food. If you find yourself obsessed with the amount of food you eat, you may want to seek professional advice. Realize that food is the fuel for your body. Take the time to follow the advice in this book, and you will leave college with good eating habits to carry you through a healthy lifetime.

# Unhealthy Practices

## Anorexia nervosa

Anorexia nervosa, also called anorexia, is a potentially life-threatening eating disorder in which the individual refuses to maintain a normal body weight. They tend to be more than 15 percent below their normal weight for their height. Women and girls are affected more often, with almost 1 percent of the female population suffering from this disorder.

## Symptoms

- Restriction of food intake. Individuals skip meals and tend to consume only diet foods, such as diet drinks, carrots, and lettuce. They do not eat in front of others, or tend to just move food around on their plate instead of eating.

- Obsession with food. They think constantly about food, what they will eat next, and how many calories it contains.

- Distorted body image. Although they are quite thin, they see themselves as "fat."

- They have an intense fear of gaining weight and may weigh themselves several times a day.

- Females lose their menstrual cycle as the disorder becomes severe.

- Electrolyte problems and malnourishment lead to fainting; weakness; moodiness; and dry, brittle hair and nails. Their skin may be dry or yellow.

- They are frequently cold.

## Who is susceptible?

While anyone of either sex or any age can fall victim, the most frequent victims are:

- Individuals in occupations that glorify or require thinness, such as modeling, acting, jockeying, dancing, or other athletics.

- Individuals in families with anorexic family members.

- Individuals with other mental health problems.

- Individuals with parents who criticize their weight.

- Individuals who undergo very stressful events.

- Individuals who tend to be very hard on themselves. They are perfectionists and set unrealistic goals.

### What causes anorexia?

It is believed to be caused by a multitude of factors, including genetics, chemicals, and hormones. It is much more common in cultures where thinness is applauded in the media.

Anorexia can lead to death or permanent disability. The bones lose calcium, and the heart, brain, and kidneys can become damaged. The individual may literally starve themselves to death.

Medical care and mental health treatment are critical to control of anorexia. If you feel that you may suffer from this disorder, seek help. If you feel that a friend may be anorexic, talk with them in a non-threatening manner.

## Bulimia nervosa

Bulimia nervosa, also called bulimia, involves eating or overeating and then purging oneself. Its victims are generally adolescent or young adult females with low self-esteem and a feeling of lack of control. It can happen to males, but is seen in lower rates. Victims are usually normal weight or overweight. Bulimics may also resort to laxative use. These activities are devastating physically, with tooth enamel being damaged, damage to the gastrointestinal tract, and occasional malnutrition and electrolyte imbalances.

People with bulimia are not as delusional as those with anorexia nervosa, in that they generally realize their true weight and tend to be aware they have a problem. They tend to believe that everyone is focused on their weight and body size and judging them accordingly. They lose awareness of their intrinsic worth as human beings as they worry about pleasing others.

Symptoms of bulimia to watch for in friends include being of normal weight or overweight but never eating in front of others, or always going to the bathroom alone after eating. They may binge eat, followed by remorse. They may have an obvious smell of vomit, or they may use breath mints or gum after returning from the bathroom.

Treatment is aimed at improving their self-esteem. It also involves careful monitoring as the person gets their behavior under control. As people learn to develop a healthy relationship with food, positive reinforcement is critical to successful recovery.

## Binge eating

Binge eaters may eat 10,000 to 20,000 calories at one time. They usually have certain foods that they overeat, such as ice cream. There is a large emotional component to the binges, and they may be precipitated by a relationship crisis or other stressor. Common emotions that precipitate a binge can include sadness, despair, guilt, worry, loneliness, and occasionally, anger or fear. The overeating becomes a coping mechanism and is typically followed by remorse and self-loathing. Binge eaters are generally overweight, but can be of normal weight. Needless to say, this behavior is harmful to the body as it tries to process the many calories at once. For a few people, avoiding the foods that are used to binge will correct the problem. For most, however, learning and practicing new coping mechanisms is required for successful recovery.

## Emotional eating

Do you head toward chocolate when you feel upset, or toward chips when you are stressed? Many of us have a pattern of emotional eating. The chemicals in the food give us a temporary mental boost. The problem, of course, is that the boost leads to a later crash, and the extra calories translate into extra pounds. It is not always easy to recognize oneself as an emotional eater. It feels the same as "I'm hungry." Stay in tune with your emotions, and you can learn when you are eating for emotional reasons. This can be compounded if you grew up in a home where you were encouraged to eat to make yourself feel better. Parents who said, "Here, some ice cream will make it all better" did us no favors over the long term. But you can overcome these tendencies by recognizing them and taking other actions to pacify your moods.

## Yo-yo Dieting

Do you know people who yo-yo diet? They are on a diet, then off, then back on. They lose pounds, only to regain them. Sometimes, they gain more than they lost to begin with. Medical experts agree that this type of behavior is harmful to the body and has long-term detrimental effects. It is often the after-effect of a fad diet or a sudden strenuous exercise program. Most of the people who lose weight do regain it. The best way to avoid this is to diet in a slow and steady manner. While it is safe to lose two to three pounds per week, in reality, most of the people who lose weight and keep it off lose their weight at a rate of around one pound per week. Continued exercise is also critical to maintain weight loss. The U.S. government now recommends one hour of exercise most days for people trying to maintain a healthy weight loss.

## Diet pills

There are several categories of diet pills. The most dangerous kinds appear to be stimulants. While they may boost your metabolism, they overwork the heart and other organs. Some weight-loss drugs are designed to trick the body into thinking it is full. Clinical studies on these type of drugs often fail to prove efficacy. A new type of pill, called Orlistat or Alli®, works by keeping your intestine from absorbing one quarter of the fat you consume with the meal you take the pill with. It claims to stay in the digestive tract and not affect you systemically at all.

Of course, it is always best not to take medication unless it is necessary, but this method seems to be safer than the alternatives. You can develop issues relative to diarrhea, or possibly malabsorption of fat-soluble nutrients, from these drugs. For some people, the benefits will outweigh the risks, and if you are significantly overweight, you may want to ask your primary care provider about the best options for you. The future of bariatric science will no doubt give us new innovations over the years. For now, the most important advice to follow is simply to eat a healthy diet.

# Where to Turn if You Need Help

If you feel you may need help with an eating disorder, contact your school counseling department or your primary care provider. A variety of professionals are available to help, including psychologists, psychiatrists, clinical nurse specialists, nurse practitioners, physician assistants, licensed clinical social workers, licensed professional counselors, and dieticians. Whom you choose to help you will depend on the specifics of the issues you are having. The school counselor or your primary care provider can point you in the right direction. Treatment centers exist for those who need inpatient care. Most people can resolve their problems as an outpatient. Support groups, such as Overeaters Anonymous, can also be invaluable in recovery and maintenance. Realize that millions of others have faced the same issues that you are, and do not feel ashamed of the problems you are having. It shows great strength to seek help, and you can expect to be treated with dignity and respect.

If you feel that a friend may have an eating disorder, talk to them about it, even if it feels uncomfortable. Tell them of the resources you are aware of, and ask them to make a plan to seek help if needed. If they deny having a problem, tell them that it is easy to get an evaluation and find out for sure. If a friend loses weight to an unhealthy level, you may have to seek assistance from their family or the school counseling service. Do not be afraid to get involved.

## Keeping It All in Perspective

It is not always easy to know how much emphasis to place upon your weight. If you are within 10 percent of your ideal body weight, you can feel comfortable not focusing too much on your weight. If you are significantly underweight, despite trying to eat healthily, you should get professional advice, as you could have an underlying medical problem that needs to be addressed. If you are significantly overweight, it is important to monitor what you eat and how much you exercise, but obsessing about it does not help. Consider it one part of who you are, and not a sole judgment of your character. Your weight is never associated with your worth. It is one component of your physical health, no more and no less.

# CHAPTER 17

## Special Needs

**M**any of us have special needs regarding our food intake. We will discuss some of the more common ones here.

## Food Allergies

Food allergies can develop at any time and can range from mildly annoying to lethal. The only criterion to developing a food allergy is that you must have eaten the food, or something similar, at least one time before. While you can become allergic to any food, some of the most common ones include nuts, especially peanuts; wheat; and shellfish. If you have a food allergy, avoid the products that make you ill, even if your previous reaction has been minor. There are some exceptions to this, but only if you are being treated by a physician who is desensitizing you to the food. Read labels and be aware of the dishes in restaurants that typically contain the allergens. Each type of food allergy has its own specifics, and you should have solid medical advice if you have one.

Nut allergies can be especially dangerous. They tend to create situations where the throat can swell closed, or other serious problems may occur. Avoid nut butters, candy chocolate, and foods made where nuts are processed if you have this problem.

Wheat allergies are problematic because wheat is found in so many foods in the United States. You will need to learn good substitutes for breads and desserts, and exactly what to avoid in restaurants. Many pastas are made of wheat also, and can turn up in Italian dishes or even soups.

Egg allergies can be tricky, as eggs can be added to so many recipes. If you are at someone's house, ask whether any of the offered dishes contain eggs. Learn what to avoid at restaurants.

Seafood allergies are somewhat easier, as you can still find many safe foods to eat.

You may wish to consult an allergist to see whether you can be desensitized to the allergen. Avoid practitioners who are not licensed medical professionals when undergoing medical procedures such as this.

# Vegetarianism

People frequently become vegetarians for religious or cultural reasons. They may also believe it is being compassionate to animals. Others feel it is a healthier diet. Whatever your reasons, you must be careful to get the proper nutrients if you do not eat meat.

Lacto-vegetarians do not eat meat, but do consume milk and milk products. Milk contains complete protein and allows your body to get the amino acids it needs. Ovo-vegetarians avoid meat but do eat eggs, which also gives them complete protein. It is trickier for vegans, who avoid all animal products. The following foods, eaten together, will help you get the amino acids your body requires:

- Wheat with peanuts or beans
- Beans with corn
- Soybeans with seeds and nuts
- Peas with rye

A popular theory in the past was that you needed to consume these foods at the same time, but it is now commonly agreed that it is adequate to consume them in the same day. Nonetheless, it is simple to make a peanut butter sandwich on whole-wheat bread, or to eat a bowl of peas with rye bread.

Another concern for vegans includes getting an adequate supply of vitamin B12. This can be accomplished by drinking soybean milk that has been fortified with the vitamin. You may also find vegetarian meat substitutes that are fortified with vitamin B12. An alternative is to take a daily supplement of it under your tongue. Vegans and ovo-vegetarians who do not consume milk products may become deficient in riboflavin and vitamin D. Vitamin D requirements can easily be met by getting 15 to 20 minutes of sunshine most days. Riboflavin can be found in fortified cereals and other fortified grains. Iron and zinc can be found in vegetables and grains, but you should consciously be seeking out the foods that will give you your daily requirements. Zinc can be found in whole grains, legumes, and nuts. Iron can be found in beans, peas, raisins, figs, molasses, lentils, and greens. Eat citrus to ensure you are getting the vitamin C needed to process the iron. It used to be thought that vegans could easily become deficient in calcium, but new research suggests most vegans get adequate calcium from a varied diet. If you are concerned, you can consume calcium-fortified orange juice.

A wide array of meat substitutes is available for vegetarians. They include artificial bacon, sausage, hamburgers, hotdogs, meatballs, and the many items made with tofu. New products come on the market each year, adding to the choices. Artificial cheese and soy milk products are also widely available.

There are many health benefits to eating a vegetarian diet, including a decreased risk of heart disease, stroke, obesity, and certain cancers. Studies of the long-term effects of these diets have found little to be concerned about, but it is a good idea to follow the latest medical research over the years for guidance.

# Cultural and Religious Dietary Restrictions

Many religions of the world practice varying dietary restrictions. A few religions avoid all meat, while others avoid certain meats, alcohol, meat byproducts, yeast, or caffeine. It is not difficult to create a healthy diet despite most dietary restrictions. Creativity is key. Some religions also observe periods of fasting, in which no solid food is consumed. This may also include liquids. The healthy adult body can adjust to fasts of short duration. Fasts of longer duration, such as the Muslim practice of fasting from sun-up until sun-down for a month, can be fraught with medical complications. Hypoglycemia can occur as well as deficiencies of nutrients. Concentration can be difficult when one has not eaten for many hours. An early morning breakfast is helpful in these situations. Approach any long periods of fasting with good medical advice and a careful plan.

# Medical Diets

### Diabetic diets

People with type I and type II diabetes have dietary restrictions tailored to their bodies' needs. Concentrated sugars and starches are generally avoided. Diets are centered around a calorie count, such as 1,200, 1,400 or 1,600 calories consumed per day. The glycemic index — a measure of the effect of carbohydrates on blood glucose levels — is also factored in the daily choices. Carbohydrates that trickle glucose into your bloodstream over time have a lower glycemic index, while foods that cause larger amounts of glucose to be dumped into your bloodstream have a higher glycemic index. Foods with a low glycemic index help keep diabetes under control, while foods with a high glycemic index are hard on your body.

Some foods with a high glycemic index include:

- White rice
- Potatoes
- High fructose corn syrup
- Dates
- Parsnips
- Cornflakes and many other breakfast cereals
- Energy drinks
- Popcorn
- Honey
- Pretzels
- Granola bars
- Tapioca
- Ice cream
- Jelly beans and other candy
- Watermelon
- Sweet potatoes
- Licorice
- Doughnuts
- Waffles
- Pumpkin
- Cheese puff snacks
- Cornbread
- Millet
- Pop-tart-type snacks
- Cantaloupe
- Fruity gummy snacks

Foods with a low glycemic index include:

- Hummus
- Nuts
- Chickpeas
- Beans
- Lentils
- Milk
- Cherries
- Barley
- Peas
- Fat-free, sugar-free yogurt

- Pears
- Grapefruit
- Apples
- Peaches
- Lasagna
- Prunes
- Rye
- All-bran cereal
- Apricots
- Tortillas

Only foods with carbohydrates can be rated on the glycemic index. Foods that are predominantly proteins or fats are excluded. Vegetables (other than potatoes) and fruits (other than watermelon) tend to be good choices on diabetic diets. Beans, nuts, whole grains, lentils, and milk are also helpful. White flour, white rice, corn flakes, and sugary snacks should be avoided when possible.

Diabetics need to consume an adequate amount of protein, which can be achieved by eating meat, poultry, fish, eggs, beans, lentils, and nuts. While fat is not harmful to blood sugar, it is currently felt that diabetics should not consume large amounts of fat, as they are more susceptible to heart disease and stroke than the rest of the population. It is best to stick with the healthy fats from nuts, fish, olive oil, canola oil, and corn oil.

Diabetics' food needs can vary when they are under stress. Illness can greatly affect blood sugar and cause your daily needs to change. Mental stress can affect blood sugar as well. Keep your blood sugar levels as stable as possible by avoiding illness when possible and not allowing your stress levels to rise. It is very important to avoid skipping meals or bingeing. Diabetics should consume small meals, and snack throughout the day. Have a small snack at bedtime to keep blood sugar stable during the night. A healthy diabetic diet does not really differ from any healthy diet. We should all be watching our calories, avoiding high-calorie sweets, and eating plenty of vegetables, grains, and lean protein.

Exercise is an important component of a healthy diabetic life style. If you begin a new exercise program, consult your primary care provide to see whether your caloric intake should be modified. Monitoring your blood sugar, following your diet, taking prescribed medications, and keeping a healthy activity level can allow you to have a long, healthy life with diabetes.

## Crohn's disease

If you suffer from Crohn's disease, you likely know you need to avoid the foods that trigger problems for you. But do you fully understand what you should be eating? While your primary care provider can advise you best, we will discuss some general rules to follow.

- Eat three regular meals each day, plus two or three snacks.
- Follow a high-calorie, high-protein diet.
- Take vitamin and mineral supplements as advised by your primary care provider.
- You may benefit from a low-fiber, low-residue diet that avoids nuts, popcorn, seeds, and raw fruits and vegetables.
- High-calorie beverages, such as milkshakes (if you can tolerate lactose) can be beneficial, as they can rest your intestines and give you needed calories.

Consider how you feel after eating various foods. You may need to avoid foods that cause pain or severe diarrhea. Likewise, you will discover many foods that tend to agree with you.

## Other medical diets

Following a prescribed medical diet is critical to physical health. Whether you are avoiding certain foods (such as caffeinated foods) or certain nutrients (such as fiber), your body will function at its best when given the specific foods you need. Take the time to learn what you should be eating, as well as what you should not, and you can create many alternatives you may not have thought of.

# Do I Need a Supplement?

An entire industry has developed to convince us that we need nutritional supplements but for the healthy adult who eats a varied diet, this is simply not true. If you suffer health problems, your primary care provider may order supplementation. If you do not eat one or more of the foods groups that are found in the USDA food pyramid, you may need a supplement. If you tend to eat poorly and skip meals or you are significantly underweight, you will want to take appropriate supplementation. People who consume alcohol can become deficient of B vitamins and will want a supplement. Ensure-type drinks that meet all your nutritional needs can be ideal. For the average young adult, it is not harmful to take a simple vitamin/mineral supplement if you are concerned. Do not regularly take supplements that give you much more than 200 percent of the U.S. RDA for a particular nutrient without your primary care provider's approval.

# CHAPTER 18

# Entertaining

**A**lmost everyone enjoys entertaining now and then. Learn how to incorporate foods into your gatherings.

## Party Foods

Party foods are remembered by your guests long after the party. Here are some memorable, fun ideas for you.

### Appetizers

Creating good appetizers is fun and simple. Fruit is an excellent place to begin. A hollowed out watermelon or honeydew makes an attractive bowl for berries and melon balls. Fancy toothpicks add flair to fruit. They can be purchased at the grocery store or party goods store, and can hold apple wedges or skewered berries. Raw vegetables also make a nice appetizer plate. You can serve cherry tomatoes, baby carrots, celery slices, broccoli florets, pepper slices, cauliflower florets, mushrooms, and cucumber slices. Add a ranch dip or your own favorite dip in a bowl in the center of the plate.

A low-cost appetizer idea is deviled eggs. Boil the eggs as described in the Breakfast section in Chapter 6, and allow them to cool. Peel and rinse the egg well, and continue with the other eggs. When all the eggs are out of their shells, take a sharp knife and slice each one lengthwise. Carefully remove the yolk of each and place in a small bowl. This can usually be accomplished by holding the egg upside-down and squeezing it slightly. Do not be concerned if you ruin one or two of them; it takes practice to perfect making deviled eggs.

Add mayonnaise or Miracle Whip-type salad dressing to the yolks. Add around one tablespoon for every three whole eggs. Add a small amount of mustard, if desired, and a sprinkle of salt. Some people like to add chopped sweet or dill pickles or a bit of relish. Mash the yolks together with the other ingredients until all the lumps are gone. Make sure you like the flavor. With a small spoon, place the mixture where you removed the yolks, dividing evenly. Add a sprinkle of paprika, if you have some. It can often be purchased for $1 or less at dollar stores.

Other attractive appetizers include fancy crackers topped with turkey or ham slices. Be creative in cutting up the meat slices, and add a fancy cheese slice if desired. You can top some of the appetizers with a sweet pickle slice or a slice of Roma tomato. It is a good idea to vary the appetizers, as different people will prefer different tastes.

For more substantial appetizers, you may still want to think of finger foods. Mini muffins are tasty and simple. Do not be afraid to serve purchased items, such as pizza rolls or frozen appetizers. Chicken fingers served with a dip can make a light meal, when offered with veggies or fruit. Sausage balls make good appetizers in the winter. Notice the appetizers you like at gatherings of friends or establishments, and write down the ideas for your next party.

## Full meals

If you are having a party and wish to prepare a full meal, you will want to consider the following:

1. How many guests do you expect? You may wish to start small the first time you prepare a large meal. Four to eight guests is ideal.
2. What is the atmosphere of the party? Will people be casually dressed? A casual party can have casual, fun food offerings. A more formal party will require a more serious meal.
3. What is the theme of the party? Will you have luau decorations hanging everywhere? Western? Exotic? Plan your menu accordingly.
4. What is your budget? How much can you spend per expected attendee?

Here are a few menu ideas to get you started:

A hot dog bar – Supply: the best hot dogs you can find, hot dog buns, two varieties of potato chips, a dip for the chips, diced onions, diced tomatoes, and shredded cheddar cheese. Provide mustard, ketchup, and relish. Optional items include chili, baked beans, and coleslaw.

A taco bar – Supply: Warm taco meat made from lean hamburger meat and seasoning mix, taco shells, nacho chips, diced white onions, shredded lettuce, diced tomatoes, sour cream, shredded cheddar cheese, and refried beans. Optional items include black olives, warm nacho cheese, salsa, guacamole, and jalapeno peppers.

Grilled chicken with a baked potato bar – Supply: Grilled bone-less chicken breasts; large baked potatoes wrapped in foil; margarine served in chilled, medium-size balls; shredded cheddar cheese; sour cream; chives; bacon cut into small bits; and steamed broccoli florets. Have salt and pepper available. Optional items include nacho cheese; butter pats; and chili.

Shrimp – Supply shrimp served hot (prepared your favorite way) and your choice of fish fillets, hush puppies, French fries, cole-slaw, cocktail sauce, tartar sauce, and ketchup. Optional items include corn on the cob with margarine and green beans.

Picnic-themed meal – Supply fried chicken in a variety of pieces, potato salad, baked beans, coleslaw, and rolls or biscuits.

Spaghetti – Supply a light spaghetti noodle variety, such as ver-micelli or "thin spaghetti," spaghetti sauce, meatballs, and a canister of Parmesan cheese. Serve garlic breadsticks, Texas toast, or French bread. Optional items include sautéed mushrooms and olive oil dipping sauce for the bread. Consider offering a simple salad, such as a bag of mixed greens with sliced tomato and various salad dressings.

Steak – Supply grilled steaks; small-to-medium baked potatoes wrapped in foil; grilled mixed vegetables; margarine or butter served in chilled, medium-size balls; sour cream; and various steak sauces.

Vegetarian dinner – Supply potatoes fixed your favorite way; corn on the cob; a mixture of broccoli, cauliflower, and carrots; tomatoes vinaigrette; cottage cheese or macaroni and cheese; vegetarian baked beans; one casserole, such as squash or sweet potato; and one fancy vegetable, such as an eggplant dish or portobello mushrooms. Add margarine and rolls or Italian bread.

You will probably want to enlist help with your dinner. Consider whether you want to use someone whom you are inviting as a guest to the party, or perhaps a parent, sibling, or roommate. Here are some dinner-time issues to consider:

- What time do people tend to eat the meal you are preparing? You may want to serve the meal at 6 or 7 p.m. instead of 8 or 9 p.m. Lunchtime is also a possibility. State in your invitation that a meal will be served.
- Do you have seating for your guests? Will people be sitting at one table, in one room, or scattered throughout two or more rooms? Do you need to borrow chairs?
- Do you want a pretty tablecloth? Will you be using disposable dishes and napkins? Are the plates sturdy enough for the food you are serving?
- Do you have the means to serve the hot foods hot and the cold foods cold? Think of what bowl, plate, or platter each food will be served in, and what utensil will be used to serve it.
- Do you have an empty, large garbage can ready for after the meal?
- Consider the ambience of the meal. Do you want light music playing? How about the lighting?
- Do you need a centerpiece for your table? Candles and candlesticks (if allowed where you live)?

### Drinks

Do you want to serve a variety of sodas, tea, lemonade, milk, bottled water, or juice? Make sure you have plenty of ice for cold drinks. You can purchase ice, make your own, or get it from a friend. If you want to serve punch, do you need a punch bowl? Will you serve hot drinks, such as coffee? You may want Styrofoam cups. Make sure you have additives if serving coffee or other hot drinks, such as cocoa or tea.

### Dessert

Unless you are feeling especially brave, it is a good idea to keep dessert simple. Many people are full from dinner and may not eat dessert. A simple ice cream works well. If it is a birthday, you will want to serve the honoree's favorite cake and vanilla or Neapolitan ice cream. Homemade or bakery-made cookies make excellent desserts. Also consider a simple variety of fruit slices.

# Ball Game Menus

For a tailgate party, consider taking prepared foods from a deli. They are generally well-wrapped and less messy to move. If you are taking foods that you make yourself, have everyone pitch in and bring a dish. Consider chicken strips with dip, potato chips, bowls of hot chili, cheese poppers, and cookies. This is not the time most people are thinking about nutritious eating. Remember drinks, disposable dishes, and plenty of napkins.

If you are planning a ball-game-watching party at your home, sandwiches are ideal. Take sub rolls and cut into three-inch rolls. Offer these with a variety of meats, such as turkey, chicken, ham, sliced beef, and salami. Have at least two sliced cheeses, such as cheddar, Swiss, American, provolone, or Muenster. Offer tomato slices, lettuce slices, red onion slices, pickles, mayonnaise, and mustard. Have around three 3-inch rolls for each person. You will want to serve some sort of potato, such as tater tots or potato chips, with the appropriate ketchup or dip. Have some fruit, such as apple slices, orange wedges cut from the whole orange, and/ or strawberries. A variety of sodas and bottled water should be fine with this meal. If the guests will be there for several hours, you may want to also pop popcorn and have a special drink, such as punch, cocoa, or apple cider.

# Holiday Foods on a Budget

## New Year's Day

Traditional foods to eat on New Year's Day include black-eyed peas and "something green," such as turnip greens or spinach. Cornbread is a natural accompaniment. To prepare black-eyed peas for company:

> Sort 1 pound of black-eyed peas and soak overnight in a saucepan with 4 cups water. The next morning, pour off the water and add 4 cups of fresh water. Add a piece of ham or two raw slices of bacon, if desired. Bring to a boil with lid on at medium-high heat. Reduce heat to medium-low and allow to simmer with lid on. One hour after the peas have begun to boil, add 1 tablespoon of sugar. Dice half of a small white or yellow onion and add. Continue to cook for 30 minutes, and add 2 teaspoons of salt. Cook another 30 minutes, and test for softness. When they are done, remove from heat and serve. Some cooks offer this dish with white rice and call it "hoppin' John."

Fresh turnip greens are often not available at New Years, so you may need to prepare the canned variety:

> Add 1 tablespoon of margarine or bacon grease per can. Have vinegar or apple cider vinegar available on the table for the turnip greens. Alternatively, serve frozen creamed spinach. Prepare either dish according to directions, and serve with the black-eyed peas.

## Cornbread

Cornbread can be prepared in an iron skillet, baking dish, muffin pan, or pone pan. Since you are most likely to use a baking dish, we will discuss that method:

> Take 2 tablespoons bacon grease and place in dish. Put on middle rack of oven and preheat oven to 400 degrees. Remove pan after 5 minutes, or when grease is melted and hot. If you do not wish to use bacon grease, simply eliminate that step. Pour 2 cups corn meal mix in a large bowl. You can use white or yellow mix, and regular milk or buttermilk. Purists generally prefer white, while yellow makes a prettier presentation. Add 1 tablespoon of salt and stir. Add ¼ cup softened bacon grease or your favorite oil (not olive oil). Mix together and add two eggs. Stir and add ½ cup milk or buttermilk. Blend together and pour in baking dish. If you made the hot bacon grease, pour the batter right over it. Place the dish in the oven on the lowest rack. Cook for 20 minutes and check. If the top is not beginning to brown, move to the middle rack. Cook for another 10 to 15 minutes, until top is nicely browned. Cut into slices and serve hot.

You can add various things to cornbread batter. After you have mastered making traditional cornbread, consider adding ½ cup creamed-style corn, 2 tablespoons sugar, or ¼ cup of diced peppers.

This inexpensive New Year's Day meal can be served with milk or iced tea. If you wish to add dessert, consider angel food cake topped with canned peach slices or thawed frozen strawberries.

## Valentine's Day

For Valentine's Day, simply think red. Pretty butter or sugar cookies, cut into heart shapes and decorated with white, pink, or red icing, make a beautiful offering. Red velvet cake is another option. Sweets signify the special day, and you will want to avoid spicy offerings. If you wish to prepare a full meal, consider the ideas in the Romantic Dinners section in this chapter, or try this dinner:

What you need to buy or have on hand:

> 2 boneless, skinless chicken breasts
> ½ cup pineapple juice
> ¼ cup honey
> 2 large carrots
> 1 cup frozen peas
> 1 cup dried cranberries
> ¼ cup sugar or your favorite sweetener
> margarine or butter
> dash of cinnamon, nutmeg, or allspice
> can of crescent roll dough
> can of sliced pineapple in its own juice
> salt

Create a marinade of ½ cup pineapple juice, ¼ cup honey, and 1 teaspoon salt. Take a fork and pierce holes in two boneless, skinless chicken breasts. Place them in the marinade and allow to sit in the refrigerator for at least 2 hours. Change the positions of the breasts halfway through the marinating process, keeping both breasts covered at all times. Meanwhile, take one cup of dried cranberries and place in a small saucepan with 1 cup of water. Bring to a boil over medium high heat and add ¼ cup sugar or your favorite sweetener. Add 1 teaspoon margarine or butter. Add a dash of cinnamon, nutmeg, or allspice. Lower heat to low and simmer until cranberries are soft and almost all the liquid is absorbed. Place in a bowl and refrigerate. Peel two large carrots and cut into carrot wheels. Place in a small saucepan and add 1 cup water. Boil over medium-high heat with the lid on. When the carrots have been boiling for 25 minutes, add 1 cup of frozen peas and boil an additional 10 minutes. Add ½ teaspoon salt and 1 teaspoon margarine or butter, stir, and remove from heat. Reheat for 2 minutes just before serving.

Prepare crescent rolls according to the package directions. Heat the Foreman-type grill, remove the chicken from the marinade, and place it on the grill as the rolls cook. Grill until completely done and remove. Place two pineapple slices on the grill and cook briefly, until they have nice grill marks. Take the juice from the canned pineapple and pour into a small, microwave-safe bowl. Heat for 45 seconds, or until hot. Reheat the vegetables while you are taking up the rest of the food.

Place the chicken on the plates, add a pineapple slice, and pour the warmed juice over both. Add the peas and carrots to the side. Place the cranberries on the plates and offer the crescent rolls with margarine or butter. Serve with iced tea.

## Easter

A traditional Easter meal includes ham. Find the smallest ham that will feed your guests and prepare according to directions. As your ham bakes, you may want to baste it with any mixture of the following: honey, pineapple (fruit and/or juice), black pepper, brown sugar, butter, coca cola, salt, or cloves (a small amount).

Prepare mashed potatoes according to the following recipe:

Place 4 cups of water in a large saucepan, cover pan, and bring to a boil over medium-high heat. Peel one potato for each expected attendee. Cut into 2-inch cubes, and carefully add to the boiling water. Boil 20 minutes or until potatoes are soft but not falling apart. Place in a large bowl, add 1 teaspoon of margarine or butter for each guest, and mash with a potato masher or mix with a blender on low. Add whole milk until potatoes are of desired consistency, and mix. Salt to taste, and stir.

Serve with whole cranberry sauce and either green beans or peas. Add traditional rolls and margarine or butter. Offer any fruit pie for dessert. Top the hot pie with whipped cream or vanilla ice cream. If you are on a budget, compare prices. It is often less expensive to buy a frozen fruit pie than to make one from scratch.

## Independence Day

The Fourth of July calls for hot dogs or hamburgers. The most fun way to prepare these is on a traditional grill. If you have access to one, here are some ideas:

> Hot dogs – Buy the best hot dogs you can afford, buns, mustard, ketchup, relish, and onions.

> Hamburgers – Purchase lean hamburger meat (around 85 to 90 percent lean), seeded buns, mustard, mayonnaise, ketchup, lettuce, tomato, pickles, onions, and American cheese. You may want to make your hamburger patties with all beef, or you may want to add salt, pepper, or other seasonings to the meat as you make the patties.

For side dishes, add potato chips, coleslaw, baked beans, and optionally, potato salad. Offer a variety of sodas, iced tea, and lemonade. Have watermelon for dessert.

## Labor Day

Labor Day is a traditional day to have hamburgers, hotdogs, or barbecue. Many options exist for barbecue.

You can bake various pieces of chicken in the oven until 15 minutes from done, and add barbecue sauce to the entire pieces of chicken. Continue to cook until completely done.

You can take sliced or shredded beef or shredded pork or chicken and add barbecue sauce in a saucepan, and cook covered on medium-low for 15 minutes. This type of barbecue should be served on large, seeded buns.

You can bake a rack of pork or beef ribs in the oven and baste in barbecue sauce during the last hour. This can be expensive.

Some items to consider serving with barbecue include coleslaw, potato salad, baked beans, and corn on the cob. For dessert, consider watermelon or ice cream.

## Halloween

Food prepared for Halloween generally has a humorous or spooky theme. Meatballs with noodles (such as spaghetti or stroganoff) are appropriate, as are cakes, muffins, or cookies designed with spooky patterns or shapes. It is also a good time to think of the autumn harvest and serve candied apples, hot apple cider, or pumpkin pie with whipped cream.

## Thanksgiving and Christmas

It could be quite difficult to prepare a large dinner if you are in a small kitchen with limited supplies. If you wish to do so, here are some ideas that will not break your budget:

Instead of a large turkey, have a turkey breast. It is smaller and will cook more quickly. Cook according to directions, and keep it well-basted with margarine or butter. Add your favorite herbs to the baste if desired.

Prepare mashed potatoes according to the recipe in the Easter section. Serve frozen corn. It can be cream-style or regular, white, or yellow. Prepare instant stuffing. Offer canned whole cranberry sauce. Have a green vegetable — either green beans or peas. Prepare a sweet potato casserole according to the following recipe:

Add four cups water to a large saucepan. Cover and bring to a boil over medium-high heat. Peel one sweet potato for every two attendees. Cut into 2-inch cubes and carefully add to the boiling water. Boil with the lid on for 25 minutes or until soft. Drain well and place potatoes in a large bowl. Add 1 tablespoon of butter for every potato. Add 4 tablespoons of sugar for every potato. Add salt and cinnamon as desired. Mix with the blender on low speed until thoroughly mixed. Pour into baking dish and add marshmallows to completely cover the potatoes. Place on bottom rack of oven, preheated to 300 degrees. Watch carefully and remove when marshmallows barely begin to brown.

Serve with traditional rolls and butter. Offer milk, iced tea, and your favorite beverages to drink. Have a fruit pie, pecan pie, or cake for dessert, depending on your family's tradition. Offer eggnog after dinner.

When preparing special meals, you may want to serve and cook with real unsalted butter instead of margarine. Serve and use whole milk in your recipes. Do not buy sugar-free or fat-free items unless you need to for health reasons; traditional meals are best prepared traditionally.

## New Year's Eve

Are you planning a New Year's Eve party? For your menu, anything goes. Because these parties are long, it is a good time to get your guests involved in the cooking. Consider making homemade pizzas, either making the crust or buying ready-to-use crusts. Make or prepare pizza sauce. Purchase different pre-cooked toppings, such as pepperoni, beef, sausage, and ham. Have a variety of veggies, such as mushrooms, red onions, black olives, and tomatoes. Consider diced pineapple. Have plenty of shredded mozzarella cheese. Get everyone involved in the fun of preparing the pizzas. Bake according to the crust directions, and serve. You may have to prepare one at a time, and that is fine, as you have several hours from party beginning to end.

Should you decide to order pizza instead of making it, or you have a different menu, make cookies together during the last two hours. The idea is to get everyone involved in the process. Have plenty of towels or napkins handy. For beverages, consider milk (for the cookies), a variety of sodas, or punch. Offer cocoa and eggnog late in the evening.

# Romantic dinners

Preparing a special dinner for two can be scary as well as fun. You will want to think out your menu carefully. Prepare foods that you know your guest enjoys. Avoid foods that cause bad breath or gastrointestinal upset, such as sweet potatoes, beans, boiled eggs, hot sauce, onions, and garlic. Do not try to get too complicated, especially on an early date. Chicken, steak, or salmon is often a safe bet. You may want to venture into Oriental dishes when you get comfortable with both your date and your cooking skills.

A romantic chicken dinner can include grilled skinless, boneless chicken with homemade French fries with the skin on, and mixed Italian vegetables baked in aluminum foil. Serve crescent rolls with this meal.

A steak dinner can include steak, a baked potato served in aluminum foil with margarine and sour cream, and green beans with crisp bacon pieces. Serve yeast rolls with this meal.

A salmon dinner can include flavored rice and steamed mixed vegetables, including mushrooms, squash, zucchini, and snow peas. Serve breadsticks.

For dessert, have something fun, such as strawberries dipped in chocolate or ice cream sundaes. Serve iced tea or your guest's favorite soda. Do not be afraid to add garnishes to your dishes, such as fresh parsley or a slice of whole orange or lemon.

## Be a hit at potluck dinners

When you get invited to a potluck dinner, try to find out what the theme is and what main dishes are expected. If you have time or budget constraints, consider offering to bring the sodas. Your host is often happy for someone to take over that task. If you are bringing a dish, your next consideration is healthy or traditional. Do you want to set a good example and take grilled veggies, or do you want to knock them out with your green bean casserole or banana pudding?

If you do not have a large glass baking dish with a cover and a carry bag, ask for one for the next gift-giving occasion. They are indispensable for potluck dinners and many other times in life. Following are a few ideas to make you the hit of the potluck dinner.

## Banana pudding

Purchase six ripe bananas, a box of vanilla wafers, two boxes of vanilla pudding mix to be cooked, whole milk, 1 teaspoon of sugar, and two eggs. Follow the instructions on the box to make the two boxes of pudding. Allow to cool to room temperature. Place a row of wafers on the bottom of your baking dish. Spoon vanilla pudding to barely cover the wafers. Slice the bananas into wheels and place on top of the pudding. Layer another level of pudding and add another layer of wafers. Continue to add bananas, pudding, and wafers until eight wafers remain.

Take an egg and carefully crack it over a medium-size bowl. Move the yolk back and forth from one cracked shell piece to the other, as the egg white goes into the bowl. When all the white has left the yolk, discard the shell and yolk. Continue with the other egg. Take the egg whites and beat with the mixer on high until they begin to get stiff. Add 1 teaspoon of sugar and continue to beat until stiff. Add the meringue to the top of the pudding in the baking dish. Place the dish in the middle rack of the oven that you have preheated to 350 degrees. Watch carefully, and remove when the meringue begins to brown slightly. Add the last eight wafers to the top in an attractive design. Chill until time to serve.

When you master this dish, you can begin to make pudding from scratch, which will use the discarded egg yolks.

## Green bean casserole

Purchase 1½ pounds of frozen green beans, two cans of condensed cream of mushroom soup, whole milk, and a large can of French fried onions.

Preheat oven to 325 degrees. Thaw 1½ pounds of green beans. Place in a large baking dish and add the two cans of soup. Add

⅔ cup of whole milk and stir. Add pepper if desired. Add half of the can of onions and stir again. Place in the oven on the middle rack and cook for 20 minutes. If the dish is getting too brown on the top, stir and place on the bottom rack. Cook another 10 minutes and check. Continue to cook, checking every 5 minutes until the green beans are soft and the top is lightly browning. Add the rest of the onions to the top and cook another 5 minutes. Do not allow the onions to overbrown.

## Mixed vegetables

If you wish to take a healthy dish, purchase a roll of heavy-duty aluminum foil or an aluminum foil baking bag, two bags of your favorite frozen mixed vegetables, margarine, and seasoning mix.

Thaw the vegetables. Preheat the oven to 375 degrees. Layer the bottom of a large baking dish with the foil, leaving a 12-inch length coming up both sides. Place the vegetables on the foil and add 2 tablespoons of margarine. Season liberally with the seasoning mix. Close the foil packet, folding all the ends closed so it will be entirely closed.

Alternatively, use the foil baking bag and close according to directions. Place in the middle rack of the oven for 35 minutes and check to see if well done. Some of the vegetables should be browning. If they are not, continue to cook, and check every 10 minutes. Leave the vegetables in the packet or bag until time to go to the dinner, and reheat at 375 degrees for 10 minutes before you go.

It is rewarding to create your own dishes to take to potluck dinners. Soon, hosts may be asking you if you can bring that special dish you make.

# CHAPTER 19

## Preparing for Life after College

## What Now?

College is ending, and you are headed into the work force. Your cooking skills, honed over the past few years, will serve you well as you enter this stage of your life. You can now spend more resources, and hopefully more time, in creating your meals.

## Shopping with a Bigger Budget

Only you know what having a bigger budget will mean to your grocery buying. Will you purchase more organic items, either for health reasons or ecological reasons? Do you have a list of "never eat again" items, such as ramen noodles? Will you purchase better grades of meat, leaner hamburger, fresh fish, and more produce? Consider your goals as your budget changes. Let us look at one example:

In the past, you had $40 to spend per week at the grocery store. You can now spend $100 per week.

- You continue to spend ¼ of your budget on fresh produce — from $10 to $25 a week. Consider organic options, a bigger variety of fruits and vegetables, and more vegetarian main courses. Purchase fresh herbs and spices.

- In the grocery aisles, look at items that you never buy. Spend some time in the ethnic cuisine aisle, and look carefully at the vegetable and bean sections. Make sure that any changes you make are nutritional upgrades. For example, if you used to buy the cheapest potato chips, now, purchase the baked ones. Buy cereals and breads with whole grains. Find grains you have never tried, as well as healthy pastas.

- In the meat and seafood departments, search for lean cuts of meat and fresh fish. Buy chicken breasts instead of thighs or drumsticks.

- In the frozen department, if you have been buying the cheapest frozen dinners, upgrade to the healthier options that have restricted fat and calories. Buy frozen fruit, especially berries, when you cannot obtain good, fresh, seasonal fruit.

- In the dairy and ice cream departments, buy skim products and fat-free items. Try the fat-free frozen yogurt instead of the cheapest ice cream.

This should give you some ideas on how to expand your food budget wisely. The key words are fresh, healthy, and variety.

## Keeping It Healthy

Resist the urge to overeat now that your budget is larger. Also, beware of upgrading at restaurants in a way that includes more calories instead of more nutrition. Remember to only eat half of entrées at restaurants, and take the rest home for the next day. If you must splurge, do so only briefly, and then continue on your healthy lifestyle plan. You can now avoid fast food, unless you wish to find a salad or a healthy grilled option.

Encourage your friends to join you at healthy restaurants, and set a good example by bringing salads and healthy sandwiches when you bring food with you. This is a good principle that is also self-serving, as it is known that our friends' eating habits rub off on us. Friends of overweight people are more likely to be overweight themselves, and you can help yourself and your friends work toward a healthy life by setting a good example.

# Expanding Your Culinary Knowledge

Eventually, you will replace your existing pots and pans with a brand new set. There is a dizzying array of copper-bottomed cookware, stainless steel utensils, and more. You will add new appliances, plates, silverware, tools, and other exciting items. Keep in mind that your tastes in food should dictate what you purchase. If you cook daily, you may want a different set of cookware than the person who cooks once a week. Likewise, do not purchase appliances to make dishes you do not like or seldom eat. Consider your desires, and work to meet them.

Someone who cooks frequently will want to consider adding the following to their basic cookware and appliances:

- A large iron skillet with lid
- A small iron skillet
- Ceramic bowls that can go in the oven
- Glass bowls of various sizes
- A stock pot
- A double boiler
- Extra cookie sheets
- A Bundt cake pan or other specialty pan

- A pressure cooker
- A food processor
- A bread maker
- A coffeemaker
- A mini-muffin pan

You will also want to expand your spices and seasonings. Base your purchases on your own tastes. A fairly basic set will include:

- Salt
- Kosher salt or sea salt
- Black pepper
- White pepper
- Red pepper flakes
- Parsley
- Oregano
- Onion powder
- Paprika
- Lemon pepper
- Chicken bullion
- Beef bullion
- Meat tenderizer
- Basil
- Rosemary
- Cumin
- Cloves
- Sage
- Garlic salt
- Garlic powder
- Cinnamon
- Vanilla extract
- Almond extract
- Toppings for cupcakes
- Nutmeg
- Allspice

Purchase small quantities of the spices you use infrequently, as they do not stay fresh indefinitely. Many other spices exist, and you will find new favorites as you expand your cooking. Purchase fresh herbs and spices for the week's menu, when possible.

When you purchase new plates, cups, and bowls, it is a good idea to keep practicality in mind. Items that can be used in the microwave are ideal. They should be dishwasher-safe as well. Avoid any items that seem fragile or thin. A nice set of silverware will last for many years. Find spoons that are resilient enough to remove hard ice cream from the container, for example. You will purchase many spatulas and similar plastic items over the years and do not need to spend extra money on expensive models.

When searching for a new home, carefully consider the kitchen. If you cook frequently, you will want to have a dishwasher and plenty of cabinet and counter space.

## Cooking courses

Consider taking a cooking course, either in an area where you feel you are deficient, or to learn a new style of cooking. Cooking classes are fun and will teach you skills for a lifetime. Going with a friend or relative can enhance the experience.

### Basic courses

If you still do not have the required confidence in egg boiling and soup cooking, take a beginner's course, and watch things being made firsthand. Take a course that lasts at least ten hours total and covers a variety of topics that you are interested in. Find out whether you will be participating or just watching and also see whether there will be an opportunity to ask questions. Take notes if there is not a book or video to purchase.

### Advanced courses

Famous chefs often offer advanced cooking courses. These courses can equip you to prepare gourmet meals with ease. Choose a course of at least 12 hours, and purchase the book or video if possible.

### Specialty courses

Do you wish to bake better pies and cakes? Take a specialty course in baking. Want to learn to prepare Oriental or Italian dishes? Find an appropriate course. These courses can be especially fun as you taste the finished products. Do not forget to treat yourself to these kinds of courses over the years to expand your culinary palate.

Another alternative you may wish to consider is to have a family member teach you to cook your family's traditional dishes. Remember holiday favorites as well as seasonal, party, and picnic traditions. These lessons usually take place in their kitchen, where they have access to everything needed. Take plenty of notes, or have someone make a video for you. A video of your grandmother preparing family pies or stuffing will be invaluable to you and your descendants for many years.

A different idea is to advertise for someone to teach you a certain aspect of cooking. You can find wonderful chefs who work every day in their own homes but never venture into professional cooking. These lessons can occur at their home or yours.

## New methods of cooking

As the years pass, you will hear about new methods of cooking. A fairly recent development involves convection cooking, which cooks food much more quickly than the traditional oven. Explore all the different griddles and surfaces available, and pizza ovens, quesadilla makers, ice cream makers, and other things that might interest you. Ask friends how they cook particular foods, and watch cooking shows occasionally to learn new ideas. You will be cooking for many years of your life and want to have the broadest range of choices available.

# CHAPTER 20

## Senior Year Recipes

## Cooked Cabbage

**Ingredients:**

> ½ head of cabbage
> 1 tablespoon margarine
> 1 tablespoon canola, corn,
>    or olive oil
> 1 teaspoon bacon grease
>    (optional)
> 2 tablespoons sugar
>    or your favorite
>    sweetener
> Salt

**Instructions:**

Fill a 3-quart saucepan ⅔ full of water and heat on medium-high with the lid on. As it heats,

| Nutrition Facts | |
|---|---|
| per serving | |
| makes 1 serving | |
| **Amount per serving** | |
| **Calories** | 451 |
| Calories from fat | 231 |
| | **% Daily Value \*** |
| **Total Fat 25.6g** | 39% |
| Saturated Fat 4g | 20% |
| **Cholesterol 0mg** | 0% |
| **Sodium 377mg** | 16% |
| **Total Carbohydrate 49.5g** | 16% |
| Dietary Fiber 10.4g | 42% |
| **Protein 5.6g** | |
| Percent values are based on a 2,000 calorie per day diet. Your daily values may differ. | |
| <u>**Additional Information**</u> 51.2% of calories from Fat 43.9% from Carbohydrates 5% from Protein | |

cut half the head of cabbage and divide it into various-size pieces. Making around six cuts is ideal. Carefully add to the water when it begins to boil. Replace the lid and allow to cook for 20 minutes on medium-high, stirring occasionally. Turn heat to medium and add the oil. Cook another 15 minutes, and add the margarine. Turn to medium-low and cook for 15 minutes. Add 1 teaspoon of salt and the bacon grease if desired. Cook for 10 minutes, or until very soft. Pour off all but 1 cup of the liquid and add the sugar or sweetener. Cook on medium with the lid off for 3 minutes and remove from heat. Serve in bowls, distributing the juice evenly. Salt as desired.

**Accompaniments:**

This dish is traditionally served with cornbread. It is filling enough to be a meal on its own. Serve with a small piece of fruit pie or angel food cake if desired.

**Tips:**

*If you do not have a 3-quart saucepan, use the largest that you have, and reduce the ingredients accordingly.*

# Crock-Pot Chili

## Ingredients:

- 1½ pounds extra lean ground beef
- 2 cans chili beans
- 1 can light red kidney beans, drained
- 1 large onion, white, or yellow
- 1 large can diced tomatoes in juice
- 1 can tomato sauce — around 8 ounces
- 1 tablespoon cumin
- 1 tablespoon oregano
- 1 tablespoon salt
- 1 teaspoon hot chili powder
- 2 tablespoons chili powder
- 2 tablespoons sugar
- 1 tablespoon masa harina, optional

| Nutrition Facts | |
|---|---|
| per serving | |
| makes 8 servings | |
| **Amount per serving** | |
| **Calories** | 426 |
| Calories from fat | 192 |
| **% Daily Value \*** | |
| **Total Fat 21.3g** | 33% |
| Saturated Fat 8.4g | 42% |
| **Cholesterol 78mg** | 26% |
| **Sodium 1886mg** | 79% |
| **Total Carbohydrate 32.2g** | 11% |
| Dietary Fiber 9g | 36% |
| **Protein 26.4g** | |
| Percent values are based on a 2,000 calorie per day diet. Your daily values may differ. | |
| **Additional Information** 45% of calories from Fat 30.2% from Carbohydrates 24.8% from Protein | |

## Instructions:

Place the ground beef in a medium-size skillet over medium heat. Crumble the meat with a fork to leave some large pieces along with the crumbles. When no longer pink, drain the grease into a bowl or cup for later disposal. Place the beef in a Crock-Pot. Add chili beans, drained kidney beans, can of diced tomatoes, tomato sauce, and 1 cup of water. Cover and cook on the highest setting until boiling and place heat on low. Begin timing at this point. Keep the cover on, other than stirring occasionally. Cut the onion into large pieces and add at the 1-hour mark. At the 1½-hour mark, add the cumin, oregano, hot chili powder, chili powder, and paprika. Continue to cook, and stir occasionally. If the chili is not bubbling lightly, increase the heat to medium. At the 3-hour mark, add the salt and sugar. Add ½ cup of water if needed at any point during the cooking. At the 3½-hour mark, place the masa harina into a small bowl and mix with 3 tablespoons of hot water. Stir well. Add to the chili and stir. Taste test the chili at the 4-hour mark and add salt, chili powder, or hot chili powder if necessary. If you add additional ingredients, cook 10 more minutes before turning off the heat. Makes 8 servings.

## Accompaniments:

Serve with saltine crackers or cornbread. Have a cold beverage and a cold, light dessert, such as chilled mandarin oranges, if desired.

**Tips:**

*Chili can be served year-round, but it is especially comforting on a cold winter day. Buy a box of saltines and invite friends over for a chili supper. You can also freeze the leftover chili for later use.*

# Barbecued Chicken

## Ingredients:

    1 piece of chicken — any
        cut, skin on, with bone
    ¼ cup barbecue sauce

## Instructions:

Preheat the oven to 400 degrees. Place the chicken in a baking dish and heat on the lowest rack of the oven for 20 minutes. Turn the chicken over and place on the middle rack of the over for 15 minutes. Check to see if chicken is done. Check every 10

| Nutrition Facts | |
|---|---|
| per serving | |
| makes 1 serving | |
| **Amount per serving** | |
| **Calories** | 458 |
| Calories from fat | 257 |
| **% Daily Value *** | |
| **Total Fat 28.6g** | 44% |
| Saturated Fat 7.9g | 40% |
| **Cholesterol 189mg** | 63% |
| **Sodium 688mg** | 29% |
| **Total Carbohydrate 8g** | 3% |
| Dietary Fiber 0.8g | 3% |
| **Protein 42.3g** | |
| Percent values are based on a 2,000 calorie per day diet. Your daily values may differ. | |
| **Additional Information** 56.1% of calories from Fat 7% from Carbohydrates 36.9% from Protein | |

minutes until done. Carefully remove the skin. Put 2 tablespoons of barbecue sauce on the chicken and cook for 5 minutes. Turn the chicken over, add 2 tablespoons of sauce, and return to the oven for another 5 minutes. Serve with the additional barbecue sauce on the side.

## Accompaniments:

Serve with oven-baked fries or potato salad. You can add cole-slaw, baked beans, barbecue beans, or pork and beans, if desired. This goes well with a cornbread muffin or hushpuppies. For dessert, have a small scoop of low-fat vanilla frozen yogurt. Serve with iced tea or lemonade.

**Tips:**

*This dish is a fun treat. You can easily prepare 2 or 3 pieces of chicken at once, if desired. Refrigerate and reheat the leftovers for additional meals.*

# Easy Blackberry Cobbler

### Ingredients:

1 cup fresh blackberries

¼ cup plus 1 teaspoon sugar

¼ cup self-rising flour

1 tablespoon margarine

2 tablespoons milk

¼ teaspoon salt

### Instructions:

Place the berries in a small sauce-pan with ¾ cup of water. Heat on medium-high until boiling, and reduce the heat to medium.

| Nutrition Facts | |
|---|---|
| per serving | |
| makes 2 servings | |
| **Amount per serving** | |
| **Calories** | 262 |
| Calories from fat | 58 |
| % Daily Value * | |
| **Total Fat 6.5g** | 10% |
| Saturated Fat 1.3g | 6% |
| **Cholesterol 1mg** | 0% |
| **Sodium 501mg** | 21% |
| **Total Carbohydrate 48.6g** | 16% |
| Dietary Fiber 4.2g | 17% |
| **Protein 2.5g** | |
| Percent values are based on a 2,000 calorie per day diet. Your daily values may differ. | |
| **Additional Information** | |
| 22.1% of calories from Fat 74.1% from Carbohydrates 3.8% from Protein | |

Add ¼ cup of sugar. Cook for 12 minutes, beyond the time it begins to boil.

Preheat the oven to 350 degrees. Pour the berries and water into a medium-size baking dish. Place the flour, salt, and sugar into a small bowl and stir together. Add margarine and stir with a fork until coarse and crumbly. Add milk and stir. Take the batter and add by teaspoons to the berries, scattering throughout. Place the baking dish on the bottom rack of the oven. Remove after 15 minutes, turn the dough patties upside down, and return the dish to the oven. Check for doneness after 10 minutes. When the dough is no longer raw, remove from the oven. Makes 2 servings.

### Accompaniments:

Serve blackberry cobbler alone or with a very light meal, such as a salad. Traditional toppings include a pat of margarine, a dollop of whipped cream, or a scoop of low-fat vanilla ice cream. Offer milk.

**Tips:**
*Serve warm for a rare college-days indulgence.*

# Peach Cobbler

### Ingredients:

9 fresh peaches

1 cup sugar

1 cup self-rising flour

1 tablespoon lemon juice

½ teaspoon salt

1 egg

6 tablespoons margarine

Dash cinnamon

Dash nutmeg

| Nutrition Facts | |
|---|---|
| per serving | |
| makes 8 servings | |
| **Amount per serving** | |
| **Calories** | 333 |
| Calories from fat | 85 |
| % Daily Value * | |
| **Total Fat 9.5g** | 15% |
| Saturated Fat 1.8g | 9% |
| **Cholesterol 27mg** | 9% |
| **Sodium 353mg** | 15% |
| **Total Carbohydrate 58.2g** | 19% |
| Dietary Fiber 4.2g | 17% |
| **Protein 3.7g** | |
| Percent values are based on a 2,000 calorie per day diet. Your daily values may differ. | |
| **Additional Information** 25.6% of calories from Fat 70% from Carbohydrates 4.4% from Protein | |

### Instructions:

Peel the peaches and dice into medium-size pieces. Place in a medium-size saucepan. Add 1½ cups of water, ¼ cup of sugar, cinnamon, and nutmeg. Cover and bring to a boil on medium high. Remove lid and cook on medium for 20 minutes, or until peaches are soft. Preheat the oven to 375 degrees. Pour hot peaches and water into the bottom of a baking dish. Put the remainder of the sugar, flour, and salt in a medium-size bowl and stir together. Crack the egg into a small bowl and beat with a fork. Pour into the dry ingredients and toss until crumbly. Sprinkle with lemon juice. Melt the margarine in the microwave on high for 35 seconds in a small bowl. Pour the margarine over the peaches. Take the flour mixture and add with a spoon to the peaches, distributing throughout. Place the baking dish on the middle rack of the oven. Check after 15 minutes, and cover with foil if the top is beginning to brown too quickly. After 30 minutes of total cooking time, check for doneness. Remove from oven when done and serve. Makes 8 servings.

## Accompaniments:

Serve peach cobbler alone or after a traditional country meal, such as chicken, mashed potatoes, and green beans. Offer milk and low-fat vanilla ice cream.

**Tips:**

*This high-calorie dessert should be a rare treat. It can be taken warm to a potluck dinner.*

# Grilled Shrimp

### Ingredients:

8 ounces peeled, large
    shrimp
1 cup orange juice
¼ cup honey
1 teaspoon garlic powder

### Instructions:

In a medium-size bowl, mix together the orange juice, honey, and garlic powder. Add the shrimp, making sure each piece is covered. Place in the refrigerator for 1 hour. Remove and stir lightly. Return to the refrigerator for at least 1 hour.

| Nutrition Facts | |
|---|---|
| per serving makes 2 servings | |
| **Amount per serving** | |
| **Calories** | 316 |
| Calories from fat | 20 |
| **% Daily Value \*** | |
| **Total Fat 2.2g** | 3% |
| Saturated Fat 0.4g | 2% |
| **Cholesterol 170mg** | 57% |
| **Sodium 171mg** | 7% |
| **Total Carbohydrate 49.8g** | 17% |
| Dietary Fiber 0.4g | 2% |
| **Protein 24.2g** | |
| Percent values are based on a 2,000 calorie per day diet. Your daily values may differ. | |
| **Additional Information** 6.3% of calories from Fat 63% from Carbohydrates 30.6% from Protein | |

Spray the Foreman-type grill with spray oil and preheat. Place pieces of shrimp on the grill surface and cook for 2½ to 4 minutes until done. Prepare in batches until all the shrimp is cooked. Makes 2 servings.

## Accompaniments:

For a traditional flair, add baked onion rings, hushpuppies, and a green vegetable, such as asparagus. For a modern meal, add a side of wild rice, corn on the cob, and a breadstick. Serve with iced tea and a small piece of white cake, if desired.

**Tips:**

*If you are using frozen shrimp, make sure the shrimp stays in the marinade for at least 2 hours after it is thawed. This dish is not ideal as a leftover. Make only the amount you and any guests will be eating.*

# Oatmeal Raisin Cookies

### Ingredients:

1½ cups oats

¾ cup raisins

¾ cup plain flour

½ cup sugar

½ cup brown sugar

1 stick unsalted butter

1 egg

1 teaspoon salt

½ teaspoon baking soda

1 teaspoon cinnamon

½ teaspoon nutmeg

2 teaspoons vanilla

| Nutrition Facts | |
|---|---|
| per serving | |
| makes 12 servings | |
| **Amount per serving** | |
| **Calories** | 285 |
| Calories from fat | 86 |
| **% Daily Value \*** | |
| **Total Fat 9.5g** | 15% |
| Saturated Fat 5.1g | 25% |
| **Cholesterol 39mg** | 13% |
| **Sodium 259mg** | 11% |
| **Total Carbohydrate 44.7g** | 15% |
| Dietary Fiber 2.8g | 11% |
| **Protein 5g** | |
| Percent values are based on a 2,000 calorie per day diet. Your daily values may differ. | |
| **Additional Information** | |
| 30.2% of calories from Fat | |
| 62.8% from Carbohydrates | |
| 7% from Protein | |

### Instructions:

Preheat the oven to 350 degrees. In a large bowl, mix together the butter and sugars. Beat on medium with a mixer for 2 minutes, or by hand for 4 minutes. In a separate medium bowl, combine the flour, salt, and baking soda. Stir well and set aside. Add the egg to the bowl with the sugar and mix thoroughly. Add the flour mixture to the bowl with the sugar. Mix for 1 minute with the mixer on medium, or 2 minutes by hand. Stir in the oats, cinnamon, nutmeg, and vanilla. Mix for 1 minute with the mixer on medium, or by hand for 2 minutes. Add the raisins and stir with a large spoon. Drop by spoonfuls onto a cookie sheet with the sides not touching. You will need to use at least two cookie sheets, or you can cook in batches, allowing the sheet to cool thoroughly and the batter to be refrigerated in between batches. Place on the middle rack of the oven and begin watching closely after 10 minutes. Remove when done and serve warm or cooled. Makes 2 dozen cookies.

**Accompaniments:**

These cookies are best accompanied by one thing: a large glass of milk. They can be served after a light lunch or dinner if desired; salad is ideal.

**Tips:**

*These cookies are fantastic when you feel homesick. They make good treats for a sick friend, or if you need to make a peace offering. A half-cup of chopped walnuts can be mixed in when the raisins are added.*

# Roasted Vegetable Pasta

## Ingredients:

¼ red onion, chopped

1 cup cauliflower

1 cup squash — yellow or butternut

¼ cup frozen baby spinach, thawed

Sprinkle Parmesan cheese

2 ounces tri-colored corkscrew pasta

1 tablespoon olive oil

1 teaspoon minced garlic

1 teaspoon Italian seasoning

| Nutrition Facts | |
|---|---|
| per serving makes 2 servings | |
| **Amount per serving** | |
| **Calories** | 221 |
| Calories from fat | 71 |
| | **% Daily Value \*** |
| **Total Fat 7.9g** | 12% |
| Saturated Fat 1g | 5% |
| **Cholesterol 0mg** | 0% |
| **Sodium 37mg** | 2% |
| **Total Carbohydrate 32.3g** | 11% |
| Dietary Fiber 7g | 28% |
| **Protein 5.1g** | |
| Percent values are based on a 2,000 calorie per day diet. Your daily values may differ. | |
| **Additional Information** 32.2% of calories from Fat 58.6% from Carbohydrates 9.2% from Protein | |

## Instructions:

Add 2 cups of water to a medium-size saucepan and heat covered on medium-high. When boiling, add pasta and cook for 10 minutes. Add spinach and cook an additional 4 minutes uncovered. Pasta should be soft. Drain and set aside in a large bowl.

Preheat oven to 450 degrees. Spray a baking dish with spray oil and add onion, cauliflower, and squash. Add garlic and seasoning and stir. Add olive oil and toss. Place the baking dish on the middle rack of the oven and cook for 30 minutes. Check often and move to the lowest rack of the oven if the vegetables begin to brown too quickly. Remove vegetables when done and stir into the pasta. Place on two plates and sprinkle with Parmesan cheese. Makes 2 servings.

## Accompaniments:

This dish should be eaten as a meatless main course. Add a breadstick if desired. Serve with iced tea or fruit juice.

**Tips:**
*Experiment with a variety of veggies, such as zucchini, bell peppers, or fresh black olives.*

# Pecan Sweet Potatoes

## Ingredients:

1 large sweet potato

¼ cup brown sugar

¼ cup orange juice

1 tablespoon margarine

½ teaspoon vanilla

2 tablespoon pecans

## Instructions:

Peel sweet potato. Cut into medium-size cubes. Place cubes in a small saucepan and add 1½ cups of water. Cover and heat on medium-high. Water will begin to boil. Cook until potato is soft, but not overboiled. Drain.

Preheat the oven to 350 degrees. Spray a baking dish with spray oil and add drained sweet potatoes. Place the margarine in a medium-size, microwave-safe dish and microwave on high for 25 seconds. Add the brown sugar, orange juice, vanilla, and pecans to the margarine. Stir. Pour the mixture over the sweet potatoes

| Nutrition Facts | | |
|---|---|---|
| per serving | | |
| makes 2 servings | | |
| **Amount per serving** | | |
| **Calories** | | 278 |
| Calories from fat | | 98 |
| | **% Daily Value \*** | |
| **Total Fat 10.8g** | | 17% |
| Saturated Fat 1.5g | | 8% |
| **Cholesterol 0mg** | | 0% |
| **Sodium 17mg** | | 1% |
| **Total Carbohydrate 43.5g** | | 14% |
| Dietary Fiber 2.2g | | 9% |
| **Protein 1.6g** | | |
| Percent values are based on a 2,000 calorie per day diet. Your daily values may differ. | | |
| **Additional Information** | | |
| 35.2% of calories from Fat 62.5% from Carbohydrates 2.3% from Protein | | |

and lightly blend. Place the baking dish on the middle rack of the oven for 30 minutes. Check and continue to bake until potatoes begin to brown. Remove from oven and enjoy. Makes 2 servings.

## Accompaniments:

Sweet potatoes traditionally accompany ham or pork. Add a green vegetable, such as zucchini or Brussels sprouts. Serve with a dinner roll and milk or tea. Do not have dessert with this sweet dish.

**Tips:**

*This simple dish gives your meal a gourmet flavor. Refrigerate leftovers and reheat in the microwave. The potatoes should be just as tasty the following day.*

# Foil Bag Veggies

## Ingredients:

1 cup broccoli

4 mini ears of frozen corn on the cob, thawed

1 large onion, any color

1 cup squash or zucchini

1 bell pepper, any color

6 cherry tomatoes

2 tablespoons minced garlic

1 tablespoon seasoning salt

2 tablespoons margarine

## Instructions:

Preheat the oven to 425 degrees. Spray the inside of a large foil bag. Place inside a large baking dish. Cut up vegetables except corn and tomatoes. Add all vegetables and disperse pieces of mar-

| Nutrition Facts | |
|---|---|
| per serving | |
| makes 2 servings | |
| **Amount per serving** | |
| **Calories** | 265 |
| Calories from fat | 115 |
| **% Daily Value \*** | |
| **Total Fat 12.8g** | 20% |
| Saturated Fat 2.3g | 11% |
| **Cholesterol 0mg** | 0% |
| **Sodium 297mg** | 12% |
| **Total Carbohydrate 31g** | 10% |
| Dietary Fiber 7.4g | 30% |
| **Protein 6.5g** | |
| Percent values are based on a 2,000 calorie per day diet. Your daily values may differ. | |
| **Additional Information** | |
| 43.4% of calories from Fat | |
| 46.8% from Carbohydrates | |
| 9.8% from Protein | |

garine throughout. Sprinkle the seasoning salt and garlic over the vegetables. Close the bag and place the baking dish on the middle rack of the oven. Cook for 45 minutes and let the bag sit for 5 minutes. Open carefully and enjoy. Makes 2 large servings.

## Accompaniments:

Serve as a meatless main dish, or with boneless grilled chicken or fish. Add a slice of toast. Have fresh watermelon or other seasonal fruit for dessert.

**Tips:**
*These types of recipes help you to enjoy preparing and eating veggies. Find other ways to experiment and keep healthy eating fun.*

# Foil Bag Chicken

## Ingredients:

1 boneless, skinless chicken
   breast
1 tablespoon olive oil
¼ teaspoon Mrs. Dash®-
   type seasoning, any
   flavor

## Instructions:

Preheat the oven to 425 degrees. Place a small foil bag in a baking dish and spray the inside with cooking oil. Place the chicken breast inside and pour the oil over the breast. Sprinkle the seasoning evenly over

| Nutrition Facts | |
| --- | --- |
| per serving | |
| makes 1 serving | |
| **Amount per serving** | |
| **Calories** | 241 |
| Calories from fat | 135 |
| **% Daily Value \*** | |
| **Total Fat 14.9g** | 23% |
| Saturated Fat 2.2g | 11% |
| **Cholesterol 65mg** | 22% |
| **Sodium 74mg** | 3% |
| **Total Carbohydrate 0.4g** | 0% |
| Dietary Fiber 0.1g | 0% |
| **Protein 26.2g** | |
| Percent values are based on a 2,000 calorie per day diet. Your daily values may differ. | |
| **Additional Information** 55.9% of calories from Fat 0.7% from Carbohydrates 43.4% from Protein | |

the chicken. Close the bag and place the baking dish on the middle rack of the oven. Cook for 30 minutes and check for doneness. If not done, continue to check at 5-minute intervals.

**Accompaniments:**

This tasty chicken breast is excellent on a whole-grain roll or bun. Add romaine lettuce, two tomato slices, and condiments. Consider adding a slice of Swiss cheese, two slices of bacon, or pickles. Serve baked potato chips on the side and a half-serving of baked beans. For dessert, offer a frozen fruit sorbet. Have milk or tea as a beverage.

**Tips:**

*You can easily double or triple this recipe, making enough for friends or for extra meals. You may want to use a large foil bag for this.*

# Foil Bag Salmon

**Ingredients:**

1 salmon fillet
1 tablespoon olive oil or
    canola oil
½ teaspoon lemon pepper
1 lemon
Dash of salt — optional

**Instructions:**

Preheat the oven to 425 degrees. Spray the inside of a small foil bag lightly with spray oil. Place the fillet into the bag. Drizzle the oil over the fillet and sprinkle with lemon pepper. Cut the

| Nutrition Facts | |
| --- | --- |
| per serving | |
| makes 1 serving | |
| **Amount per serving** | |
| **Calories** | **532** |
| Calories from fat | 224 |
| | **% Daily Value \*** |
| **Total Fat 24.8g** | 38% |
| Saturated Fat 3.6g | 18% |
| **Cholesterol 166mg** | 55% |
| **Sodium 511mg** | 21% |
| **Total Carbohydrate 12.3g** | 4% |
| Dietary Fiber 5.4g | 22% |
| **Protein 64.8g** | |
| Percent values are based on a 2,000 calorie per day diet. Your daily values may differ. | |
| **Additional Information** | |
| 42.1% of calories from Fat | |
| 9.2% from Carbohydrates | |
| 48.7% from Protein | |

entire lemon into six pieces and surround the fillet with 5 of the slices. Close the bag and place the baking dish on the middle rack of the oven. Bake for 30 minutes and check for doneness. If not done, continue to check at 5-minute intervals. Add salt if desired. Place the last piece of lemon on the side.

## Accompaniments:

This salmon is well-accompanied by whole-grain rice with mushrooms. Add a crisp green vegetable, such as snow peas, and a breadstick if desired. Have tea, water, or a fruit juice as a beverage. Consider dried fruit for dessert, such as dried blueberries and cherries.

**Tips:**
You can replace the salmon with any boneless fish fillet. Make sure the fillet is "boxy" and not long. You do not want a fillet with a thick middle and thin ends for this recipe. This dish is attractive served on a large lettuce leaf.

# Foil Baked Apple

## Ingredients:

1 large apple
2 tablespoons raisins
1 tablespoon walnuts
1 tablespoon margarine
1 tablespoon sugar
Dash of salt
Dash of cinnamon

## Instructions:

Preheat the oven to 400 degrees. Take a knife and carefully remove the core of the apple while keeping the apple whole. Place

| Nutrition Facts | |
|---|---|
| per serving | |
| makes 1 serving | |
| **Amount per serving** | |
| **Calories** | 360 |
| Calories from fat | 150 |
| | **% Daily Value \*** |
| **Total Fat 16.5g** | 25% |
| Saturated Fat 2.6g | 13% |
| **Cholesterol 0mg** | 0% |
| **Sodium 299mg** | 12% |
| **Total Carbohydrate 50.4g** | 17% |
| Dietary Fiber 6.2g | 25% |
| **Protein 2.2g** | |
| Percent values are based on a 2,000 calorie per day diet. Your daily values may differ. | |
| **Additional Information** | |
| 41.6% of calories from Fat 55.9% from Carbohydrates 2.4% from Protein | |

the apple on a sheet of heavy-duty aluminum foil, 12" x 12." In a small bowl, mix together the raisins, walnuts, margarine, sugar, salt, and cinnamon. With a small spoon, put ingredients into the cavity of the apple. Bring the foil up, enclose the apple, and seal the edges. Place in a small baking dish on the middle rack of the oven. Check the apple after 30 minutes. The apple is done when it is soft all over. Continue to cook at 5-minute intervals until done.

**Accompaniments:**

This apple should be served with another fun food, such as a corn dog or hot dog with baked fries. Add milk as a beverage.

**Tips:**

*This typical fall treat is tasty year round. Once you perfect it, it is easy to make extras in their own packets for guests.*

# Mini Meatloaves

**Ingredients:**

    4 ounces extra lean
        ground beef

    1 egg

    ½ teaspoon salt

    ¼ teaspoon pepper

    ¼ cup minced or diced onion

    1 tablespoon ketchup

    ½ teaspoon oregano or
        Italian spice mix

    ¼ cup spaghetti sauce

    1 piece of bread

    2 ounces shredded cheese,
        any type

| Nutrition Facts | |
|---|---|
| per serving | |
| makes 2 servings | |
| **Amount per serving** | |
| **Calories** | 383 |
| Calories from fat | 204 |
| **% Daily Value \*** | |
| **Total Fat 22.7g** | 35% |
| Saturated Fat 10.9g | 54% |
| **Cholesterol 176mg** | 59% |
| **Sodium 1261mg** | 53% |
| **Total Carbohydrate 21g** | 7% |
| Dietary Fiber 1.9g | 8% |
| **Protein 23.8g** | |

Percent values are based on a 2,000 calorie per day diet. Your daily values may differ.

**Additional Information**
53.2% of calories from Fat
21.9% from Carbohydrates
24.8% from Protein

## Instructions:

Preheat oven to 375 degrees. Tear the bread into small pieces and place on a cookie sheet. Place the cookie sheet on the middle oven rack while the oven is preheating. Remove when the bread is lightly toasted. Mix the first seven ingredients together in a medium-size bowl. Add the bread crumbs and mix. Spray four muffin cups with spray oil. Press the meatloaf mixture into the cups. Using the back of a teaspoon, hollow out a place in each loaf. Evenly distribute the spaghetti sauce between the loaves, into each hollow. Place the muffin tin on the middle oven rack and cook for 30 minutes, or until the loaves are thoroughly done. Sprinkle cheese on top of each well and return to the oven until the cheese is melted. Makes 2 servings of two mini meatloaves each.

## Accompaniments:

Serve with mashed potatoes, green beans or peas, and a small roll. Offer milk, buttermilk, or iced tea to drink. If dessert is desired, serve with a traditional dessert, such as pound cake or a fruit pie.

**Tips:**

*These easy meatloaves make wonderful comfort food when you are homesick for your family's cooking. Find out what your family adds to meatloaf and incorporate it into the recipe if you like. You can add ¼ cup of minced green bell peppers or celery if desired.*

# Pork Chop with Pineapple Slices

## Ingredients:

1 six-ounce pork chop (with
or without bone)
1 tablespoon corn or
vegetable oil
2 pineapple slices with juice
Dash of salt

## Instructions:

Add oil to a medium or large skillet and heat on medium-high. Add pork chop and allow it to brown lightly on both sides by turning it once. Reduce the heat to low and cover with lid. After 5 minutes, add the pineapple slices to the skillet. Salt both sides of the pork chop. Re-cover and cook 5 more minutes. Turn pineapple slices over. Check to see whether the pork is done. If the pork is not done, check every 5 minutes. When it is done, pour the pineapple juice over the pork chop and increase the heat to medium-high. Place the pineapple slices on top of the chop, cover with lid, and cook for 1 minute. Remove from the skillet and pour the remaining juice over the chop.

| Nutrition Facts | |
|---|---|
| per serving makes 1 serving | |
| **Amount per serving** | |
| **Calories** | 509 |
| Calories from fat | 337 |
| | **% Daily Value \*** |
| **Total Fat 37.4g** | 58% |
| Saturated Fat 10g | 50% |
| **Cholesterol 102mg** | 34% |
| **Sodium 367mg** | 15% |
| **Total Carbohydrate 8.9g** | 3% |
| Dietary Fiber 0.5g | 2% |
| **Protein 34g** | |
| Percent values are based on a 2,000 calorie per day diet. Your daily values may differ. | |
| **Additional Information** 66.3% of calories from Fat 7% from Carbohydrates 26.7% from Protein | |

## Accompaniments:

This dish can be served with white or whole-grain rice and full-length green beans. Add a crescent roll if desired. Serve with milk, iced tea, or 100-percent fruit juice. Do not serve dessert with this meal.

**Tips:**

*As with all of the recipes, you can increase the quantity of all the ingredients and make enough for leftovers the next day.*

# CHAPTER 21

## Conclusion

**H**opefully, the guidance in this book and these healthy recipes have been of benefit to you. Good self-care is the most precious gift you will ever give. It enables you to see the world through positive eyes and serve as a role model to everyone around you.

My highest wish is that I have sparked a love of cooking in you. I have been cooking since the age of 19 and enjoy sharing my love with my family by creating foods that nourish their bodies and minds. Whether you become a professional chef or simply make lunch once a week, your cooking knowledge will benefit you throughout your life. Share your knowledge with others, and constantly seek ways to expand it. As time goes by, we will learn more about the healthiest ways to prepare cuisine. I believe that in the future, many diseases will be prevented or arrested solely by eating healthy foods. Stay on the cutting edge of these trends, whether you cook or eat in restaurants.

Take good care of yourself, physically, mentally, and emotionally. Bon appétit.

# APPENDIX A

## Case Studies

### CASE STUDY: TOBY AMIDOR, MS, RD, CDN

Food, Nutrition, and Food Safety Consultant
E-mail: toby@namsko.com
Telephone: 914-588-0363

Registered dietician Toby Amidor feels that one of the biggest challenges to new college students involves keeping new hours. She advises to avoid late-night unhealthy eating. Amidor likes the idea of students getting together and learning how to cook. Her top three pieces of nutrition advice for college students include:

**1) Schedule regular exercise.** Regular exercise is also lost in the chaos of college life. Most campuses have a free gym that students can work out in and even offer classes like yoga and aerobics. Find a workout buddy, and make yourself a schedule to go to the gym. Gym classes are also offered — sign up for the ones that make you sweat, like dance and weight training.

**2) Drink responsibly.** It is no fun waking up after a night of heavy partying knowing you have a hangover; *plus,* you downed hundreds, if not thousands, of calories. Drinking tips include:

- Stick to light beer or wine.
- Rotate one drink and then one glass of water or a non-caloric beverage (i.e., diet soda).

## CASE STUDY: TOBY AMIDOR, MS, RD, CDN

- Forget those mixed drinks — they are laden with sugar and spiked with extra alcohol to get people more drunk.

- Forgo the "drunk pizza" at 5 a.m. and have a snack ready and waiting at home (e.g., a peanut butter and jelly sandwich).

**3) Scout out all the eateries and find your quiet corner.** To avoid the pressure of eating fatty foods in groups, find a nice, quiet cafeteria (or go at the off-peak hours). In my college years, I found a beautiful cafeteria that faculty went to on the other side of campus. Take time to choose the healthiest options for you without worrying about what others will think.

*Toby Amidor is a registered dietitian with a master's degree in clinical nutrition and dietetics from New York University. She is also a Certified Dietitian Nutritionist by the state of New York. Amidor is pursuing her doctoral degree in nutrition education from Teachers College - Columbia University. Amidor consults for various food-marketing and food-safety companies. Clients include Scripps Networks subsidiaries Food Network®, HGTV®, and Fine Living™. She has appeared in a variety of media outlets, including Good Day New York (WNYW Fox5 NY), Self Magazine, Us Weekly® Magazine, WebMD®, Working Mother® Magazine, The New York Daily News, and Fitness Magazine.*

## CASE STUDY: RYAN D. ANDREWS, MS, MA, RD, CSCS, NSCA-CPT, ACSM-HFS, CISS

Director of Education — Precision Nutrition
**www.precisionnutrition.com**

In his career, Ryan Andrews has noted that students should keep nutrition simple and take small steps each day to stay fit and healthy. Andrews advises students to challenge their muscles and mix some sleep into their routines. He feels that eating healthy does not require marathon kitchen sessions; instead, microwave some frozen vegetables, heat some beans, and snack on fresh fruit. Andrews' top advice to students is:

1. Eat real food (e.g., veggies, fruits, beans/legumes, whole grains, nuts/seeds, tea, and water.)

2. Do not ever go on a diet.

3. Do something physically active for at least four hours each week.

## CASE STUDY: RYAN D. ANDREWS, MS, MA, RD, CSCS, NSCA-CPT, ACSM-HFS, CISS

*Ryan D. Andrews, former dietitian at the Johns Hopkins Weight Management Center, is trained in Exercise Physiology (BS, MA, CSCS), Nutrition (MS), and Dietetics (RD, LD). After leaving Johns Hopkins, Andrews began working with Dr. John Berardi as the Director of Education for Precision Nutrition, Inc.*

## CASE STUDY: LAURIE BEEBE, MS, RD

Diet Coach, Owner of Shaping Your Future
**www.mycoachlaurie.com**

Laurie Beebe said that students have so many new responsibilities that they frequently put nutrition too far down on their list of priorities. She realizes that students often socialize around food and may also turn to food for comfort when feeling homesick or to cope with new stressors.

Beebe suggests that learning to cook a little bit and maintaining a regular eating pattern will help you to achieve success. She reminds us all to incorporate exercise into our daily routines.

When Beebe was in college, she was part of a group of students who prepared meals together, taking turns to buy food, cook, and clean up. She suggests posting a notice on the dorm bulletin board that expresses an interest in starting a small group of three or four people to share dinner three or four nights per week.

Beebe's advice to students is:

1. Eat three meals a day and limit "treats" (like candy bars from vending machines, late-night eating, and high-calorie fast foods) to just one instance every other day or so.

2. Find something you like that you can have for breakfast, no matter how much you are in a hurry, to start your metabolism going and stave off late-day hunger.

3. Get in plenty of walking for exercise if you do not have a regular exercise routine.

"I would teach students that for every extra 100 calories they eat in a day, this can add up to gaining a pound at the end of the month. So if they do not want to go home with an extra five pounds at the end of the semester, keep an eye on those extras/treats/junk foods, and just say no once in a while," she said.

## CASE STUDY: LAURIE BEEBE, MS, RD

*A registered dietitian for more than 25 years, Beebe became certified in Adult Weight Management in 2006, and then completed the core essential coaching courses at Coach U in 2007. Her mission is to help people lose weight permanently by making small changes, one at a time, to develop lasting, healthy habits. Beebe's Web site is **www.my-coachlaurie.com**, and she hosts two blogs to provide you* with weight loss tips *(**lifedietbalance.blogspot.com**)* and nutrition information *(**askthedietitian.blogspot.com**).*

## CASE STUDY: ANATOLY BELILOVSKY, M.D.

Belilovsky Pediatrics
Brooklyn, New York
**www.babydr.us**

Dr. Anatoly Belilovsky treats college students in his pediatrics practice. When asked what problems he is seeing in his college-age patients due to a poor diet, he commented:

"As with most overweight patients, diabetes is always a risk with poor diet and a sedentary life style. More basic effects of poor diet include increased fatigue, lowered brain function, and digestive irregularities. Mental health is also affected by weight gain due to a changing self-image and self-worth. Many times, students use food and alcohol to cope with new emotions over sudden independence, unfamiliar environments, and social situations. This, coupled with weight gain, can lead to depression, anxiety, and eating disorders."

He feels that students should make it a habit to get up 30 minutes earlier each day in order to go for a workout or take a brisk walk around campus. Belilovsky advises students to make a point of putting more octane in their engines with more nutritious foods. His top advice to students includes:

1. **Do not eat while doing something else** (e.g., reading, writing, computer, TV). Eating should be mindful so you actually pay attention to what foods (calories) are entering your body and when you are full. This will cut down on excessive eating and the potential to gain weight through empty calories.

2. **Do not drink your calories.** Drink water, and plenty of it. No juices (eat the whole fruit or vegetable from which juice is made), no sugary / corn syrupy sodas, and limit alcohol consumption to reduce major empty calories that cause you to overeat and gain weight.

## CASE STUDY: ANATOLY BELILOVSKY, M.D.

3. **Choose fat-free versions of whatever you like to eat.** Less caloric density means that even if you cannot control binge eating (like late at night), there are only so many calories that will fit in.

*Anatoly Belilovsky, M.D., has been a board-certified pediatrician since 1990. He is the medical director of Belilovsky Pediatrics in Brooklyn, New York. Belilovsky is a clinical instructor in pediatrics at the Weill College of Medicine and is the recipient of an Americhoice Quality of Care Award. He has a blog at **www.babydr.us**.*

## CASE STUDY: NICOLE BRITVAN, RD, CDE

Nutritionist, Certified Diabetes Educator
San Francisco, CA
415-722-2616

Nicole Britvan thinks students should not overlook the importance of at least seven hours of sleep each night, as a lack of adequate sleep can lead to weight gain. She reminds us that liquid calories add up quickly and to be mindful of what our body needs versus wants. Britvan encourages students to aim to get at least 30 minutes of exercise each day. She has noted in her practice that, when we are stressed, we crave fat, salt, and sugar. Her top advice to students is:

1. Water (plain or sparkling) — Make it your main beverage. An extra 100 calories a day is 10 lbs. of weight gain in one year — easy to do with juice, energy drinks, and other sugary drinks.

2. Eat fruit and vegetables whenever possible.

3. Be careful about late-night eating due to stress, anxiety, or boredom.

## CASE STUDY: ELIZABETH DEROBERTIS, MS, RD, CDN, CDE

Registered Dietitian, Certified Diabetes Educator
Scarsdale Medical Group, Scarsdale New York
**www.nutritionistliz.com**

Elizabeth DeRobertis said that college students need to make healthy eating a priority. She believes in starting each day with a balanced breakfast, even if it means grabbing a

## CASE STUDY: ELIZABETH DEROBERTIS, MS, RD, CDN, CDE

granola or cereal-type bar and a piece of fruit on their way out the door. She encourages us to get eight hours of sleep each night. DeRobertis sees students eat in response to stress, obtain high-calorie snacks from vending machines, and go too long without eating. She would like to see a short healthy cooking class added to school orientations and recipe cards being made available year-round. DeRobertis' advice to students includes:

1.  Keep tabs on your calorie intake and prioritize where you want to spend your calories. I often think of the analogy between calories and money. Just like college kids need to be mindful of how and when they spend money, they should use the same strategic thinking when deciding how and where to spend their calories. They should look up the calorie and fat content of the foods they commonly eat if they do not have a nutrition label. Most restaurants offer their calories online. It is important not to drink empty calories. Juice, soda, Gatorade®, Vitamin Water®, and high-calorie, sugared coffee drinks can contribute hundreds of extra calories to the day, and many unwanted pounds to their waistlines.

2.  Choose deli sandwiches more often than other types of "fast food" choices. Stock up on lean cold cuts, such as turkey, ham, roast beef, and chicken. This will always be fewer calories than a hamburger and fries or a piece of pizza. Buy low-fat condiments, so if they make things like a standard tuna sandwich, the calories and fat will be less if it is made with low-fat or fat-free mayo.

3.  Start as many meals as possible with a big salad or a broth-based soup. This will help with portion control and to meet nutrient needs. I read a story once about a freshman starting college who wanted to lose weight. He made a point of having a big salad each time he entered the cafeteria, and then he let himself eat what he wanted after he finished his salad. He lost 50 pounds his first year in college by doing this.

## CASE STUDY: EVE KECSKES, MS, RD

Nutrition by Eve, LLC
303 5th Avenue Suite 603
New York, NY 10016
**www.nutritionbyeve.com**
eve@nutritionbyeve.com

Eve Kecskes is a registered dietician who believes strongly that college students should incorporate daily activity into their lives. Hertop

## CASE STUDY: EVE KECSKES, MS, RD

ideas include going to the gym and working out with friends, going for a swim in the pool, running around the track, playing basketball, or joining a sport. She encourages at least seven hours of sleep each night and never skipping meals. Kecskes would like to see healthy cooking clubs started on campuses or resident assistants being trained in healthy cooking to assist freshmen in getting together weekly for a healthy meal. She also suggests a column in the college newspaper devoted to healthy eating tips and sample recipes. Her nutritional advice for college students includes:

1. Try to look for lower-fat options when you have the choice.
   - Grilled chicken instead of fried chicken/chicken tenders
   - Baked potato instead of French fries
   - Pita chips instead of potato chips
   - Mustard instead of mayo
   - Veggie pizza instead of pepperoni pizza
   - Low-fat salad dressing instead of full-fat
   - Marinara sauce instead of vodka or Alfredo sauce
   - Low-fat cheese instead of full-fat
   - Turkey, chicken, ham, or fish instead of hamburgers, sausage, pepperoni, salami, bacon, or steak.

2. Start learning about portion sizes, and cut back.
   - When you buy a packaged food, look at the label and see what consists of a serving. It is easy to overdo it on crackers, cookies, candy, chips, and other foods that have multiple servings in a box/bag.
   - Cut back on portions of carbohydrates, such as bread, pasta, rice, and potatoes. While these foods are naturally low in fat, the calories add up quickly.
   - A normal dinner plate should consist of:
     i. ½ fruits and vegetables
     ii. ¼ lean protein
     iii. ¼ carbohydrates

3. There are many more suggestions that should be made as well:
   - Choose whole grains, such as oatmeal, high-fiber cereal, brown rice, whole-wheat pasta, whole-wheat bread, and popcorn, when given the option.
   - Always eat breakfast. Incorporate one of each of the following:

## CASE STUDY: EVE KECSKES, MS, RD

   i.   Low-fat dairy (skim or 1 percent milk, non-fat yogurt, low-fat cheese, or low-fat cottage cheese)
   ii.  Fruit (one cup)
   iii. Whole grains (whole-wheat bread/English muffin/bagel, high-fiber cereal, or oatmeal)
- Choose unsaturated fats instead of saturated/trans fats.
   i.   Unsaturated (vegetable oil, nuts/seeds, fatty fish, avocado, and olives)
   ii.  Saturated (butter, whole fat dairy, red meat, poultry skin, cheese, cream, coconut, and palm oil)
   iii. Trans fat (partially hydrogenated oil)
- Limit sugar intake.
   i.   Added sugars should be no more than 10 percent of daily caloric intake
   ii.  Fruit should be eaten for sweets instead of candy and cookies
- Drink at least eight glasses of water each day, and limit sugary drinks, such as sweetened coffee, soda, and juice.
- Do not overdo caffeine.
   i.   Energy drinks should not be used to stay up late
   ii.  Limit coffee and other caffeinated drinks to two per day

4. Eat at least one vegetable or one fruit with each meal and snack.

*Kecskes (formerly Salik) is the president of Nutrition by Eve, LLC, a private nutrition practice located in Manhattan. She is a registered dietitian (RD) with the American Dietetic Association who uses an individualized approach based on lifestyle, eating habits, and nutritional goals to achieve optimal health and well being. She specializes in disease prevention and management, weight loss, sports nutrition, pre- and post-natal nutrition, and general wellness.*

## CASE STUDY: AUDREY A. KOLTUN, RD, CDE, CDN

askoltun@hotmail.com

Koltun is a registered dietician, and she believes time management is a paramount concern for college students, especially making time for regular meals, including breakfast. She states: "Even a quick bite in the morning is very beneficial for energy and academic achievement, and it helps prevent overeating later in the day from increased hunger. Eating a meal or a healthy snack every four to five hours is important."

## CASE STUDY: AUDREY A. KOLTUN, RD, CDE, CDN

Koltun reminds us to schedule time for physical activity and to be conscientious of food portion sizes. She would like to see nutrition information be given as part of college orientation and also suggests "taste tests" to encourage healthy eating in the dining hall. Her top advice to students includes:

1. Try to eat fruits and vegetables every day, and try to consume plenty of water.

2. Do not linger in the dining hall. The longer you are there, the more you will eat.

3. Keep healthy snacks handy — in the dorm and with you in class. This can prevent overeating by avoiding extreme hunger when you are not eating for extended periods of time.

*Koltun works in the New York metropolitan area providing nutrition counseling to clients of all ages, from children and adolescents to adults. She provides medical nutrition therapy in various areas, including weight management, type 1 and type 2 diabetes, cardiovascular nutrition, and general nutrition and wellness. Koltun also does workshops and lectures on matters relating to nutrition and health.*

## CASE STUDY: SANDRA MEYEROWITZ, MPH, RD, LD

Nutrition Works
**www.smartnutritionworks**

Meyerowitz feels that we all need to remain tuned in to our physical hunger and not eat along with the crowd or for emotional reasons. She feels that students should schedule exercise into their day, as if it were a class. Meyerowitz would like to see college students keep their rooms stocked with healthy snacks. To facilitate students cooking for themselves, she suggests special cooking utensils that are convenient and easy to use, very easy recipes that are "cool," and people to share the experience with. Meyerowitz believes we should all portray eating right as the means to give students the image they like — healthy, vibrant, sexy, athletic, chic, and smart. Her top nutrition advice includes:

1. Listen to your body. Learn what feels right, and pay attention to your intuition.

2. Do not skip meals.

## CASE STUDY: SANDRA MEYEROWITZ, MPH, RD, LD

3. Do not fall prey to portion distortion.

4. Avoid the fads.

*Sandra Meyerowitz, MPH., RD, LD is the owner of Nutrition Works, a health promotion company specializing in weight loss, wellness, and sports nutrition. She offers individual consultations, team and corporate seminars, and online nutrition services.*

## CASE STUDY: MICHELLE PLUMMER, MS, RD, CD

Relationship Specialist
American Dairy Association of Indiana, Inc.
Dairy & Nutrition Council, Inc.
plummer@mpsiinc.com
Telephone: 317-842-7133
Fax: 317-842-3065

Michelle Plummer advises students that what they drink matters; they should try to limit the amount of Gatorade® and other soda-type beverages in favor of water, milk, and other healthier beverages. Plummer encourages moderation as a long-term goal. She states that she would like to see "colleges set up programs for students to participate in 'cooking classes' on campus with local 'food people;' not only chefs, but professional cooks and celebrity cooks. Make it fun and exciting." Her top nutrition advice includes:

1. Eat only when hungry.

2. Seek out the best selections at each eating location on campus.

3. Do not *diet,* but eat with color and moderation in mind.

## CASE STUDY: PEGGY SPENCER, M.D.

University of New Mexico Student Health and Counseling

Dr. Peggy Spencer treats college students in her medical practice and sees considerable obesity among her patients. When asked about the major nutritional problems she sees, she said that obesity is a big one. Overeating leads to obesity, which leads to a decreased willingness to exercise, because it is more difficult to move when you are

## CASE STUDY: PEGGY SPENCER, M.D.

heavy. Obesity can lead to other health problems, like skin rashes (in fat folds), joint pain, and even diabetes, if it goes on long enough. Weight gain of any significant amount can be upsetting for a student, who might feel socially isolated and ashamed. Under-eating or skipping meals can lead to fatigue and fainting episodes. Inadequate nutrition can lead to anemia. Irregular eating can cause uneven energy, focus, and concentration, resulting in poor performance and mood swings. Eating disorders are sadly too common among college students.

Spencer encourages students to exercise daily and make their health their top priority. Her top nutritional advice includes:

1. Avoid fast food.

2. Carry healthy snacks with you, like fruit and nuts. This can help maintain your energy level throughout the day without resorting to machine candy or other high-calorie, high-sugar snacks.

3. Eat slowly and mindfully. The abundance of the cafeteria, with "all you can eat" access, often results in overeating. Control your portion size and minimize desserts.

One of her suggestions in the cafeteria is to take fresh spinach from a salad bar and microwave it. Then, add it to a simple pasta dish for increased nutritional value. Dr. Spencer would like to see students take turns rotating dinner responsibility to facilitate healthy eating. She feels that students should be allowed to snack during long classes.

*Spencer is a graduate of the University of California with a BA in Biology with Honors, and of the University of Arizona College of Medicine with an MD. She is certified by the American Board of Family Practice. She has worked as a staff physician at the University of New Mexico (UNM) Student Health and Counseling for 17 years and holds an adjunct faculty position at the UNM School of Medicine.*

## CASE STUDY: DEIRDRE WILLIAMS, MS, RD, LDN

8 Melton Road
Brighton, MA 02135
williams_deirdre@yahoo.com

Deirdre Williams says that balance is important for college students: "I think college students need to focus on balance. College can be a time of a tremendous amount of stress from numerous factors: academic demands, poor diet, social pressures, poor sleeping patterns, time constraints, managing parental expectations, financial issues, and many more. Finding a healthy balance by setting priorities and managing time efficiently, keeping expectations realistic, getting adequate sleep, exercising on a regular and consistent basis, eating a healthful and complete diet, seeking support when necessary, and managing finances are essential. This is by no means an easy task."

Her top advice includes:

1. **Exercise is essential.** Regular physical activity helps to maintain weight in many ways. The more you move, the more calories you use, which keeps weight in check. In addition, regular exercise has been shown to help manage stress, regulate sleep patterns, improve energy levels, sharpen mental acuity, and boost self-confidence.

2. **Focus on fluid.** Drinking plenty of water is crucial. Aim for at least six to eight glasses per day, and even more if you are highly active or live in a hot climate. Inadequate fluid intake can result in headaches, fatigue, chapped lips, dizziness, and dehydration. Furthermore, limiting sugary drinks, caffeine-laced liquids, and nutrient-poor libations is a healthy habit for all college students. These beverages are full of nutrient-poor "empty" calories, which can lead to weight gain. Caffeine and alcohol also disrupt sleep patterns and can exacerbate stress.

3. **Eat regular meals.** Try to consume at least four to six small meals or snacks each day. Do not skip meals, as this can diminish energy levels and mental sharpness, decrease metabolism, and lead to overeating later in the day. Late night eating often consists of pizza, fried foods, burritos, and other high-calorie, high-fat foods. Eating small meals at regular intervals during the day can help reduce the urge to eat high-calorie foods late at night.

*Deirdre Williams has an MS in nutrition from Boston University. She is a registered and licensed dietitian, currently practicing in Boston, Massachusetts.*

# APPENDIX B

## Resources

United States Department of Agriculture **www.mypyramid.org**
This Web site provides a huge amount of healthy eating resources. You will also find exercise data.

American Dietetic Association **www.eatright.org**
This organization can help you find a registered dietician to work with you on improving your diet. They provide plenty of nutrition advice, such as how to eat healthfully on a budget.

Overeaters Anonymous **www.overeatersanonymous.org**
These support groups provide a 12-step program for compulsive eaters.

ANAD — The National Association of Anorexia Nervosa and Associated Eating Disorders **www.anad.org**
This organization can provide information, support groups, and therapists who specialize in eating disorders.

American Psychological Association **www.apa.org**
This organization provides information about various mental health concerns and can provide you with a psychologist who specializes in specific issues.

All Recipes **www.allrecipes.com**
This Web site, along with thousands of others, can provide you with healthy, simple recipes to continue your cooking journey.

# BIBLIOGRAPHY

Albers, Susan, *Mindful Eating 101: A Guide to Healthy Eating in College and Beyond*, Routledge, New York, 2006.

Bowen, Carol, *The Microwave Kitchen Bible*, Hermes House, London, 2003.

James, Shelly Vaughan, *The Complete Idiot's Guide to the College Diet Cookbook*, Alpha, New York, 2007.

Litt, Ann Selkowitz, *The College Student's Guide to Eating Well on Campus*, Tulip Hill Press, Bethesda, MD, 2005.

**www.MyPyramid.gov**, United States Department of Agriculture – Home, 2009.

Nimetz, Alexandra, Jason Stanley and Emeline Starr, *The Healthy College Cookbook: Quick, Cheap, Easy*, Storey Publishing, North Adams, MA, 1999.

Oz, Daphne, *The Dorm Room Diet*, Newmarket Press, New York, 2006.

Tribole, Evelyn, *Eating on the Run*, 3rd Ed., Human Kinetics, Champaign, IL, 2004.

Smith, M. J. and Fred Smith, *The Smart Student's Guide to Healthy Living: How to Survive Stress, Late Nights, and the College Cafeteria*, New Harbinger Publications, Inc., Oakland, CA, 2006.

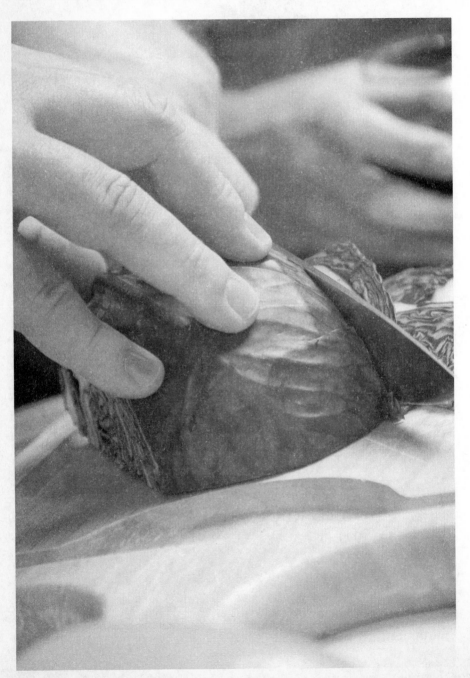

# AUTHOR BIOGRAPHY

J. Lucy Boyd, RN, BSN has practiced nursing since 1991. She has treated many adolescent and young adult populations for eating disorders and has counseled hundreds of patients on principles of sound nutrition. Now a registered nurse and full-time writer, she enjoys sharing her medical and culinary wisdom with new generations.

Boyd was valedictorian of her class at the Livingston School of Practical Nursing and later graduated Summa Cum Laude from the University of the State of New York – Regents College with a Bachelor of Science degree in Nursing. She is a proud native of Chattanooga, Tennessee, where she can be found cooking in her spare time.

Boyd is also the author of *101 Ways to Score Higher on Your NCLEX: What You Need to Know About the National Council Licensure Examination Explained Simply* (**www.atlantic-pub.com**).

# INDEX

# C